BRITAIN
AND IRELAND
1914-23

SHEILA LAWLOR

GILL AND MACMILLAN

BARNES & NOBLE BOOKS
Totowa, New Jersey

First published 1983 by
Gill and Macmillan Ltd
Goldenbridge
Dublin 8
with associated companies in
London, New York, Delhi, Hong Kong,
Johannesburg, Lagos, Melbourne,
Singapore, Tokyo

© Sheila Lawlor 1983

7171 1147 4

Library of Congress Cataloging in Publication Data

Lawlor, Sheila.
  Britain and Ireland 1914-23.

  Bibliography: p.273
  Includes index.
  1. Ireland—History—1910-1921.   2. Irish question.   3. Ireland—History—
Sinn Féin Rebellion, 1916—Causes.   4. Great Britain—Foreign relations—
Ireland.   5. Ireland—Foreign relations—Great Britain.   6. Great Britain—
Foreign relations—1910-1936.   I. Title.
DA962.L34 1983   941.5082'1   83-10015
ISBN 0–389–20409–9

Origination by Galaxy Reproductions Limited, Dublin
Printed and bound in Great Britain by Biddles Limited
Guildford and King's Lynn

To my parents

NOTE ON TERMINOLOGY

According to publishing convention, the names of political affiliations and institutions (for example, Conservatives, Volunteers) have been capitalised. This should not be taken to suggest a greater cohesion than in fact, existed. Capitalisation has also been standardised within quotations.

Contents

Preface

There have been any number of accounts written about all — or part of — the 1914-23 period. Many have been based on or have been the memoirs or recollections of those involved, both British and Irish. They have been mainly written after the event, and have been affected by the attitude adopted by the author, if not at the time then subsequently. There have also been the less partisan, but no more illuminating, accounts, written very often by academic historians. These, though more general in scope, have been limited to providing interpretative essays on aspects of the period and have drawn in the main on the memoir material, or on the newspapers of the day. In addition there have been the more ambitious investigations into particular themes: Irish nationalism; the Irish question in British politics; biographies of individual figures. None of these is based exclusively on contemporary written evidence; and even where the more recent studies have used unpublished documentary evidence, their authors have tended to restrict their examinations to specific problems, such as the British campaign in Ireland, or the origins of the Free State. None is concerned with determining exactly how and why events occurred, at the highest level, on the British and Irish sides.

This book differs in that it is primarily concerned with events and interventions as they occurred at the time at the highest level on all sides and in the context of the period as a whole, from great war to civil war; it also differs in that it is based entirely on contemporary documents, most of which have never been published, or have not been examined in the context of the 'higher' and complicated developments of events between 1914 and 1923. As a result the account which emerges is more complicated than those traditionally accepted.

On the *British* side Ireland was an important, but not unique problem. The attitudes and interventions of those involved can only be understood in the context of British party politics — which were affected (and dominated) by the great war, until 1918, as they subsequently were by its implications. Whereas before war broke out in August 1914 Asquith, a Liberal, was prime minister of a Liberal government with the support of the Liberal party and of Redmond's Irish party, after the war Lloyd George was prime minister; and though a Liberal himself, he led a coalition in which he depended on Conservative support. Lloyd George's attitude to Ireland and the Irish question in the years after 1918 was, therefore, affected by the complex and changing balance, conveyed by those on whose support he counted — the Conservatives led by Law (and later Chamberlain), and to a lesser degree his own Liberals, whose 'conscience' on the Irish matter was maintained in the government by Montagu and Fisher particularly. Moreover, the views and attitudes of those involved differed at any given time, and continued to change. Fisher, Montagu and Churchill urged, for example, that a measure of fiscal autonomy should be included in any proposal to settle the Irish question — although Churchill simultaneously warned that it should not be offered until the timing was right. Law and Long continued to oppose fiscal autonomy as did Lloyd George, whose position remained that of a 'Gladstonian home ruler', or so he maintained. There were other and constant divisions — over, for example, the area to be included in the jurisdiction of the northern parliament; over the nature and extent of military rule in the south; and over the fundamental question as to whether there could ever be a settlement which would satisfy any of the main parties involved. Moreover, the problem for Lloyd George was complicated by the way in which the advice and appreciations of the professional soldiers often conflicted with the demands of the Conservatives or the sentiments of the Liberals, as they did also with their individual positions. In addition it should be stressed that Ireland was only one of many issues after (or arising out of) the war, which reflected the conflicts between and amongst the politicians in the coalition; but it was one, the deterioration of which tended to coincide with, and provoke, disenchantment amongst those who supported Lloyd George's coalition.

Similarly, the issue on the *Irish* side was complex. Instead of, for example, the hitherto alleged categorical division between those who accepted the 1921 treaty and those who did not, it has become clear from the documents that many divisions were in existence in Ireland long before that treaty; and that the additional ideological differences which it provoked merely served to complicate further those already there. Such differences had existed throughout the 1914-18 period, though they had been obscured after 1917 by the organisation of Sinn Féin. But as early as the summer of 1918, for example, Collins had noted with some bitterness the predominance of non-militant (and indeed anti-militant) leaders in the Sinn Féin movement. From 1919 onwards, there was the further distinction between the fighting (Volunteers) and non-fighting (political) men; this distinction was complicated in turn because certain leaders belonged to both the Volunteer and the political movements, or that in addition members of one (or both) were members of the secret Irish Republican Brotherhood. Local rivalries also mattered: the Corkmen, for example, worried their own and the headquarters' leaders long before the treaty was signed, on account of their 'vanity' and 'indiscipline', or their contempt for the 'politicians'. The treaty exacerbated local rivalries when the prospect of jobs, or of holding the various barracks now being evacuated by the British, began to matter. In early 1922, this led to incidents in Limerick, Kilkenny and Tipperary, which although linked to the question of republican allegiance, had more to them than just that.

If the post-treaty period was complicated by local rivalries, by divisions between the 'political' and the 'military' groups, it also was by Collins's attitude to what should or might be done concerning the north — a matter inseparable from his own views on the republican Volunteers. Throughout the whole period the confusions and complexities were emphasised by the ambiguous position of de Valera: ambiguous at least from the time of his return from America in December 1920, until the outbreak of civil war in June 1922. It was never quite clear what de Valera stood for; or with whom he stood; and this became particularly evident during the period before and after the treaty, when matters were further confused by the absence of any close connection between de Valera and the men with the guns. This was true as late as March 1922; and even after the outbreak of civil war it remained to some extent the case, as Lynch and the IRA staff resolved to keep themselves apart from de Valera and his republican 'politicians'.

The story, therefore, is more complicated and unpredictable than any previous account has suggested. There was no one position on either side before or after the treaty; and the commonplace assumptions suggested by the terms 'Irish' or 'British', and adopted by historians since then, are misleading. Instead of one, or two views, there were many — which continued to change in the context of events, domestic and international, and in the context of the interventions and attitudes of those involved.

Such a book as this could not have been written without access to the archives and documents of those principally involved at the time, British and Irish. (Though in regard to the latter it must be stressed that the documentary evidence is more fragmentary, as much of it has been destroyed; much, of course, was never committed to paper.) I am therefore indebted to the owners, custodians and archivists of the manuscript collections listed in the bibliography for permission to use the material listed; and I am also indebted to the owners and trustees of copyright material for permission to reproduce extracts from those collections listed: the Bodleian Library, Oxford; the trustees of the Beaverbrook Foundation; Mr Mark Bonham Carter; Lord Derby; the Clerk of the Records, the Record Office, the House of Lords; the Liverpool City Library; the owner and trustees of the Mulcahy papers; the director of the National Library of Ireland and the Keeper of Manuscripts; the owner and trustees of the O'Malley papers; the Keeper of State Papers,

State Paper Office, Dublin; the Master and Fellows of Trinity College, Cambridge. Transcripts of crown-copyright records in the Public Record Office appear by permission of the Controller of HM Stationery Office.

I owe a particular debt to the staff of the House of Lords Record Office, as I also do the archivists and staff of the Department of Archives, University College, Dublin. I am grateful to the staff of the Bodleian Library, Oxford; the Cambridge University Library; the Liverpool City Library; the National Library of Ireland; the Public Record Office, London; the State Paper Office, Dublin; the Library, Trinity College, Cambridge.

I am indebted to Professor Desmond Williams who supervised my master's thesis, submitted to the National University of Ireland in 1976, *Civil-Military Relations in Ireland, 1921-23,* for his consistently generous advice, expertise and help.

My thanks are due to the Robert Gardiner Memorial foundation for financial help.

Mr John Marenbon very kindly read the manuscript and made many valuable suggestions, as did Professor Derek Beales. Professor and Mrs Dudley Edwards, Dr E. R. Norman, Mr P. Williamson, Mr S. MacBride and the late Mrs C. MacBride have made suggestions and given advice.

I am grateful to the Master and Fellows of Sidney Sussex College for their generous support since 1976, for their congenial company, and for providing conditions conducive to research and writing.

I continue to be grateful to my parents, to whom this book is dedicated.

1
Introductory, 1914-18

The outbreak of war in August 1914 had a consequence for Ireland as dramatic as its implications for the ultimate settlement of Europe. Before August 1914, the solution to the Irish question 'belonged' to Asquith's Liberal government, but the combination of Ulster Unionists and Conservative opposition denied it to him. After that date, the importance of the Irish question became almost negligible by contrast with the gravity of the grand political and strategic issues arising out of the war. Before August 1914 Redmond's party of Irish MPs was prepared, with varying degrees of enthusiasm and reluctance, to recommend to their voters Asquith's schemes for home rule, notwithstanding their diminishing scope. Subsequently, the implications – both direct and indirect – of the war on Ireland, changed the ostensible context of the demand in Ireland. Instead of home rule, the Irish wanted independence; instead of negotiation, they resorted to the use of force, both physical and moral. Asquith and Redmond, the names before the war, were replaced by Lloyd George and de Valera. Lloyd George was dependent on Conservative support, and de Valera on that of the gunmen.

In the months preceding August 1914, Asquith had been determined to proceed with the Irish government bill. But from a position of dominance in the House of Commons in 1906, when his party had won 400 seats at the general election (as against the Conservatives' 157), that strength had been eroded; and following the last general election in 1910, Asquith's Liberal party had been reduced to a strength of 272 MPs (the same number as the Conservatives). It was in this context that the support of the Irish nationalist MPs – of

whom there were 84 — was vital. The Irish party's MPs had
had been led by John Redmond since 1900; their object was
to secure, through constitutional means, home rule for
Ireland — that is its own legislature in Dublin. They were
nationalist, but not republican; and they attended Westminster
in order to secure the necessary legislation to remain away
from it. Once Asquith became dependent on their support,
it seemed that in return he would have to concede home
rule. The third home rule bill was therefore introduced in
April 1912. This proposed to set up an Irish parliament of
two houses, with an executive responsible to it; responsibility
for matters affecting the crown, defence, foreign relations,
coinage and taxation would remain vested in Westminster,
although the lower house might raise or reduce existing duties
by ten per cent. In essence, the home rule bill did not differ
from previous bills, and the supremacy of the imperial
parliament over the proposed Irish parliament was reiterated
throughout by Asquith. Redmond's party supported the
measure, but the Ulster Unionists, and their unionist champions in the Conservative party, rejected it. If a home rule
parliament were forced upon them, they would 'refuse to
recognise its authority'.

This opposition, combined with threats of 'civil war',
bloodshed and armed resistance, resulted in substantial
modification of the terms of the bill — though it did not
undermine Asquith's resolution to proceed with home rule.
Yet no modification which Asquith might concede could be
sufficient for Carson, the southern unionist and one-time
solicitor-general who had become the champion of the
Ulster men, or for Law, the leader of the Conservative (or)
Unionist party.

Asquith's proposal of December 1913 — that no legislation passed by the Irish parliament need become effective
in the Ulster area against the majority will of Ulster
representatives, unless submitted and approved by the
imperial parliament — had made little impression on Carson.
He continued to refuse 'any negotiation which does not
proceed upon the basis of Ulster being altogether excluded . . .
from the proposed Irish legislature'.[1] Asquith and his
colleagues, while looking upon each concession made to the

Unionist opposition as representing the 'extreme limit' to which they would go, nonetheless continued to alter the bill in order to mollify Ulster and its champions. By 4 March 1914, the Irish party leaders had been persuaded 'as the price of a peaceful settlement' to agree to a plan to give the Ulster counties 'the right, by plebiscite, of excluding themselves for a term of years'.[2] The temporary nature of this solution did little to remove the anxieties of the Ulstermen, who whether in earnest or bluff, within a week were reported to be preparing to seize police and military barracks, and depôts of arms and munitions.[3] Next came the Ulster gun-running. It seemed increasingly to be the case throughout the spring and early summer of 1914 that no home rule bill might be passed unless it had the blessing of Ulster, as interpreted by Carson, and the acquiescence of the Conservative party, as conveyed by Law.

Carson and Law continued to be consulted by Asquith. Carson warned of the need to find, and publicly announce, that a basis of settlement would be reached, without which there would be demonstrations in Ulster 'with inevitable collisions and bloodshed leading to a general outburst'.[4] Law feared that his party who were 'growing adverse to any kind of settlement', would 'kick over the traces, and that subsequent negotiation would become impossible'.[5] Both insisted that no settlement was possible which 'purported to proceed on temporary exclusion with compulsory inclusion at the end of the term'.[6] Nonetheless, the bill, which was to be introduced with an amending bill into the house of lords in June, provided for a county option in Ulster, for a term of six years, in accordance with the proposals which Asquith put before the house of commons on 9 March. During its passage through the house of lords, the amending bill — intended to preclude the possibility of any part of Ulster 'being forcibly brought under the jurisdiction of the new Irish parliament' — had been transformed into a measure which excluded from the home rule government 'the whole province of Ulster'.[7]

In Asquith's view, such an exclusion was 'inequitable' and would be rejected by the house of commons — particularly because out of the nine Ulster counties, whereas four

were predominantly protestant, 'three are as unmistakeably
Catholic', and in the remaining two (Fermanagh and Tyrone)
'the division between the two creeds is fairly even, but with a
perceptible Catholic majority'.[8] By that stage, mid-July
1914, Asquith was not prepared to compromise on the
amending bill and in view of 'the dominating opinion' of
their respective followers, neither the government nor the
opposition could 'at the moment publicly offer any acceptable form of compromise'.[9] Carson, for example, had
threatened that 'the government will learn wisdom when a
few days after we move the big banks in London begin
putting up their shutters'.[10] Before the crisis became 'acute'
Asquith proposed to the king that he should invite all parties
concerned to a conference at Buckingham Palace 'for a free
and full discussion', which, even if it did not attain a definite
settlement, would postpone and might 'arrest . . . dangerous
and possibly irreparable action. By 24 July the conference
had done its work; the cabinet decided to proceed with the
amending bill, to propose the restoration of the county
option, but with the omission of automatic inclusion after a
term of years, and the substitution of a 'fresh power of
option' as suggested by Sir Edward Carson.[11]

This was not the solution of Asquith's choosing; yet by
late July, he had reached the position of allowing himself
consider that he simply had no other choice. Whatever
objections he had had to modifying the bill — because of
the difficulties which that might cause for Redmond's
party on account of the 'principle' involved — had been
superseded by the implication of unionist intransigence
and by the anxieties about violence, civil war, bloodshed.
Ten days later Britain was at war; and what might have
become protracted dissensions amongst the groups involved
in the Irish issue were superseded by the exigencies of the
international situation. The home rule bill, in its modified
form, was put on the statute book, with a provision that its
operation might be suspended for a period involving at least
one year.[12] At that stage it was hoped that the time involved
would be long enough for 'ample negotiation'; but it was
neither envisaged nor admitted that instead of resolution
by 'ample negotiation', not only Ulster, but the whole of

Ireland, would eventually defy settlement in the context obtaining in August 1914.[13]

The outbreak of war precipitated a series of crises for the Liberals as the party of government. Asquith, from the outset, had to contend on the one hand with demands, particularly from the Conservative opposition and from those within his own party like Lloyd George and Churchill, that he should organise the country more rigorously for war. Yet at the same time the feeling persisted amongst certain members, not only of the Liberal party, but of the government, that there should not be more organisation, but less. Even on the day when Britain went to war on 3 August, four members of his cabinet resigned; and although three of these rescinded their decision, the incident was symptomatic of the difficulties which persisted for Asquith throughout his remaining period of office. Faced as he was with those discontented Liberals who begrudged and resented any measure taken to put the country on 'wartime organisation', he was simultaneously criticised by others who demanded that the Conservatives, the 'patriotic' party, should be included in government; for they, unlike the Liberals, would put themselves wholeheartedly to winning the war.

Asquith did include the Conservatives in May 1915: Law, Balfour, Chamberlain, Lansdowne, Long, Curzon, Selborne and Carson all joined the war cabinet — as did Henderson for the Labour party. Redmond refused to. But the divisions persisted, both inside and outside the cabinet, as to the best means of winning the war — reflected for example in the controversy over conscription — and that provoked by the differing views as to what size the cabinet should be, to be at its best to conduct affairs. Both of these issues, which were to some extent 'resolved' in 1916, were symptomatic, not only of the impact of the great war on British domestic politics, but of its implications, and those of British political developments, for an Irish settlement. The meeting of the demand for conscription in 1916, and the replacement of Asquith's cabinet with, at first, a smaller war committee, and then by a war cabinet in December 1916 led by Lloyd George, had repercussions in Ireland, every bit as significant as those they had in Britain.

Asquith's reconstruction of May 1915 had no great effect in dispelling the doubts about his management of the war. By October of that year, Kitchener, in charge of recruitment, estimated that he would need to recruit an average of 35,000 men each week until December 1916. This number would be essential in order to reach his proposed army of 3,000,000, a figure which allowed 1,400,000 for the field army, 350,000 for home defence and a reservoir of 1,200,000.[14] When the cabinet considered these estimates, the Liberal party members, McKenna and Runciman, not only opposed recruitment at the rate of 'anything like' 35,000 per week, but would not admit that so large an army in the field was either required or could be maintained.[15] However, the Conservatives Curzon and Long, together with two Liberals, Churchill and Lloyd George, not only accepted the Kitchener figures, but urged that voluntary recruiting would not produce the required results, that it 'could not . . . fill the gap'.[16] At that stage Asquith was not prepared to advocate conscription, particularly as various schemes for additional recruitment were being investigated; with Balfour and Grey he 'provisionally' accepted Kitchener's figures, but claimed at the same time that it was 'by no means clear' that 'any form of compulsion yet suggested would be found capable of producing a better result'.[17]

However, Asquith's position in the cabinet continued to weaken. By November 1915 he was prepared to form a war committee consisting of himself, Balfour, Lloyd George and McKenna. By January 1916 he was prepared to introduce a measure of compulsion and by April, full military conscription. By the end of April, despite the opposition of Runciman and McKenna, he believed that 'in the circumstances the government have no alternative but to proceed with legislation for general compulsion'.[18] The circumstances of the decision reflected the demise of the Liberal party under its last prime minister. Its announcement at the cabinet came with demands from Cecil that the government should resign or reconstruct, from Chamberlain and Curzon that it should show 'more vigour in self defence', while coinciding with a malaise amongst certain Liberals, like Montagu, who felt, nevertheless, that a prime minister must not 'down tools'. Moreover, the decision on conscription not only reflected the implications of the war on British domestic politics, but its implications for the Irish question in Ireland itself. For the combination of the cabinet's reaction to the events of Easter 1916, the prospect of extending conscription to Ireland, and the replacement of Asquith by Lloyd George in December 1916, finally transformed the context of the Irish question from being one of home rule to one of independence.

If the war had removed Ireland from Asquith's problems in August 1914, its prolongation, far from making a solution more likely (in view of the prospect of 'ample negotiation') complicated further the Irish issue. In Ireland, the involvement of Britain in war with Germany had given some nationalists a cause for hope. England's difficulty had traditionally been Ireland's opportunity; and the opportunities afforded by the war, when England was preoccupied elsewhere, were seized by Irishmen in Easter 1916 to rise in arms and proclaim the Irish republic. The rising itself was a small unrepresentative affair; in all, about 1,600 took part. Although there were incidents throughout the country — such as the ambush of police by Ashe's Volunteers in Co. Meath, the holding of Enniscorthy by Volunteers and its subsequent surrender without firing a shot, the mobilisation of a hundred Volunteers in Limerick, and of a thousand in Galway under Mellows whose action included the capture of police barracks but who eventually dispersed — it was mainly confined to Dublin. Here on Easter Monday, a group of about a hundred Volunteers and Citizen Army men occupied the General Post Office in Sackville (O'Connell) Street, hoisted the traditional green flag with the golden harp and another 'tricolour', while one of their leaders, Patrick Pearse, read aloud from the steps the proclamation of the provisional government of the Irish republic: he summoned the Irish people to her flag and exhorted them to strike for her freedom. Most Dubliners were out of the city, many at the races on the bank holiday Monday; and those in the street seemed to pay little attention to the proclamation. Indeed, according to some accounts they preferred to exploit the confusion to loot the shops. Elsewhere in Dublin other leaders occupied 'strategic' positions. Michael Mallin and Countess Markievicz, revolver in hand, led a small band of Volunteers and Citizen Army men to occupy St Stephen's Green, but then retreated to the College of Surgeons; Daly took the Four Courts; de Valera, Boland's Mills — and indeed a group under his command successfully ambushed the first reinforcements of British troops marching into town from Kingstown harbour (four officers were killed, fourteen wounded and 216 other ranks killed or wounded).

This ambush was the most successful operation. Otherwise the numbers throughout the country, as in Dublin, were few; and they were hampered by the lack of arms — on account of the discovery of the gun-running operation from Germany on the *Aud* beforehand — and by the confusion surrounding the order to the Volunteers to come out, which had been issued and then countermanded before the rising. By Thursday, the rising in Dublin was over. On Saturday Pearse surrendered; and orders were sent by him and Connolly to the other positions to surrender, though some of these had not ever been involved in any serious fighting.

The rising, therefore, was not in any sense a national insurrection; though it later assumed a place of momentous importance in Irish nationalist historiography, as the manifestation of popular and republican sentiment from which all subsequent developments followed. In England it acquired a notoriety for the same reason, and because the Irish rebels were thought to be in league with the Germans, with whom the country was at war. Yet, at the time, and despite the spread of national and nationalist movements in Ireland before the outbreak of war — the Gaelic League, the Gaelic Athletic Association (GAA), Cumann na mBan, the Irish Volunteers, the Irish Republican Brotherhood (IRB), Sinn Féin, the Irish Nation League — the rising itself was not ostensibly representative of a united nationalist movement, but rather of elements of two of the many organisations which had developed before the war, namely the IRB and the Volunteers. In one sense, it could be argued that because of these characteristics, it was paradoxically representative:

that is, of the haphazard and disunited bodies which abounded in nationalist Ireland, an amalgam which embraced social and socialist, literary, cultural and gaelic, sporting, ideological, political and non-political, military or volunteer, and republican concerns. Although the leaders of those movements with a political aim had dissociated themselves from Redmond's party before the rising, it was not clear that popularly Redmond had been ditched. Youngsters in Dublin of nationally minded parents sang, throughout the war, the Redmondite verse, to the effect that once the war ended, there would be an Irish parliament in College Green.* Redmond's 'people' had been 'strongly against the rebellion while it lasted'.[19] But once General Maxwell's policy of executing the leaders began, then 'hundreds' 'veered completely round'.[20] In fact 'nothing' could have been 'better calculated to revive the spirit of the "jail journal" than General Maxwell's performance'.[21]

Maxwell, who had been sent to Ireland after the rebellion with full plenary powers under martial law, had been authorised to use his 'discretion' by Asquith's government, though with certain provisos: on the one hand the capital sentence was not 'to be carried out in the case of any women', and on the other it should not be inflicted 'except upon ringleaders and proved murderers'.[22] Furthermore Maxwell was to 'bring the executions to a close as soon as possible'.[23] Although Maxwell had been 'anxious not to have any incident' which would 'disturb public opinion', and would 'confirm no death sentence . . . without reference' to Asquith, the combination of the executions, imprisonments and internments, disturbed both 'public opinion' and Asquith's government.[24] By June 1916, although Ireland seemed to be 'quietening down', there was nonetheless 'considerable feeling against the internment of the Sinn Féiners', which in Maxwell's view was 'fostered by the young priests and women'; and on the anniversary of Wolfe Tone's death on 17 June, after the requiem masses in Dublin, the congregations from the quayside churches

---

*When I am a Member of Parl-i-a-ment,
The War will be over I ween,
You'll never see me in Westminster,
I'll be sitting in old College Green.

'joined up spontaneously and marched in procession waving small Irish republican flags' and '"booed" at officers and soldiers'.[25] By October 1916 Asquith had decided to remove Maxwell from Ireland, and find a command 'elsewhere'.[26]

The rising itself was therefore neither a cause nor a manifestation of the unpopularity of Redmond's party, whereas the executions which followed did contribute somewhat to Redmond's decline, although the measure was probably overestimated by Redmond's enemies. The Irish lawyer, Gavan Duffy, who was himself one of the leaders of a nationalist group, the Irish Nation League, believed that Redmond's initial unpopularity had been due to his reaction to the rising, and his calling 'out for blood from the first' — it being alleged that Redmond knew of the intentions of the military'.[27] Although Redmond and his party subsequently changed their tune and appealed for clemency, on account of the 'urgent messages' he received from Ireland that 'he...[was] done for' if he did not, the change was to little avail.[28] But, although the executions may have prompted some reaction against the party, its decline was far more tied up with that of Asquith himself, to whose party its aim of, and tactics for, home rule had been bound — a decline which had had its origin in the compromises reached, even before the outbreak of war, over the nature and extent of the home rule bill.

But it was not at all clear to whom the party would lose its support, and least of all that it would go to Sinn Féin. Founded in 1905, Sinn Féin had been one of many popular national movements. Its policy had been based on Arthur Griffith's 'Hungarian policy'. Griffith's vision for Ireland had been influenced by his understanding of the Austro-Hungarian model of dual monarchy. Under Griffith, Sinn Féin, meaning 'We Ourselves', sought for Ireland a constitutional position analogous to that of Hungary in the Austro-Hungarian monarchy. Although membership of Sinn Féin may have, and often did, overlap with membership of other national organisations like the Gaelic League (a nonpolitical 'gaelic' organisation) or, later on, the Volunteers (a military type organisation, whose members drilled and wore uniform, set up before the war to 'guard' Ireland's independence, and as a counter to Ulster Volunteers),

Sinn Féin advocated an extreme policy neither before Easter 1916 nor afterwards. Moreover, it was not until late in 1917 and early 1918 that Sinn Féin assumed some of the characteristics believed to have been assumed after the rising, and attributed to it by the British leaders. For it was not until 1917-18 that it adopted as its aim constitutional separation and alluded to the 'Irish Republic' proclaimed in 1916, while simultaneously setting out for itself a set of rules to govern the expanding organisation, which only then began to embrace the allegiance of more and more people (see below pp.13-14).

In the aftermath of the rising and the executions, although the imprisonments and deportations would not help John Redmond, there was no reason to believe they would specially benefit Sinn Féin, as opposed to the other movements.[29] The various movements not only lacked unity, but they were without any radical political attraction, over and above that of Redmond's party. The Irish Nation League, for example, and Sinn Féin were at one only in the opposition of their leaders to Redmond and, paradoxically, in their initial rejection of a course of abstention from Westminster. Throughout 1917 moves for the fusion of both bodies took place. The moves were complicated by the divisions in the Irish Nation League between those who favoured amalgamation, and those who preferred dissolution — though the issues became irrelevant from October 1917, when the new Sinn Féin organisation took off.[30]

The similarities between both organisations, and the confusion as to object and policy between Easter 1916 and October 1917 is best illustrated by the attitudes to the candidacy and election of Count Plunkett as MP for North Roscommon in February 1917.

Count Plunkett's son Joseph had been executed in 1916, and two others had been imprisoned in England. He stood for North Roscommon partly as a Sinn Féin candidate, but partly with the help of the Irish Nation League. Members of the Irish Nation League Council helped him during the election, and claimed that 'the principle of abstention from Westminster' had not been an issue put before the electors during the contest.[31] The matter became important after the election on account of Plunkett's decision, once elected, that he would abstain from Westminster. This decision was not only unpopular with the Irish Nation League, but was — contrary to the assumptions of historians since then — apparently unpopular with Griffith of Sinn Féin and with other national leaders. Plunkett not only persisted with a policy of abstention in his own case, but urged a similar policy for others, despite the wholesale opposition of most of the anti-Redmondite nationalist leaders.

Gavan Duffy, for example, deplored Plunkett's obstinacy and feared that the abstention policy would 'seriously handicap future candidates'.[32] The secretary of the Irish Nation League urged Plunkett to drop his abstention.[33] Other national leaders were dubious about abstention. Sean T. O'Kelly 'emphatically' did not think it would carry; Figgis thought 'it would go in the west' though MacBride said 'no'; McCartan, though personally an abstentionist, did not feel that a radical programme would 'catch on', and if the Nation League did 'go further' then 'we shall only do ourselves harm'.[34] The feeling was that 'no constituency could be carried on that policy'.[35] Griffith's position was unclear, though the rumours suggested he was more against the Plunkett course than for it. Initially it was thought that he 'fell in' with Plunkett's plan, but that he was later 'repenting at leisure' yet failed 'to move' the Count and then claimed he was 'not a safe guide in Irish National matters'.[36] Plunkett, who persisted, determined to organise an assembly which would 'oppose the sitting of the Irish party at Westminster, refusing to recognise any foreign authority over Ireland'; and by May 1917, he was 'certainly gaining ground in Dublin and he and the young volunteers behind him seem to have a much bigger pull than Griffith'.[37] 'In other words the montagne [*sic*] is on top and Griffith is probably being squeezed'.[38] By that stage Plunkett had his own organisation, the Liberty League. However accurate were rumours of a split between Griffith and Plunkett, a settlement had been reached by June 1917: the Liberty League and the Sinn Féin organisation were to be amalgamated under a temporary provisional executive known as the Mansion House Committee 'until a convention of Sinn

Féin Clubs is held which may determine the future policy of Sinn Féin'.[39] On 10 June the Mansion House Committee invited the Irish Nation League to amalgamate with Sinn Féin on the same terms, and the members of the League divided over amalgamation or dissolution.[40]

Besides the Plunkett by-election, there were three other by-elections — in May, June and July — when the anti-Redmondite candidate won. The 'issue', as in the Plunkett case, may not have been clear, but the appeal of the candidates was. In South Longford in May, the candidate, Joe McGuinness, was in Lewes jail for his part in the rising, and the electors were urged to 'Put him in to get him out!' which they duly did. In East Clare in June, the only surviving commandant of the Easter rising, recently released from jail to a bonanza of a popular welcome in Ireland, Eamon de Valera, was returned. In Kilkenny in July, William Cosgrave won. But though candidates may have been 'Sinn Féin', it was not yet absolutely clear what Sinn Féin stood for.

In October 1917 the position changed, when the Sinn Féin convention began on the 25th. A scheme of rules governing the organisational framework of Sinn Féin was adopted, and the scheme affirmed that the aims of Sinn Féin, as set out in the 'Constitution', might not be altered, except by a two-thirds majority vote of the 'supreme governing and legislative body' — the ard fheis.[41] The constitution, in its preamble, referred to the claim of the people of Ireland to 'separate nationhood', to the 'Provisional Government of the Irish Republic' of Easter 1916, and reasserted the 'inalienable right' of 'the Irish Nation to Sovereign Independence'.[42] It alluded to the way in which the proclamation 'of an Irish Republic' in Easter 1916 together with the courage and sacrifices of those 'who gave their lives to maintain it' had 'united the people of Ireland under the Flag of the Irish Republic'.[43]

The preamble referred to those present as 'we, the delegated representatives of the Irish people in Convention, as assembled' and proceeded to 'declare the following to be the Constitution of Sinn Féin'.[44] The 'following' indicated that the name of the organisation would be 'Sinn Féin', that

it aimed at 'securing the international recognition of Ireland
as an Independent Irish Republic', that once that status had
been achieved 'the Irish people may by referendum freely
choose their own form of Government'.[45] It claimed that the
object would be obtained 'through the Sinn Féin organisation'
which would in the name of the sovereign Irish people 'deny
and oppose the will of the British parliament and British
Crown, or any other foreign government' to legislate for
Ireland; and that the Sinn Féin organisation would 'make use
of any and every means available to render impotent the
power of England to hold Ireland in subjection by military
force or otherwise'.[46] It then affirmed that 'in accordance'
with the resolution of Sinn Féin, adopted in 1905, a
constituent assembly should be convoked 'comprising persons
chosen by the Irish constituencies' as the 'Supreme National
Authority to speak and act in the name of the Irish people'
and to 'devise and formulate measures for the welfare of the
whole people of Ireland'.[47]

The Sinn Féin Convention, therefore, not only claimed to
be 'the delegated representatives of the Irish people', but
reaffirmed that the people of Ireland had been united 'under
the Flag of the Irish Republic', by the proclamation of that
republic in Easter 1916 and by the sacrifices of the men 'who
gave their lives to maintain it'.[48]

Developments between May 1916 and October 1917
hardly suggest that radical nationalist leaders or their followers were united about anything, except perhaps their
opposition to John Redmond; in particular, there was no
unity based on allegiance to the 'republican' flag. After
October 1917 the position began to change. Sinn Féin
started to embrace a more significant proportion of the
population, assisted partly by its expanding organisation,
but particularly by its identification with a policy of resistance to the extension of conscription to Ireland, threatened
by Asquith's successor, Lloyd George.

In Ireland, the rising and its aftermath helped to turn nationalist or barely nationalist Ireland to sympathy for the rebels, if
not support for their cause, on account of the measures taken
by Asquith's government to deal with the problem; martial law,
executions, deportations, and imprisonment resulted in the

emergence of heroes and leaders, and in sufficient strength of feeling to bind the various organisations and their members into a 'movement', which became known, inaccurately, in England as 'Sinn Féin'. But it was not merely Redmondite Ireland that had begun to come to an end. In England, shortly before the rising, Asquith had indicated that he would introduce conscription; and this decision, combined with the circumstances under which it came, marked to put it dramatically, the end of Asquithean England. By December 1916 Asquith, even in the aftermath of the rising, had refused to allow the extension of conscription to Ireland, Lloyd George did not.[49] Conscription reflected the divisions which existed in Asquith's government in England. More successfully than anything else, the prospect of its introduction to Ireland promoted the claims of Sinn Féin, rather than Redmond's party, to be the party of nationalist Ireland.

Before he had become prime minister, Lloyd George had been entrusted by Asquith with an attempt to find some kind of Irish settlement which would have the approval of Redmond and Carson. Although the proposals (which provided that the twenty-six counties should have home rule at once and that the six should remain part of Great Britain until after the war) won the support of both Redmond and Carson, ultimately they came to nothing. Initially they were rejected by the Unionists — Lansdowne, Long and Curzon — and they simultaneously failed to dispel doubts as to whether they would, in fact, satisfy nationalist Ireland.[50] Although the proposals had been promoted by Lloyd George, they had fallen within the terms of Asquithean home rule; the settlement proposed would have been accepted, or so Asquith told his colleagues, before the war, and should be accepted now.[51] This should not be forgotten when examining Lloyd George's subsequent interventions in the Irish problem: not only had his proposals been on the basis of pre-1914, but the principle behind them continued to be that which determined Lloyd George's attitude as far as Ireland went. He was then, as he continued to be, and as he admitted to being even as late as 1920, 'still a Gladstonian Home Ruler';[52] having failed in 1916 to find a settlement in that context, he lost interest in doing so subsequently. But for the moment, his only concern was to find more men for the war, and if it were necessary, he would find them in Ireland, in return for the gesture of a settlement.

By January 1917 he was being pressed to do so, on account of the acute shortages expected. Derby, at the war office, thought that conscription in Ireland 'really ... must be considered'.[53] Midleton thought that the matter should have immediate consideration; and that the government 'if they act at all should act speedily: recruitment would most likely fall below the war office estimates, and every month's delay in 'adopting compulsion' in Ireland, would 'render it more difficult to change the present policy'.[54] By 26 January it seemed to Lloyd George, in view of his being worried by the military authorities on the matter, that 'we shall soon have to discuss the best methods of utilising the man power of Ireland'.[55]   Accordingly,   he   instructed   the   Irish   under secretary, H.E. Duke, to submit his 'latest views' as to the 'practicability and advisability of conscription for Ireland'.[56]

Duke believed it would be an 'error in policy' to impose military service in Ireland, without first 'disposing ... of Home Rule'.[57] Whereas conscription 'could be applied without grave risks' with a national settlement, without one, it could only be done 'at the cost of much disturbance ... some bloodshed now and intensified animosities' later.[58]

This view, that the introduction of conscription should be accompanied by a further attempt to offer a national settlement, was one which determined Lloyd George's inclinations until   May   1918.   Contemporaneously   with   proposals   to extend conscription to Ireland there would be a fresh attempt to reach a settlement, and one which, by May 1917, would be left to the Irish themselves to find. Lloyd George, having discussed the matter with Asquith, decided to summon a convention, calling Irishmen 'of all creeds and parties' together, to draft a constitution for their country, which might 'secure a just balance of all the opposing interests' and 'compose' the 'unhappy discords' which had 'so long distracted Ireland'.[59]

If Lloyd George had entertained private doubts as to the prospects of the conference, he kept them to himself. Others did not. From the outset its representative character was suspect. It was alleged, for example, that the proposal merely amounted to a showy gesture of the government's sincerity *vis-à-vis* the Irish, made particularly for the benefit of the Americans. From London, Law was 'not sanguine of anything coming of the attempt'; and in Ireland, by late May there were rumours that Sinn Féin would not be represented, rumours which subsequently became 'fact'.[60] The Ulstermen were reluctant to 'come in'; and in the rest of the country the 'people', according to Dunraven, the unionist peer, remained 'suspicious of a trap', fearing 'failure on the part of a not truly representative body', or dreading 'some arrangement between the Ulster Covenanters and the Irish parliamentary party, involving partition of some kind'.[61] The terms of reference for the convention posed difficulties, as did the selection for the chairmanship. Anxieties and recriminations were provoked, particularly amongst the southern unionists, by Lloyd George's release of the prisoners — amongst whom was de Valera, who then went on to stand for, and win, the East Clare seat.[62] Moreover Midleton feared an 'open and bitter' debate on the matter, for the southern unionists resented the likely predominance of nationalists at the convention, and the government's refusal to appoint additional unionists.[63]

The nationalists to whom Midleton referred included twenty-eight chairmen of the Irish county councils. As Dunraven had noted, they did not include Sinn Féiners, nor would they include representatives of Redmond's party. The proposed convention was seen by its critics as a 'government trick' to 'gain time and stave off foreign pressure', particularly in the United States.[64] In any case Lloyd George determined to proceed; and the convention was summoned to meet in Trinity College on Wednesday 23 July, with a promise that if agreement were reached on proposals, and if there were grounds to believe that these proposals 'met with support from the Irish people', then the government 'would do their best to give them legislative sanction'.[65]

The convention, which began its deliberations in July 1917, continued them until April 1918 — considerations of the final report being due on the tenth. Neither the convention itself, nor the promises to give 'legislative sanction' to its proposals made any impact on Sinn Féin Ireland. Its deliberations began against the background of the four by-elections of 1917 — February, May, June and July — when the anti-Redmondite candidates, Plunkett, McGuinness, de Valera and Cosgrave had won, but when the issues were not quite clear. These have since become known as Sinn Féin victories, but Sinn Féin was not then what it later became. The success of the candidates owed something to their association with 1916, whose impact was increasingly acquiring its disproportionate proportions. There were still many objects for the 'movement', and the convention called by Lloyd George in July 1917 provided another means of identity: the right-minded men would reject it, though the grounds for doing so revealed the confusion of object. For whereas the Irish Nation League joined Sinn Féin in repudiating the 'Lloyd George Convention' in June 1917 (on the grounds that it could have no authority to adopt a constitution for the Irish nation, unless it had been 'elected for that purpose by the Irish people', and was 'free to adopt any form of government decided upon by a majority of its members', a decision which must be 'final and binding') there was no unanimity as to what an acceptable convention might propose.[66] When AE suggested in his pamphlet 'Thoughts for a Convention' that the only satisfactory compromise at present would be 'Colonial Home Rule', Gavan Duffy agreed to sign a manifesto supporting the AE conclusions; while the circular describing the objects of Sinn Féin urged a 'strong campaign' on 'sovereign independence', on putting Ireland's claim for that before the 'peace conference', and on 'abstention from the British Parliament'.[67]

But none of this was clear to Lloyd George's Irish executive. In September 1917, Thomas Ashe, a prisoner in Mountjoy jail, died on hunger strike; thousands paid their respects when his body was laid out in City Hall, Dublin. Ashe had been an IRB man. During the laying out in City Hall, and again during the funeral to Glasnevin cemetery, uniformed Volunteers were prominent. By that stage the drilling of what seemed to Duke to be 'Sinn Féin' men had become widespread, and the activity seemed to him to be serious 'because the . . . leaders intend the drilled men to be a menace to the Union and . . . the imperial connexion'.[68] Despite the drilling and the display at Ashe's funeral, for which Michael Collins, Ashe's friend and fellow IRB member bore much responsibility, the fears of Duke were as yet premature. Although the Sinn Féin convention resolved the inconsistencies of its former position in October 1917, it required more than the presidency of Eamon de Valera, or the new constitution with its declared object of and methods for achieving an independent Irish republic, for the movement to become the Sinn Féin which its enemies thought it already was.

The growth and development of Sinn Féin seemed to co-incide with what struck those involved as the disintegration of effective British administration in Ireland. Although by late 1917 Sinn Féin stood for 'a rupture of the Union', as Duke had put it, it was not clear that it was responsible for, or could be associated with, the condition which alarmed those engaged in the administration of the country. The Irish peers, Midleton, Dunraven and Desart, suffered 'anxiety' at what they considered to be 'the unchecked lawlessness . . . in certain parts of the country'.[69] Midleton warned that the Irish executive, 'by allowing Sinn Féin to go forward practically unchecked', were 'conniving at the entire demoralisation of large parts of the country'.[70] The arch-bishop of Dublin feared that the condition of the country would 'shortly be like that of Russia if our Irish Bolshevists are allowed to run amok' and prominent Irish unionists considered the country to be 'in a more dangerous state' than it had been 'prior to . . . 1916' — its condition deterior-ating with 'cattle drives and unlawful seizures of land'.[71] Dunraven had never, during a 'very long experience of Ireland', seen the law 'so openly derided, or the people in so dangerous a mood'; it would be 'impossible to exaggerate the contempt for authority and the complete indifference to government action' which existed; and the country was 'so completely out of hand' that no executive 'dealing with sporadic cases by the ordinary means at its disposal' would be 'capable of handling the situation'.[72]

Although Lloyd George seemed to be anxious about the unhelpful consequences of these conditions for the convention (which was not due to end until April 1918) there is no evidence that they made any impact on his attitude. His object was to press for 'a settlement in and through the convention' to which end he urged 'concessions on all sides'; in his view the 'only hope of agreement' lay in a solution which provided both 'for the unity of Ireland under a single legislature' and for the preservation of the 'well being of the empire and the fundamental unity of the UK'.[73] By April 1918 he had determined, on the one hand, to announce a measure of home rule after the convention ended, and simultaneously to press conscription through. But because of the urgency of imposing compulsion, compulsion would have to precede home rule; for the completion of the register would need time, and the new parliament could not meet before October at the earliest.[74] He resolved, therefore, to press the proposals for conscription through the house of commons 'with all the support at our command, on the ground that the military need is overwhelming';[75] and he simultaneously decided to change the administration in Ireland on which Midleton had definite views,[76] and in connection with which he had already sounded out Duke.[77]

Three lords justices (of whom one would be Midleton) would be appointed to carry on the government of Ireland, and enforce conscription. Preparations were put on foot for both the government bill and conscription; but Lloyd George was determined that even if his proposals for home rule were rejected by the nationalists, there would be no delay: for the government would then simply see itself 'absolved from proceeding with it' i.e. home rule.[78] By 4 May the Liberals had accepted Lloyd George's plan to issue the order in council simultaneously with the first reading of the Irish home rule bill, which 'must be hurried up for we need the men'.[79]

Both policies, whether to be introduced separately or as a 'package', had their critics. From within the government, Fisher, the Liberal president of the board of education, urged against introducing one without the other; he warned that no conscription should take place before home rule had been 'placed on the statute book' and an Irish executive formed; although it was 'obvious' that conscription would have to be put into operation before an Irish parliament could possibly meet in Dublin.[80] Hankey, the secretary to the cabinet, sent a 'strong appeal' for a 'peaceful solution'. Londonderry, Long and Carson, the Unionists, denounced the package. 'Contingent conscription and home rule' was, in Londonderry's view, a move which 'for folly has never been equalled', and an Irish parliament *'now'* [*sic*] would be a 'Sinn Féin parliament'; Long did not believe in a 'bargain' for that would give Law the 'worst situation' as leader of the Conservatives; it would mean 'a row with both sides' and 'no satisfaction'; instead the two issues should be dealt with separately; the government should announce conscription 'bluntly and plainly'; and although there would be a row, it would soon 'come to an end'; Carson feared that if conscription were to depend on home rule, it would serve as an 'invitation' to the nationalists to make their demands 'so extreme' that they could not be entertained.[81]

If the English critics were confused as to whether the appearance of introducing home rule with conscription should be maintained, or whether the policies would bring greater disorder, or lead to a Sinn Féin parliament, hostile reaction in Ireland was far more straightforward.

By 10 April 1918 plans were being made for an all-party meeting in Ireland 'to formulate a national policy to defeat this menace' i.e., conscription.[82] The plan had been proposed at a meeting of the Dublin Corporation, when it had been suggested that the lord mayor, Laurence O'Neill, should call 'a conference of prominent Irishmen' to arrange 'united opposition to the proposals of the government'.[83] Sinn Féin, the Irish Trades Union Congress, Tim Healy, the Irish party, William O'Brien — all were invited to be represented.[84] Meanwhile the standing committee of Sinn Féin had already decided that on the day when the order in council was issued, 'everyone throughout the country' should 'refuse to purchase any commodities, with the exception of necessary foods, on which the British government levies any tax'; and they should also refuse to pay instalments 'due in respect of land purchase' and 'every and any direct or indirect tax'.[85]

By the end of April two main recommendations had been made to Lloyd George — either to abandon or impose conscription.

It seemed to Duke by 16 April that Lloyd George should abandon conscription. He warned the war cabinet that already a 'complete organisation of resistance to conscription' existed; interference with the railways and the police had 'already begun' and the 'Nationalist Labour leaders' were reported to be making arrangements for a general strike, with a view to 'stoppage of transport and isolation of troops and police'.[86] The measures envisaged by opponents of conscription — passive resistance and a general strike — would effectively prevent 'the calling up of men for service'; while even the parliamentary party leaders intended to discontinue attendance in the house of commons and 'join forces with the revolutionists'.[87]

Midleton disagreed with Duke. He urged immediate conscription. In view of the 'great' and urgent 'need for recruits on the West [*sic*] Front', not only should conscription be applied to Ireland, but the action must be prompt, and must follow 'at once' upon the appointment of the lords justices, of whom Midleton would be one.[88] Midleton recommended that in order to enforce conscription, measures should be taken against its opponents: the leading 'Sinn Féiners' responsible for 'seditious speeches' should be arrested 'at once'; anti-conscription meetings should be prohibited and restrained; newspapers which published anti-conscription articles or speeches should be suppressed.[89] Was the war cabinet prepared for 'immediate action' to deal with conscientious objection? Was it prepared to suppress, if necessary, the *Freeman's Journal* and the *Independent*; to find sufficient labour to carry on the transport service; and in 'the last resort' to come to such an arrangement with Ulster regarding the time and nature of home rule, as would 'prevent Ulster joining the south in resistance to Conscription'?[90]

It remained unclear what exactly the government would do; and 'every day of delay', in Midleton's opinion, rendered the operation 'more difficult'; the 'national organisation becomes more complete' and the 'number of people . . . prepared to join in resistance because they believe the govern-

ment will not face such an organisation becomes greater'.[91]
The difficulty, as Law saw it, was for the British to have an
organisation which would 'make the Irish believe that we are
in earnest'.[92]

In Ireland resistance gathered momentum. By 17 May, the
instructions to be issued to the various branches of Sinn
Féin — the cumainn — were made ready. In general the
country was 'to have nothing to do with any of the . . .
Derby scheme', and they should follow the rule 'No
Attestation' 'No Registration' 'No Exemptions', adopting
throughout a 'negative' attitude.[93] The bishops and priests
should 'advise the people to lay in stocks of food supplies'
and general directions should be issued as to the action of
'individual Sinn Féinidhe' after the move of the order in
council, and if captures should be made.[94]

These developments led to increased doubt and speculation amongst the politicians in London as to the benefits
— or indeed prospects — of either introducing home rule or
imposing conscription; and the doubts were exacerbated by
the rumours circulating about nationalist implications in
German activity. Whether such reports were deliberately put
out in order to damage the prospect of home rule is not
clear; but it is clear that they were employed by those who
had views about what should or should not be done with
Ireland.

Carson, for example, had been apprised of information
recently procured that 'the Sinn Féiners are co-operating
even more with Germany'; and he also warned that if home
rule were 'set on foot' it might not be possible subsequently
'to enforce conscription if the Home Rule Government is
opposed to it'.[95] Austin Chamberlain (who had resigned from
the war cabinet in 1917, but rejoined it in 1918 when he
urged a 'federal' solution of the Irish problem) now pressed
that the government should move against Sinn Féin in connection with the 'German conspiracy'.[96] Chamberlain felt
that even if the evidence for a conspiracy between Sinn Féin
and the Germans were insufficient for a jury, it would be
'sufficient for America'.[97] It should be published 'simultaneously' with the arrival in Ireland of the new lord lieutenant,
Lord French — which was imminent — or with his 'first

definite action against de Valera and other Sinn Féin leaders'.[98] Walter Long, who opposed the 'dual proposals of conscription and home rule', urged on 7 May that the duty of the government 'at this moment' was to deal with 'the German menace in the three southern provinces of Ireland'.[99]

These allusions to a Sinn Féin conspiracy with the Germans in late April and early May 1918 coincided therefore with the doubts as to whether or not home rule would resolve the conscription issue; as they also did with the escalating opposition, for that and other reasons to granting any measure of home rule. Londonderry, for example, warned that 'an Irish parliament *now* is a Sinn Féin parliament'; and Lord Robert Cecil wrote to Law that once the cabinet resolved on a home rule bill, he would 'resign'; for apart from the 'pledges' (i.e. those given to Ulster) the 'price' of conscription had been said to be home rule, whereas it now seemed that home rule would make conscription 'not easier but more difficult'.[100] On 15 May Salisbury submitted a minute to Law signed by nineteen unionist peers reiterating that a home rule bill had no possibility of settling the Irish question; but that its introduction would 'destroy the Unionist party' and 'our friends throughout the country' would consider their leaders had 'abandoned their principles and broken faith with Ulster'.[101]

Although Law initially told Carson, as he did on 28 April, that so far there was no evidence about Sinn Féin 'relations with Germany' which would be 'proof in court', he was less forthright regarding the objections to home rule, promising Cecil, for example, that the matter would not arise 'till after the recess' and in the meantime he would 'discuss the subject' with him.[102] But by 9 May Long's cabinet committee on the Irish government bill had resolved that as a preliminary to its introduction, the Irish administration should restore respect for government, 'enforce the law and above all, put down, with a stern hand, the Irish-German conspiracy which appears to be widespread in Ireland'.[103] Lloyd George agreed that the 'first thing' was 'to enforce the law'; and in the event of a possible 'insurrection in Ireland', the government had its 'counter plans'.[104] On 17, 18 and 19 May the arrest and deportation of the Sinn Féin leaders took place: Griffith, de Valera, McGuinness, Cosgrave, Plunkett, Figgis and many more.[105]

In Ireland the arrests were denounced by those delegated to replace the Sinn Féin standing committee, who issued a public proclamation that England was merely trying to confuse the issue of conscription ('a declaration of war on the Irish people') by 'the pretence that Ireland's attitude is due to a German plot'.[106] Under that 'pretence' Sinn Féin had been 'struck' at.[107] But the Irish people were determined 'to die at home rather than fight for freedom' elsewhere and 'slavery in Ireland'; and the rousing document concluded with the declaration that 'England's will shall be broken' and 'Ireland's honour thereby upheld'.[108] The substitute standing committee continued the work begun in 1917: departments analogous to government departments, 'responsible' for finance, propaganda, food, agriculture, foreign affairs, local government were organised; frequent discussions and decisions took place regarding practical matters such as preparations for by-elections and payment of organisers; serious 'policy' was laid down on matters such as hunger striking prisoners, or, as mentioned earlier (p.18) denunciation of the 'Lloyd George Convention'.[109] The substitute standing committee, now chaired by Alderman Kelly or Fr O'Flanagan, proclaimed that no matter how many leaders might be arrested, there would always be men and women to take their places.[110]

Despite the views of the substitutes, the reasons behind the arrests had been more complicated and confused than Sinn Féin conceded. The objections of certain unionists to proceeding with home rule might not have been taken seriously or might have been overcome were it not for the obvious validity of their criticisms; home rule would not facilitate conscription; and therefore the basis on which the bargain had been settled no longer existed. Moreover, the arrests may have been partly designed to show that the government was determined to 'do something' in reaction to the increasing resistance in Ireland to conscription, and in view of the implications for the government of the events of spring 1918: the shortages on the fronts; the German offensives of the Somme and Marne; the simultaneous defeat of the Asquithean 'opposition' during the 'Maurice debate' on 9 May and the resistance of certain Unionists to the 'dual' proposals of home rule and conscription, and the general clamour that something must be done to enforce the law in Ireland.

But the arrests did not resolve the problem of imposing conscription in Ireland, or gaining unanimous support amongst the Conservatives in England for setting its 'price' at home rule. On 3 June conscription was abandoned; an alternative scheme was published by Lord French indicating that Ireland would be divided into ten districts for the purpose of recruiting, each of which would be asked to provide 50,000 recruits by 1 October.[111] On 4 June when the cabinet's Irish committee met, Chamberlain summed up its feeling as being that the immediate application of both policies was 'out of the question'.[112] Throughout the summer the Liberals — particularly Shortt, Addison and Fisher — hoped and implied that home rule was at least not 'out of the question', despite the reiteration by certain Unionists that it was and would be.[113]

In Ireland the threat of conscription had been of the greatest advantage to the development of Sinn Féin and its popularity, as had been the arrests and deportations of 17-19 May.

Throughout the remainder of the summer of 1918 Sinn Féin included the 'release of the prisoners' in its demands and protested 'against the manner in which the [imprisoned] men were treated'.[114] Despite the British decision of early June to postpone conscription in Ireland at least until October, Sinn Féin did not cease to exploit the threat; and it continued to urge 'the people of Ireland' to make 'every . . . preparation for active resistance'.[115] Its success in having identified itself as a more popular, if not more nationalist, party than John Redmond's, was reflected in the result of the East Cavan by-election result published on 22 June.

Arthur Griffith, founder of the early Sinn Féin and vice-president of the reorganised movement since 1917, was returned with a majority of 1,200 odd over the Irish party candidate. When the Cavan men voted for Griffith, rather than for Mr Redmond's man, they may not have been voting for the complicated and sophisticated separatist organisation to which Sinn Féin aspired under its 1917 constitution; but they were voting for a man whose name had become synonymous with dignified patriotism; who was one of the leaders of Sinn Féin, the party which had become particularly identified with popular resistance to conscription, and who had now been captured and incarcerated in England.

2
November 1918 — October 1920

On 11 November 1918 the armistice began and Britain was
no longer at war. If the war had had an impact on British
domestic politics, the implications of that impact did not
end with it. At its crudest, Asquith had had to include
Conservatives in his government, which he had done in May
1915; and the Liberals, for whom the wholehearted organisation and conduct of the war had provoked a series of
crises, had further differences when Lloyd George replaced
Asquith in December 1916, although it cannot be said that
two definite 'camps' emerged at that stage in support of the
respective leaders. But when in December 1918 Lloyd George
with some Liberal support went to the country on a 'ticket'
with the Conservatives, the divisions began to emerge as
between those Liberals who supported Lloyd George and the
coalition, and those who supported Asquith. Lloyd George
won the election. But his government would depend on
the support of the coalition Conservatives, who had won
338 seats, while those Liberals who supported him had won
136. The opposition, on the other hand, comprised independent Conservatives, Asquithean Liberals, the Labour
party, and Sinn Féin. The Asquitheans had only 26 seats;
Sinn Féin had 73.

The Sinn Féin members would not, of course, come to
Westminster; and although the ending of the war had, in one
sense, made the Irish question matter less, in another it began
to matter more. Over the course of the next three years,
Lloyd George's failure to resolve that question served not only
to damage his personal reputation, but also to undermine
the coalition amongst its own supporters. The Liberals
became as disenchanted with the 'moral' bankruptcy of

the government's Irish 'policy', as the Conservatives did with the government's failure either 'to come away' or 'to govern'. What was serious, however, was that dissatisfaction over Ireland, which increased in late 1920 and throughout 1921, emphasised the disenchantment with Lloyd George and the reservations about the coalition which existed even amongst its own supporters.

This disenchantment had begun to become evident in early 1919, and had been associated with the implications of the peace treaties of Versailles and Sevres. The settlement with Germany in the Versailles treaty, particularly the clauses involving the payment of reparations by Germany, provoked the criticism of both Conservatives and Liberals. In April 1919, 233 Conservative MPs signed a telegram to Lloyd George urging stronger demands on reparations; whereas certain Liberals and members of the Labour party denounced the harshness of the economic settlement as an 'act of madness' and one whose repercussions would be detrimental to Britain; and the criticism was taken up also by Keynes in his *Economic Consequences of the Peace*. There were other issues arising out of the peace treaties or the war which divided the politicians and rendered the coalition more vulnerable, such as intervention against Soviet Russia, or support for the Greeks as against the Turks. In the case of the latter, Lloyd George's interventions on behalf of the Greeks defied the traditional pro-Turk Tory policy, besides dividing him from his Liberal secretary of state for India, Montagu, on account of its adverse repercussions on the 'Moslem world'.

Although much of this was in the future, it was to reflect the way in which the implications of the war, and the peace, began to redound against Lloyd George. Moreover, at home domestic unrest and the strikes or threatened strikes, particularly those involving the triple alliance, reduced Lloyd George's radical appeal, whether to those who believed in him as a 'reformer' or to those who hoped that the coalition was a guarantee against bolshevism.

Moreover, his ministers and those who surrounded him did not inspire confidence; and the extravagant parties, whether abroad at the numerous resorts where the international conferences continued to be held, or at home, did nothing to reassure the sober that the coalition was the government they had wanted. *The Times* had described Birkenhead's appointment (as lord chancellor) as 'carrying a joke too far'; the king had also revealed his reservations about the elevations proposed under Lloyd George — whether Aitken for a peerage in 1916, Smith (later Birkenhead) to lord chancellor in 1919, or Rothermere for a viscountcy the same year.[1] Baldwin's allusion in October 1922 to the prospect of Lloyd George smashing 'to pieces' the 'old Conservative party' as he had done 'the Liberal party to which he formerly belonged', had already occurred to certain Conservatives. Even before the war ended, there were those who had entertained independent reservations about him, as well as about the association of their party with him. Londonderry, for example, had considered that Lloyd George inspired doubts as to 'veracity', and believed that the head of government 'must above all things be known to be honest'. In his view Lloyd George's position was partly due to the determination of the commons to prevent Asquith's returning to power, which gave an 'idea of enthusiasm for Lloyd George' which was 'very far from the case'.[2] Long, in July 1918, felt 'against my will' that Lloyd George was 'really determined to split our party as his own is split' and 'to destroy the old landed interests which have been the backbone of our party'.[3] In addition there had been the most recent unionist opposition to the home rule for conscription scheme; Cecil's threatened resignation; Salisbury's warnings supported by twenty-two peers, that home rule would 'destroy' the party; and Law's feeling that 'under existing conditions', i.e., in September 1918, 'it would be very difficult to justify another attempt at home rule'.[4]

Yet the Liberals, even after June 1918, had refused to abandon home rule. Mond felt the government 'must produce a home rule bill', Shortt's public statement in August 1918 alluded erroneously to the cabinet drafting a home rule bill. Montagu too wanted home rule, particularly after the war, and it seemed to him to be 'not much use' if people said they were 'home rulers' 'if they don't pass home rule'. In November Fisher 'urged' a home rule bill on Lloyd George, on 'the lines' of his letter to the convention, but Lloyd George 'would not have it' and Fisher was 'very unhappy'.[5]

The coalition, therefore, had come into power in December 1918 in the aftermath of the armistice; and the disenchantment about Lloyd George, or the reservations about the coalition amongst its own supporters, existed in some measure at the outset. It is in this context that the Irish question between the armistice in November 1918 and the treaty in December 1921 should be seen; as should the way in which individual and party differences, on the specific Irish issue, escalated during the period. Although in one sense, Ireland did not matter as it had, for example, in 1916 on account of the rebellion or in 1918 on account of conscription, the refusal of the Sinn Féin MPs to sit at Westminster, and their proclamation of an independent Irish republic in January 1919, together with their attempts to gain American and European support for their national aspirations, meant that, even at the outset of the peace, the Irish issue could not be ignored.

On 21 January 1919 the seventy-three Sinn Féin representatives who refused to attend Westminster met instead in the Mansion House in Dublin. In a declaration of independence they claimed that the Irish electorate had 'seized the first occasion to declare . . . its firm allegiance to the Irish republic' at the general election; that as the elected representatives of the 'ancient Irish people' and 'in the name of the Irish nation', 'we . . . do . . . ratify the establishment of the Irish republic and pledge ourselves and our people to make this declaration effective by every means at our command'.[6] The declaration of independence went on to 'ordain' that the 'elected representatives' of the Irish people 'alone' had the power 'to make laws binding on the people of Ireland', and that the Irish parliament was 'the only parliament to which that people will give its allegiance'.[7] It solemnly declared 'foreign governments in Ireland to be an invasion of our national right' and insisted that 'we will never tolerate, and we demand the evacuation of our country by the English garrison'.[8] It claimed 'the recognition and support of every free nation in the world' for 'our national independence' and proclaimed 'that independence' to be a 'condition precedent to international peace'.[9]

The declaration had, in its preamble, referred to English rule in Ireland as having always been based on force. It also referred to the proclamation of the Irish republic in Dublin on Easter Monday 1916 by 'the Irish Republican Army acting on behalf of the Irish people', claiming, as it were, and as the Sinn Féin convention in October 1917 had done, a metaphorical if not a literal descent from 1916. It simultaneously implicated in the declaration of the republic the Irish Republican Army, which, it claimed, was 'acting on behalf of the Irish people'.[10]

The claim was, to say the least, an exaggeration. Sinn Féin's strength and development owed little to 1916 except in that it was mistakenly implicated retrospectively in the rising. The Volunteers, now called the 'Irish Republican Army', could scarcely be said to have been acting in 1916 'on behalf of the Irish people' and certainly not at its behest. At most, what ought to be said is that events had conspired to lend popularity to Sinn Féin; that although membership of the Volunteers and Sinn Féin may have in certain cases overlapped the organisations were distinctive and separate; that while Sinn Féin's success in the December election, its setting up an independent parliament, its declaration of an 'Irish republic' for which it called for international recognition, may have suggested that Sinn Féin was now to follow a more dramatic course than hitherto, the success of that course might largely depend on the Volunteers, whether or not they acted 'on behalf of the Irish people'.

At the Dáil's first meeting on 21 January, twenty-eight representatives were present.[11] Thirty-six others were in prison, four on the run and thirty-seven described as '*as láthair*', i.e., absent. Of the latter thirty-seven, twenty-eight represented the northern counties, Queen's University and Belfast; one, Captain Redmond, represented Waterford; two represented Dublin University (i.e., Trinity College); and the last, Sir Maurice Dockrell, was the southern Unionist representative for Rath O Maighne (Rathmines).[12] On 22 January Cathal Brugha was appointed president of the ministry *pro tem*; he nominated MacNéill as minister for finance, Collins for home affairs, Plunkett for foreign affairs and Mulcahy for defence.[13]

The Dáil then adjourned and did not meet until 1 April, when Brugha submitted his resignation and that of his ministry, and proposed de Valera, now out of jail, as 'príomh aire' (first minister) or president. The proposal was accepted and the new ministry included Griffith (home affairs), Brugha (defence), Plunkett (foreign affairs), Collins (finance) and Cosgrave (local government).[14]

In his statement as príomh aire to the second session of the Dáil in April, de Valera reiterated the 'policy' laid down in January, but he introduced it with greater deliberation, and in the Irish language. The 'first duty' of the government as the 'elected government of the Irish people' would be 'to make clear to the world the position in which Ireland now stands' with 'one lawful authority' which was 'the elected government of the Irish Republic'.[15] In order to secure international recognition accredited representatives would be sent to the Paris Peace conference, the League of Nations, and as ambassadors and consuls to other countries.[16] At home the 'material interests' of Ireland would be 'looked after' by Irishmen; and the work of the government would be funded by a loan: the minister for finance would shortly be publishing a prospectus 'for the issue of a loan of one million sterling — £500,000 to be offered to the public for immediate subscription, 250,000 at home and 250,000 abroad'.[17] The details of policy would be the concern of the individual ministers and the cabinet 'as a whole' and when ready would be brought before the Dáil 'for . . . approval and sanction'.[18]

The general policy of January was reiterated. The Dáil was the sovereign government of the Irish people, and its object was to secure recognition abroad for that claim. At home individual ministries would co-operate with the details arising out of general policy. But it was not clear from the allusions to securing external recognition, and those to establishing domestic departments, precisely how this assembly intended to establish itself as the sovereign government of the Irish republic. Although reference was made to resistance being offered to those English measures which were injurious and unjust, de Valera's statement expressed the nature and limits of his views: the moral right of the Irish to self-determination, the importance of securing international recognition for that claim based on morality and justice, the simple rhetoric introduced in the Irish language for the Irish people. It was neither aggressive nor dynamic, nor was it new. It reiterated the course of January 1919, which had in turn emerged out of the rhetoric and reflections of the 1917 Sinn Féin convention, and had been made possible by the victory of the Sinn Féin candidates in December 1918.

England's right to rule Ireland against the will of the Irish people would be questioned and resisted, but not necessarily in arms. For although de Valera alluded to the Volunteers as the 'foundation of the national army' with whom Brugha, as minister for defence, was 'in close association', his statement was no more a call to arms than that made in January, or indeed any of those made by Sinn Féin.[19] He neither proposed the military overthrow of British institutions in Ireland nor any violent policy. His was a policy of attitude, of recognition or non-recognition, national and international, of Dáil Éireann as opposed to English institutions. His view was underlined by his proposal put to the Dáil before it adjourned that the 'members of the police forces . . . . of the British occupation . . . as agents of the British government, be ostracised socially by the people of Ireland'.[20] He recommended foreign recognition and domestic obstinacy, and his reference to the minister for defence being 'in close association' with the Volunteers did not suggest that the relationship was less tenuous than that which had existed between Sinn Féin and the Volunteers since their foundation in 1913.

In one sense it could be said that the leaders, or officer board, of Sinn Féin had at no stage consisted of militarists; and that the president, vice-president, honorary secretaries and standing committee consisted of nationally minded and leading citizens. The substitute president, for example, from 30 May 1918 had been Father O'Flanagan, and the standing committee had included Alderman Kelly and the prominent Labour party member, Cathal O'Shannon. On certain issues during the summer of 1918 the Sinn Féin committee considered it necessary to work with other groups, such as the Volunteers or Cumann na mBan, on the question of 'Sinn Féin prisoners' dependents', or with the Gaelic League, GAA and Cumann na mBan on maintaining a 'uniform attitude' to specific issues; but in general Sinn Féin officially had little to do with the Volunteers.[21] By August 1918 it seemed to Collins to lack 'direction'; while the men who 'ought to' have been 'directing' were too 'lax' and spent 'little or no time at no. 6' (i.e., Harcourt Street, its headquarters).[22] In Collins's view 'all' was 'not as well as it might be', and even 'officers' in the movement had been 'hob nobbing with people like James O'Connor', the allusion being to the dubious nature of O'Connor's position and his being connected with the 'enemy'.[23] The ard comhairle meeting on 20 August 1918 was 'not a very impressive gathering', or so it seemed to Collins; the attendance was poor and most items 'lacked any great force'.[24] Nor did the release in 1919 of the Sinn Féin prisoners make much difference to Sinn Féin, as far as Collins was concerned. He himself was 'only an onlooker at the standing committee now', the members of which included Drs Dillon and Lynn, Alderman Kelly and Mrs Skeffington (the last two acted as honorary secretaries for Stack and Boland, still in prison). Fr O'Flanagan and Griffith were vice-presidents and de Valera was president.[25]

By May 1919 Collins had become increasingly sceptical of the new standing committee, which seemed to him to have 'demolished' 'all precedents'. For example, instead of accepting Boland's own nomination for his substitute – Con Collins – it had elected Mrs Skeffington, as happened also with the Stack substitute 'alderman Tom' [Kelly] who was indeed elected but, as Collins put it, 'not ... because you [Stack] nominated him'.[26] The position according to Collins was 'intolerable' for 'the policy now seems to be to squeeze out anyone who is tainted with strong fighting ideas or I should say I suppose [with] ideas of the utility of fighting'.[27] None of the Dáil ministers were 'eligible for the standing committee', of whose number only one-third could belong to the Dáil. The result, according to Collins, was a 'standing committee of malcontents' whose 'first act is to appoint a pacifist secretary', and announce Boland's absence. Hence 'our own people give away in a moment what the Detective Division had been unable to find out in five weeks'.[28]

These views not only reflected Collins's objections to the 'pacifist' tendency of the Sinn Féin standing committee, but suggest that there were differences in the 'movement' as early as 1918 and 1919; that it was not 'or part of it at any rate' was not 'fully alive to the developing situation'; that Sinn Féin 'inclined to be ever less militant and more political and theoritical'; and the 'rumours, whisperings, suggestions of differences between certain people . . . rather pitiful and . . . disheartening' continued to belie the appearance of national unity implied by de Valera in the Dáil, and confuse attitudes as to how national policy could or should be achieved.[29] For, by contrast with de Valera's 'moral resistance' proposals, the Volunteers, whose reorganisation and unity had also been boosted by the conscription crisis, and of whom Collins was adjutant-general, had been conducting attacks on policemen and raids for arms.

As early as May 1917 the Volunteer executive had indicated in a letter sent out that its duty was to put the Volunteers 'in a position to complete by force of arms the work begun by the men of Easter week . . .' Throughout 1918 there had been raids for arms by individuals or groups of Volunteers. In January 1918 there had been a raid in Bansha, Co. Tipperary for 'arms for the Irish army' and the following month there had been another from Rockingham House near Boyle. Although in March Volunteer leaders spoke out against raids, they did not stop. In April a Tipperary Volunteer leader, Dan Breen, stepped up the raids, despite the prohibition of the executive; and at the same time Liam Lynch, a Cork Volunteer leader, gave up his regular job to prepare, according to his biographer, for armed struggle.[30] What should be noted about these events is that they were sporadic; that they were the result of local initiative; that after March they had been conducted against the express orders of the executive; but that that executive had as early as 1917 alluded to completing 'by force of arms' the 1916 'work'; and that some, though by no means all, of those involved in these sporadic incidents may have been looking to such an armed struggle. But what should also be stressed is that despite the formal connection between the Sinn Féin leaders and the Volunteers — Brugha was chief-of-staff and de Valera president since the Volunteer convention of 1917 — there was no indication of closer links between both. Nor was there any evidence, for example, that Sinn Féin encouraged such activity.

In January 1919 the position was altered, nominally. As the Dáil was meeting for its first session, masked Volunteers in Co. Tipperary attacked two constables carrying gelignite to a quarry at Soloheadbeg, shot them dead, and stole their arms. In Co. Cork, an attempt was made at Macroom to disarm soldiers near their camp on the initiative of local Volunteers. Although there is no evidence that the Dáil at its first session considered the matter of the Volunteers or the attacks, on 31 January a directive was issued in the Volunteer paper *An tÓglach*, edited by Beaslai, which indicated that Dáil Éireann, the national authority, was behind the Volunteers. It sanctioned them to inflict death on the state's enemies, whether British police or soldiers, whom each Volunteer was entitled 'morally and legally . . . to slay'.[31]

It is not clear whether this had been done on Brugha's initiative: Brugha was now acting president of the Dáil as well as Volunteer chief-of-staff. Collins was not involved, nor was de Valera. The latter was in Lincoln jail, and Collins was in England with Boland arranging his escape which took place successfully on 3 February. In the next, April session of the Dáil, Collins took up his post as minister for finance, and de Valera became president. By May 1919, Collins was castigating the Sinn Féin executive for being 'pacifist' and for trying 'to squeeze out the fighting' men; he was also telling the Volunteers to 'fire shots at some useful target or get to hell out of it' in his capacity of supervising the organisation of the Volunteer brigades.[32] From June 1919 onwards, the campaign against the police escalated, as did Collins's special campaign directed against the British detective and intelligence division in Dublin.

The escalation proceeded without de Valera, who in June left for America to secure recognition for the Irish republic; to float an external loan; and to influence the Americans against pledging themselves to recognise Ireland as an integral part of British territory (which they might otherwise do by supporting article ten of the covenant of the League of Nations). De Valera's mission in America does not concern us here; but suffice to say that he was out of Ireland from June 1919 until December 1920. He was therefore removed from the escalation of the raids and the attacks on policemen, and the formal decision by the Dáil in August 1919 that the Volunteers would take an oath of allegiance to it. This proposition had been Brugha's. He was now minister for defence, and he introduced a motion that various persons and 'bodies' including 'the Irish Volunteers' should 'swear allegiance to the Irish republic and to the Dáil'. He suggested that the present constitution governing the Irish Volunteers 'prevented them from being subject to any other body but their own executive'. He added that at their next convention it was proposed to ask them 'as a standing army to swear allegiance to the Dáil', for as such 'they should be subject to the government'.[33]

Although the motion was passed, it was not necessarily contentious; not did it become so until 1922, when, as will be seen, certain Volunteers demanded that control revert to their own elected executive. The campaign escalated, independently of and encouraged by headquarters. Attacks may have been the result of local initiative, or headquarters instructions; the guns may have come from Dublin; and though some of the money to finance the campaign was passed by the Dáil, it does not seem that that body — despite the 'oath' administered to the Volunteers — either interfered with or accepted formal responsibility for the campaign until March 1921.

Despite the differences of approach and the distinctions between the Volunteers who were shooting policemen and raiding arms, and de Valera who proposed resistance and moral persuasion (a position which had been reflected in Collins's resentment at the 'pacifist' nature of the Sinn Féin executive), British officials in Ireland initially did not distinguish the groups although some of the politicians in London did. The Volunteers were to them 'Sinn Féin' volunteers; and, if trouble already existed, they predicted there would soon be more and more. The lords justices (Wylie, Shaw and Ross) all thought that 'Sinn Féin, combined with the Larkin labour people, are on the eve of very serious action' and were in possession of sufficient high explosive 'to blow up every railway bridge in Ireland'. They wanted the cabinet to 'provide for an immediate emergency', so that 'prompt orders' would be carried out by the troops 'without waiting for instructions from London'.[34] Macpherson, the chief secretary, when reporting to the cabinet on 15 May concerning an incident which involved an attack on a train the previous evening in which a constable was killed, claimed it was the work of 'Sinn Féiners'.[35] He feared that there would shortly be an 'attempt at rebellion' and that more forces were now required in Ireland.[36] He was not at all clear as to the government's policy, and claimed he would 'be pressed to define' it 'generally'.[37] French, the viceroy, wrote on 19 May that 'every day' brought 'fresh proof of the underground action' by 'these Irish Volunteers' who were 'nothing more or less than a regular constituted and organised Sinn Féin army ... openly acknowledged and espoused by Mr de Valera and all the other leaders'.[38]

The problem, therefore, was clear to the officials. In Ireland the 'Sinn Féin' Volunteers engaged in 'underground activity' and would shortly attempt a rebellion. They wanted more troops and power to deal with an emergency. In addition Macpherson considered the Sinn Féin Volunteers must be proclaimed; although he did warn Law that if this were done it would mean 'OPEN WAR [*sic*] with all its horrific consequences' and reminded him that it was 'fatal' in Ireland 'to attempt ... action unless and until everything is complete to ensure its success'.[39] As a first step the Dáil could be proclaimed and, 'if need be, the Irish Volunteers'.[40]

Macpherson's contention on 15 May that he would be 'pressed to define the government's policy' on Ireland was borne out by the reactions of the politicians to his proposal that the Sinn Féin Volunteers be proclaimed. Over the course of the next four months it became clear that neither Lloyd George nor Law wanted a 'policy', or indeed had one. However, in response to demands made by the officials or the Liberals, from time to time they did claim, or appear, to have one; it was only the following October that both resolved to proceed with implementing a home rule bill — despite believing that it would not satisfy the Irish. In the meanwhile, whereas views as to what might be done continued to change, neither Lloyd George nor Law believed that anything should be done.

In May, for example, Lloyd George was in Paris when Macpherson's proposal that Sinn Féin be proclaimed was discussed. At that stage the Liberals Fisher, Shortt and Addison were both 'concerned' at the state of Ireland, and 'disturbed' by the proposed proclamation. More generally, they were reported to be 'deeply apprehensive' about certain aspects of the Paris peace settlement and 'the growing signs of criticism in this country'.[41] Yet Fisher would not say he 'would not proclaim Sinn Féin', though warned they (i.e., the ministers) must be 'very careful'.[42] Moreover, the Conservatives in the cabinet were neither certain nor steadfast. Chamberlain considered the government was 'clearly entitled to do it'.[43] Long felt that 'unless drastic action' were taken 'following on [the] proclamation', then it would be 'useless'.[44] Law, from initially considering the proclamation of Sinn Féin was 'probably . . . quite right', came to be more uncertain.[45] On the one hand he felt it would be a 'serious thing' to suppress an organisation 'which represented a great part of the south of Ireland'; and on the other that they would find 'it could not be effectively done'.[46]

In June, following the killing of a district inspector in Tipperary on the 23rd, the question was reopened to some extent. Lloyd George was again in Paris and so was Law. In their absence the cabinet was told of more specific proposals for the proclamation of Sinn Féin and its organisation in a limited area of Tipperary, for which end French wanted approval 'to take immediate steps'.[47] Curzon, who presided, was 'in favour', but Shortt was 'against', and 'probably' Fisher.[48] Long thought the Irish government should be given 'a free hand', the murders of police being 'the worst features' yet 'in the Irish situation'.[49] Fisher feared that proclamation would not 'protect the lives of constables' and warned that Sinn Féin was a 'very composite movement' embracing 'not only academic visionaries and advocates of physical force' but 'many holding ordinary nationalist views'.[50] Shortt alluded to what he thought to be the important distinction as between the Volunteers, 'the most dangerous organisation in the country' and 'responsible for these murders', and Sinn Féin who 'would be relieved . . . if the . . . Volunteers were proclaimed'.[51]

Samuel (the attorney-general) doubted that proclaiming Sinn Féin 'in Tipperary only' would be beneficial, for the counties 'adjacent to Tipperary would not be affected'. Instead he thought the Dáil might be proclaimed, and perhaps the Volunteers. Curzon indicated that he would wire French asking whether the Irish government was 'unanimous'.[52] From Paris came the news that Lloyd George, who had discussed the proposal with Law, was not prepared to oppose the decision, if taken on the basis that 'the whole of the Irish government' favoured it, and 'so long' as they considered it 'the only ... way of dealing with the question'.[53]

The views of the politicians, therefore, were somewhat confused and continued to change; and whereas there was particular confusion in May when the prospect of proclaiming Sinn Féin as a whole was raised, there was less in June when it was a case of one county — and when neither Law nor Lloyd George was in London.

Whereas it seemed that initially the views of Chamberlain, and subsequently those of Curzon, were clear — to support the course advocated by the Irish government — this was not true of their colleagues. Although the Liberals in general had been against, Fisher, for example, did want policemen to be 'protected' and only appeared 'probably' to be with Shortt (above p.40). Long was with Law; but Law considered proclamation 'right' without wanting to proceed with it, because of both its political repercussions on the south of Ireland and the difficulty, militarily, of imposing it. The 'clearly' defined policy, which he claimed the government in fact had, was nothing more or less than what it had been 'throughout — of supporting the Irish government in taking whatever measures they think necessary to secure orderly government in Ireland'.[54] For Law, until September 1919, there was a limit to the kind of measure considered necessary to preserve order.

For Lloyd George too there was also a limit. His views on Ireland, when he chose to have them, amounted to bored and resentful repulsion. He believed that 'Ireland always had hated England' and 'always would', and he seemed to have 'surrendered' to 'the most extreme anti-Irish hatred'.[55] In August, in the course of a grand review of the condition of his country after the peace, he referred to the poisoning implications of the Irish question for domestic developments.[56] It had, for example, 'more to do with the existing industrial unrest than the great majority of people imagined'. The policemen on strike, the many agitators actively engaged in various parts of the country 'were generally of Irish extraction and they were creating a vicious atmosphere'.[57] Moreover, a 'satisfactory settlement of the Irish question' was not merely 'most important from the point of view . . . of . . . the industrial world' but it also was on account of 'our relations with the dominions and the United States'.[58] Yet Lloyd George knew that there could be no 'satisfactory settlement' of the Irish question; that, as he had discovered in 1916, and again in 1917 and 1918, the Irish would not accept a settlement which was 'satisfactory'. Lloyd George, therefore, was reluctant to introduce any 'policy', knowing as he did the difficulties it would meet. He would prefer to do nothing; but if pressed, as he was for example by Grey in August when leaving to become ambassador in Washington, by Fisher, or by Macpherson, he resolved to be as vague as possible about the provisions which might ultimately be included in a bill. But the bill would not settle the matter, for that could not be done. Its objects would be to allay criticism while simultaneously avoiding antipathies. Lloyd George had told Grey, for example, on 7 August (when the latter had been urging a new scheme on Lloyd George, rather than the old home rule scheme which would 'be worse than useless politically in the U.S.') that he might tell the Americans that the government did not wish to limit itself to 'any definite policy'; and that a customs policy would receive 'careful consideration', though it might present 'considerable difficulties as long as Ireland is not united'.[59] But he did not envisage an indefinite military policy. On 5 August he had asked at the cabinet whether it was 'really necessary to retain in Ireland all the troops who were there', i.e., 'a large garrison of 60,000, each man of which cost . . . approximately £250 yearly'.[60] At that stage he was told by Churchill that the Irish government 'were engaged in ruling a country whose people wished to rebel', that more and more troops were being demanded; that all he (Churchill) could do 'was to supply the troops'; and that in any case the position would 'probably be easier' in a few months, as the people were 'beginning to lose faith in the protagonists of Sinn Féin who had carried out none of their promises'.[61] Lloyd George seemed to accept this line. One week later the 'ten year rule' was laid down: that is the rule that defence estimates for the services must be based on the assumption that 'the British Empire will not be engaged in any great war during the next ten years'. It was indicated that in regard to Ireland, although on account of 'present conditions' a 'garrison in excess of the normal' might be needed, none the less 'within twelve months there is a reasonable probability that a normal garrison will suffice'.[62]

On the 5th, although the minister of health had suggested 'we had everything to lose by postponing a decision on the Irish question' and although Fisher felt the government should 'at least announce ... that they were not going to be content with a purely negative attitude', Lloyd George demurred, supported by Churchill and Long.[63] Churchill did not believe the 'present ... a good time to look for an Irish solution' nor did Long, who remarked that Lord French had informed him 'of a considerable improvement in the temper of the country ... during the last three months'.[64] Lloyd George, for his part, reminded his colleagues that the government had 'already gone beyond' what Fisher called a 'negative attitude' in the offer they had made to Redmond before the Irish convention.[65] He pointed out that it would be 'very difficult' in any case 'to produce a policy before the recess, especially since there would be no opportunity of carrying it through before the autumn'; and the war cabinet had 'as much as they could do ... to deal with profiteering, finance and housing, as well as announce a coal policy in the next fortnight'.[66]

And that was that. By 23 August he had surrendered, or so it seemed to Spender 'to the most extreme anti-Irish hatred' and he claimed that he could 'easily govern Ireland with the sword'.[67] Within three weeks his government had proclaimed Dáil Éireann, on Macpherson's advice. Whereas Macpherson initially considered 'we had to allow these members [i.e. of parliament] to sit together *in consultation* if they wished', he had 'made up' his mind that 'we would act' 'whenever they . . . conspired by executive acts which could be clearly proved to overthrow the duly constituted authority'.[68] In his view they had 'attempted to usurp government' and he had acted; like Lloyd George, he did not believe that the Sinn Féiners would 'accept any settlement'.[69] If they did, it would be 'in their eyes, only a temporary one', for they would 'work night and day to get complete separation'.[70] But the proclamation of Dáil Éireann was not regarded as an extraordinary measure by either Law or Lloyd George. Neither believed, even in the face of frequent attacks on the Irish police, that extraordinary measures – that is, beyond 'supporting the Irish government in taking whatever measures they think necessary to secure orderly government in Ireland' – were called for.[71] Lord French had advised that 'we must be most careful not to exaggerate [the] . . . significance' of 'those isolated outrages'.[72] Both Law and Lloyd George were willing to follow such advice; whereas Lloyd George may have been prepared simply to accept that Sinn Féin was 'on the wane', Law did hope that French's views (which were 'confirmed' by Macpherson), were 'right'.[73]

This was the background against which the cabinet set up its committee 'to explore the ground' on the Irish question. Although theoretically Lloyd George would have liked a solution, he did not believe one was possible in the context of autumn 1919. Nor was he in any hurry to find one, as he had revealed as recently as August. There is no evidence that he was, or had been, impressed by the interventions of the Liberals, which were neither acrimonious nor critical; and though prepared to indicate for the benefit of the Americans that he would consider concessions on the customs issue, he would not be limited to a 'definite policy'. Although he did not like spending so much on the garrisoning of the country, it was anticipated that the present level would not be required indefinitely and in a year perhaps it could be reduced. The cabinet committee on Ireland, which had been decided upon in October 1919, might seem, therefore, to be something of an anomaly.[74] To some degree it was.

For its position was simply, as Law put it, 'to explore the ground'; and 'something' had 'to be done' because Asquith's home rule bill, postponed since before the war, would 'automatically' come into force 'on the ratification of the last treaty'.[75]

The committee was chaired by Long. French and Macpherson belonged *ex officio* and Fisher, Birkenhead, Shortt, Geddes, Horne, Worthington-Evans, as well as a Mr Roberts and a Mr Kelleway, were full members.[76] The committee would meet three times each week and would 'in the first instance' confine itself to discussing 'main principles of action'.[77] When these were agreed Lloyd George would be consulted; and if he in turn agreed 'to the main principles of action suggested by the committee' then a bill could be 'worked out'.[78]

The committee, therefore, from being appointed to 'explore' the situation, had quickly decided that once agreement had been reached on 'main principles', and once Lloyd George had concurred, a bill would be drafted. Given the prospect of the Asquithean bill automatically coming into force, there had been two alternatives: either to repeal or postpone that bill, or 'simultaneously with the suspending of the home rule act' to introduce yet another.[79] It was this last course which Lloyd George now favoured: for if the home rule bill were merely postponed, there would be, according to Law, 'violent attacks not only from the Maclean Liberals and the Labour party' but 'a large number of Liberals now supporting Lloyd George ... would turn against the government'.[80] Yet there was also the difficulty that any bill which might be introduced 'without a complete break-up of the present government' would, in Law's view, 'receive almost as much opposition in the house of commons' as a 'simple postponement' of the act, because of its seeming 'so inadequate'.[81]

In any case, by 23 October the committee had decided that rather than just repeal the 1914 act, 'some alternative policy' must be suggested.[82] The proposals discussed so far included one parliament for the whole of Ireland, with Ulster safeguards, as well as various suggestions for two parliaments.[83] By 4 November it was proposed to 'follow the peace conference' by respecting the principle 'both of respectable government and of self-determination' and to give 'to the two parts of Ireland immediately *state rights* [*sic*]' as well as 'a link between them' and 'the power to achieve Irish unity'.[84]

From the outset there were two particular problems. The first involved the prospect of Sinn Féin rejecting a bill, as well as its being unwelcome to Unionists; and the second, the area to be included in a 'northern' parliament, that is if there were to be two.

The prospect of Sinn Féin rejecting the bill would not deflect the politicians from proceeding with it. For, by November 1919, the proposed home rule bill could be seen as a purely tactical move. Worthington-Evans and Birkenhead thought it 'probable' that the Sinn Féiners would 'reject the offer with contempt' and that the Ulstermen would 'not welcome it'; but they none the less thought it 'right' to 'put forward the proposal so that the offer made . . . should be placed on record and proceded with'.[85] In addition Birkenhead considered the bill would strengthen 'our tactical position'; indeed he was 'absolutely satisfied that the Sinn Féiners will refuse it'; and he would not otherwise 'be a party to . . . the offer' which if accepted would be merely used 'for the purpose of . . . separation'.[86] Lloyd George would 'fight' to prevent 'separatism' and was determined to 'govern' Ireland if Sinn Féin proved intractable.[87] In any case something had to be done in 'view of our relations with the dominions and the United States' and on account of the 'specific pledges' given to Grey on being appointed ambassador in Washington.[88] Because it seemed that the terms of the schemes proposed were 'not likely to be acceptable' to Sinn Féin, there was a lack of urgency at the cabinet about the substance given and rather a feeling that preparations should simply proceed.[89]

As the drafting and discussions proceded throughout December, the second problem emerged. 'Ulster' had resisted home rule before the war; but it seemed that now it was more likely to accept it under a separate northern parliament. What in this case was to be the area of its jurisdiction? The question at issue was whether six of the Ulster counties, or the whole nine, should have their own parliament; and the decision, whatever the final choice, would none the less be taken in the context of the cabinet's general feeling that the 'ultimate aim' of its policy 'was a united Ireland with a separate parliament of its own . . . achieved without offending the Protestants in Ulster'.[90] 'Ulster', as Carson put it, 'must be won by kindness'.[91]

The arguments for the nine- and the six-county units continued to be made by the respective protagonists throughout December 1919. Both sides tended to invoke the currently fashionable principles of 'self' or 'national' determination, or of borders established after plebiscites, to justify the positions adopted.

There were strong arguments for the nine-county unit. These led the cabinet, on 3 December, to adopt the view that the whole of the Ulster area would be the administrative unit.[92] It seems that the arguments used were the same as those which had previously been advanced against including the six-county area in the United Kingdom when the rest of Ireland got home rule.[93] During that discussion the cabinet had been reminded that the 'Ulster Covenanters had bound themselves to treat Ulster as a unit' and would therefore 'be bound to create the strongest possible opposition to . . . this plan'. Moreover, it would be 'equally unacceptable to the Irish nationalists and all . . . moderate elements in the south and west' on whom the government 'would have to depend ultimately for support'.[94] The administrative difficulties would be 'very great', while the 'prospects of the eventual unity of Ireland would be greatly diminished by the exclusion of the six'.[95] These, then, were the considerations invoked in the decision not to permit the six counties to remain 'part of the UK'; and they were subsequently alluded to in support of the decision to support the nine-county rather than the six-county unit.[96]

On the 10th, allusion was again made to the prospect of 'a united Ireland with a single parliament' as 'the ultimate aim of the government's policy'.[97] Those present were reminded that another of 'the principal' objects was 'to produce a good effect in the self-governing dominions, as well as in the United States . . . and other foreign countries'. This could not be achieved 'by anything short of a measure' which 'paved the way for a single Irish parliament'.[98] By 19 December the relationship between the nine-county unit and the 'ultimate aim' of government policy had been more clearly set out. At that stage it had been urged that 'if' the 'ultimate aim' was indeed a 'united Ireland', then it would be 'better that the jurisdiction of the northern parliament' should extend 'over the whole of Ulster which included both Roman Catholics and Protestants ... urban and rural' and was 'by its size ... more suited to possess a separate parliament'.[99] 'Ulster' in fact was a 'geographical unit' and this area was 'more logical' and would 'in many ways' be 'easier to defend in parliament'.[100]

But against the nine counties and in favour of the six there were strong protagonists. Even on 3 December when the cabinet decided in favour of the larger unit, provision was made for the matter to be reconsidered.[101] Reference had been made to the 'principle of self-determination adopted by the allies ... and supported by the British government' at the Paris peace conference; and if the six counties desired, for example, to remain part of the UK, 'why ... should they not be permitted to decide by plebiscite'?[102] Moreover, 'the rate of increase' in the Catholic population, was such that if the nine-county unit were adopted 'the Protestants would be swamped by a ... Catholic majority'; while it was also considered desirable to make those in the northern unit 'as homogeneous as possible'.[103] In addition it became increasingly evident that the 'trend of opinion' amongst 'responsible Ulster politicians' favoured 'limiting the scheme' to the six; particularly as the idea of governing the extra three counties with a 'nationalist majority' was 'not relished'.[104]

Craig from the start preferred 'six counties'.[105] With his colleagues he indicated that they had doubts as to whether a northern parliament could 'effectively ... govern' the three nationalist counties. He suggested privately that a boundary commission be established 'to examine the distribution of population along the border of ... the six counties' and to take a vote in the districts 'on either side ... and adjoining that boundary' where a 'doubt' existed as to whether the inhabitants would prefer to be included in the northern or southern area.[106] When the cabinet was told of this suggestion on the 12th, it was pointed out that such a procedure 'would be in consonance with the principles and practice . . . at the peace conference'; for, 'whenever possible, the boundary had been adjusted on ethnological grounds'.[107] Moreover, it was recognised that in Ireland, as in 'most of the cases dealt with by the peace conference', it would be 'impossible to avoid the inclusion of isolated districts' of Protestants in the south and 'vice versa, the inclusion of Roman Catholics' in the north.[108] Balfour believed that if the peace conference had been 'delimiting the new frontier . . . we should not have included in the Protestant area so large and homogenous a Roman Catholic district as that (say) of the greater part of Donegal'.[109] Balfour continued to argue against the nine- and 'in favour of the six-county unit'.[110] He did not 'like the idea of Irish unity' and did not 'wish to encourage it'.[111] He disagreed with the 'general trend' of opinion in the cabinet (which envisaged unity as its 'ultimate aim' and adhered to the nine-county unit). He warned that if 'a *Hibernia Irredenta*' were to exist 'within the province of Ulster' the difficulties of its parliament would be added to, and 'you will repeat on a small scale the troubles' which existed in Westminster between 'the advent of Parnell . . . in 1878, and the blessed refusal of the Sinn Féiners to take the oath, . . . in 1918' – throwing on the Belfast executive 'the same embarrassments from which the executive in Dublin is now suffering'.[112]

By 19 December 1919 a final decision was needed. Lloyd George would shortly be making a statement on the bill. The cabinet, however, reached no decision in view of the objections on both sides and the additional contentions in favour of a six-county area, i.e., that unity would be best secured by a scheme 'acceptable to those who worked it' and that it would be 'difficult' for the government 'to force' one through which would be 'unacceptable to both their friends and their critics'.[113] It was simply decided that Lloyd George must explain to parliament the courses which were open: there could be the 'whole of Ulster' or the six counties 'only'; or the six counties with the additional provision for a boundary commission 'to draw the exact line of demarcation' with a view to including the Catholic or Protestant communities living near the border in the south or north respectively.[114] But he should also reveal that the government was 'inclined . . . towards the six counties solution' while prepared 'to consider favourably the appointment of a Boundary Commission if generally desired'.[115]

The details and arguments in connection with the area to fall within the jurisdiction of the northern parliament reveal that the government had not initially intended to restrict the unit to the six counties. Its 'general' attitude to the bill was that it should be framed bearing in mind its effect on the dominions, the United States, and other 'foreign' countries and that its 'ultimate aim' should be the unity of Ireland. On this basis, it held firm on 'the nine'. But following the interventions of Craig, who claimed that a northern government might not effectively govern the three 'nationalist' counties, and that the area should be limited to the six but with provision for a boundary commission, both the cabinet and Long's committee began to waver. When it came to introduce the matter into parliament, it seemed important to avoid opposition from friends and critics alike. Moral justification for the six-county unit could clearly be seen to derive from the principles laid down at the Paris peace conference. In practice the details of a six-county settlement could be worked out — as was and would be the case with the ethnic minorities and majorities in Europe from Schleswig to Istria — by plebiscites and boundary commissions. These were the means advocated and employed by the peace settlements of 1919. The inconsistencies which might result had been and continued to be acknowledged as inevitable, if not desirable (such was the case, for example, with the pockets of Germans now placed under the jurisdiction of the Poles, or under that of the new Czechoslovak state).

On 19 December it was decided at the cabinet that Lloyd George should explain to parliament that three courses lay open, but that his government 'leaned' towards the six-county parliament with, if desired, a boundary commission. What was ironical, if not indicative of the whole discussion about the delimitation of the northern area and of the bill in general, was that there would be no Irish nationalists in the house during the discussion. Their absence would be the ultimate reflection of the politicians' attitudes to the bill. From the outset there had been misgivings as to its reception by the Irish. They would reject it, or else simply use it to declare a republic.

It was an essential 'tactical' measure *vis-à-vis* world, American and dominion opinion. The initial proposal to 'explore' the whole question had been promoted by the feeling that something must be done to replace the Asquithean bill which would otherwise automatically come into force. What became important subsequently were the considerations of 'American', 'dominion' and 'foreign' opinion. Although it would not solve anything in Ireland, the *bona fides* of the government was being tested. Hence the constant reiteration of what the 'ultimate aim' of its policy was: a united Ireland which would satisfy those abroad interested in the matter, and on which account the cabinet initially resolved on the nine-county 'Ulster' unit, rather than the six. But it became clearer and clearer that the Ulstermen did not want the nine and that they might not be in a position to govern the extra three, or so they claimed. It was eventually decided that there was little sense in antagonising both the 'friends' as well as the critics of the government; while the 'principles' of the peace conference, self-determination on ethnological grounds, and its practice, which employed plebiscites and boundary commissions, seemed to afford sufficient precedent and justification for the alternative 'six-county Ulster'. By February 1920 the nine had been abandoned in favour of the six: Londonderry, Antrim, Down, Armagh, Fermanagh, Tyrone, together with the boroughs of Belfast and Londonderry.[116]

During November and December 1919, the politicians expressed reservations about the bill affording any solution to the Irish question. But once it had been drafted and introduced into parliament, those involved began to hope, if not to act on the assumption, that it might do so.

The king's speech on the opening of parliament in February 1920 would allude to the condition of Ireland as a cause for 'grave concern', but would then indicate how it was hoped that the bill shortly to be introduced would provide 'a just and generous solution'.[117] Against the ever escalating numbers of raids for arms, attacks on policemen throughout the country, and systematic undermining of the detective branch in Dublin, the two leaders, particularly Lloyd George and Law, were determined to look upon the bill as affording a solution, provided the necessary preparations for its success were made: i.e., that law and order be restored, for which purpose there would be 'new men and new measures'. Both Lloyd George and Law maintained this view, despite, or on account of, the advice of many of the new officials. Whereas these maintained that only a new initiative or a 'bold stroke' could help to provide a solution, neither Lloyd George nor Law would contemplate such a 'stroke'; for Law was a Unionist and Lloyd George was what he continued to describe himself, 'a Gladstonian home ruler'.

Even as the bill was being drafted in December 1919, the condition of the country had been worsening. Macpherson felt on 22 December that Ireland might 'have to be seriously reinforced in the next fortnight'. Henry Wilson, who considered the home rule proposals 'farcical' felt the 'only thing' to be done was 'to keep law and order . . . with police and the civil power' but 'not with soldiers'; and he impressed this view on Law.[118] French warned Lloyd George on 29 December that the situation in Ireland grew 'worse every day', though he was 'quite prepared to cope with it' provided he had the necessary authority.[119] He despatched the message, not through the post office, which he could not 'trust', but by sending it over with 'two detectives to deliver' — a means which seemed to Lloyd George to characterise 'the condition of things in Ireland'.[120] Throughout the spring of 1920, the position seemed to be 'steadily getting worse'; by February, Birkenhead wondered whether Wilson was 'ready for a rebellion'; while the condition of the police was, in Law's view, undoubtedly 'very serious' by March.[121] Fisher, who regarded the new bill 'as falling far short of the Liberal standard' but 'judged it to be of the utmost

importance that it should pass', had none the less 'no expect-
ation that it would be accepted by Sinn Féin'.[122] If 'as was
probable' they refused to work it, and attempted to set up
their own authority, 'military government would have to go
on, perhaps for two or three years' until they changed their
minds.[123] To help them change their minds, or to assist in
the restoration of 'law and order', two new appointments
were made in March and April 1920: Macready, whose most
recent position had been commissioner of the metropolitan
police, involving as it did experiences of civil disturbances,
was sent to Ireland as commander-in-chief of the forces
there, and Hamar Greenwood replaced Macpherson as chief
secretary for Ireland.

But the 'general position' had not improved. By 23 April
it seemed to Law to be 'getting worse and worse'.[124] By the
30th matters had come to such a head in French's view that
the question now was one of 'either making a truce with
the rebels or taking measures of war against them'.[125] In a
discussion with Lloyd George and Law, French described the
position as the rebels having 'declared war against us'; and it
now being 'open to us to ... arrange a truce, to ask that
[they] ... wanted, and see if we were able to satisfy them'.[126]
The Sinn Féin organisation had been taken over by the
extremists and the whole organisation was now 'imbued with
the idea of war and justified murder on that ground'.[127] The
rebels had the advantage 'of using methods of war ... denied
to us'[128] and French considered it would be 'more effective
to put the struggle on a war basis as had been done in the
Boer war' when 'the rebels were seized and put into concentration camps'.[129] The 'alternative' course would be 'to
arrange a truce to stop murders on the one hand, and arrests
on the other' and to 'enter into a conference ... to see if
some arrangement could be reached'.[130]

Greenwood, the new chief secretary, considered that there
were 'three forms of conspiracy ... agrarian, labour and
murder', and the latter was 'the spearhead of the rebellion'.[131]
He thought that the question of isolating the murderers and
dealing with them was 'quite a different thing to keeping the
country quiet'; that measures must be taken to make the
army 'more mobile'; and that more motor cars and armoured
cars 'were essential'.[132]

But Macready, the new commander-in-chief, did not think the answer lay in better mobility. On 1 May he wrote to Lloyd George that 'the moment' had come when 'a dramatic turn in policy' might have 'an instantaneous and possibly lasting effect', or so 'one person after another' had reiterated.[133] Without such a turn, 'we are drifting daily towards martial law'.[134] But although martial law might keep the country 'reasonably quiet', what would be the 'state of affairs' when 'removed'?[135] From what he called the 'soldier's standpoint, the easiest and simplest solution of present difficulties' would be martial law, although there might be difficulty, politically, in maintaining it.[136] Macready believed that within two months its repeal would be demanded; but irrespective of 'whether it be two or twenty months' the 'final result would be the same, i.e., increased bitterness on the part of the majority of the inhabitants of Ireland, and a greater resolution to resist British rule'.[137] Martial law would not afford a 'permanent solution' and if forced on the country it would accentuate the 'spirit of defiance, when removed'.[138] Instead, he urged a political solution: not the proposed bill which was 'utterly without support' in Ireland, but rather 'a broad measure of dominion home rule' for the south of Ireland, with Ulster remaining under the imperial parliament 'subject to a county plebiscite at the end of not less than two years'.[139]

Warren Fisher, the permanent secretary at the treasury, also considered that the present bill had 'no friends in Ireland' but that the Nationalists and moderate Sinn Féiners 'would apparently be content with something on the lines of dominion home rule'.[140] In the course of two reports written after a visit to Ireland, he recommended that a new under secretary, Sir John Anderson, should be appointed to work along side the present one, a man called McMahon who lacked 'initiative, force and driving power'; that Alfred Cope, a secretary at the ministry of pensions, be loaned as assistant under secretary, as a result of which the chief secretary would have 'first-class civilian advisers and assistance' for 'major issues'.[141] Regarding the police, he urged that Macready's suggestion be taken up, that is, that 'a really capable man' be introduced 'to supervise . . . both forces

and ... bring them up to date'.[142] He warned that the
morale of the RIC was 'getting shaken', while the DMP
had 'lost it entirely'.[143] He considered that the government of Ireland — with the exception of Macready — was
'almost woodenly stupid' and out of touch with opinion
of all kinds, while it resorted to the use of the phrase
'Sinn Féin' to denounce 'everyone [who is] not a loyalist'.[144]
The proclamation of Sinn Féin, the party 'representing the
great majority of Irish men' he considered 'indescribable
folly', which was 'capped by the blunders of brute force'.[145]
Fisher urged that the proscription of Sinn Féin should be
'publicly abrogated', that an announcement should be made
of bringing to a stop 'acts of violence by the executive'
against the persons and property of people 'who are politically obnoxious', and that the 'elementary human rights'
should be restored to the community at large together
with an improvement of the machine of government —
reorganisation of the police and military, improved mobility
and intelligence, and measures for the protection of life and
property.[146]

Macready and Fisher were agreed that the new bill would
please nobody, but whereas Fisher considered the political
solution 'quite outside' his province, Macready had continually
urged that a new political initiative was necessary and that
no amount of military suppression would resolve matters.[147]
French had considered that there must be either 'measures
of war' or a 'truce' 'to ask what [they] wanted'.

But Lloyd George did not believe in the 'bold experiment'; and he also rejected the suggestion of a truce, as he
did a declaration of war. By May 1920 he had come to look
on the new bill as a lesser evil than many, and one which
had come to seem necessary in view of the various 'opinions'
canvassed — world, American, foreign, dominion. Whatever
he privately considered to be its prospects of acceptance
in Ireland, he had brought himself to insist that it might
have a chance, or rather, that without the restoration of
law and order, it would have no chance. He had rejected
French's suggestion of a truce; for that would be 'an
admission that we were beaten, and it might lead to our
having to give up Ireland'.[148] There would be no truce,

but order would be restored, for home rule would be 'an utter failure unless and until' it was.[149] Greenwood should go to Ireland, obtain a preliminary view and reach some provisional conclusion. He could take it that 'the cabinet would support any demand to maintain order'.[150] On the one hand order must be restored and 'the sympathy of the moderate people' ensured; and on the other they ought in parliament to proceed 'simultaneously with the provision of remedial measures'.[151] But he would not 'declare war', which Lloyd George had reminded French 'you do not' do 'against rebels'.[152]

Law agreed with Lloyd George. The government should not 'declare war' for that 'would be a confession of failure'.[153] Although he had 'never' had 'much hope' in the bill, and had 'less than ever' after a conversation with Judge Wylie in early May, thought the position would not be made worse 'by going on'; that 'bad as the position is and doubtful as the issue must be these proposals afford in present conditions the only hope of ultimate peace'.[154] Simultaneously 'everything in our power' must be done 'to restore order', although Law believed that 'the more' order could be preserved 'by civil rather than military force the better'.[155]

Neither Law nor Lloyd George would, therefore, countenance a truce, but nor would they permit a declaration of war. By May 1920 both looked to the restoration of order: Lloyd George as a prerequisite to home rule, and Law because matters would not be made worse by 'going on' and 'doing everything' to restore order. Both Law and Lloyd George had already discussed the prospect of enlisting 'a special body of ex-Servicemen' in England 'on special terms as gendarmerie to be used in Ireland'; and on 11 May this proposal was considered at a meeting of ministers to which Macready gave a 'full appreciation' of the situation.[156] According to Henry Wilson the ministers present had been 'frankly frightened' by what they heard, and had agreed that all Macready's demands should be met.[157] Eight more battalions were to be held by the war office 'in readiness to proceed to Ireland', while signals staff and mechanical transport would be made available. A 'special officer' would be appointed to co-ordinate the RIC and DMP, with a 'small staff' and a 'first rate intelligence officer'.[158] A secret service scheme outlined by Macready was approved.[159] But in addition to all that, and in order to relieve the continued demands on the military forces, a scheme was to be prepared for raising a 'special emergency gendarmerie' as a branch of the RIC, which would be suitable for the 'present emergency in Ireland'.[160]

Thus was born the concept of the 'auxiliary' troops and the 'Black and Tans', as a special force to relieve the military, and one which might be more 'suitable' for the emergency in Ireland. Already both Law and Lloyd George had considered it; but it was not until Macready's appreciation on 11 May which 'frightened' the ministers that the proposal was approved as part of the general's overall scheme. It would, or so it was thought, help to restore order, as both Law and Lloyd George wanted without either a declaration of war or a truce; and the force would be a branch of the police, thereby promoting Law's preference (as well as Lloyd George's) for employing 'civil' rather than 'military' methods. Yet although the suggestion had generally been regarded 'with favour' by those present (Law, Chamberlain, Birkenhead, Churchill, H.A.L. Fisher, Shortt, Worthington-Evans and Long), it was none the less clear to Law that raising a special force of ex-Servicemen would 'cause a great row politically' from 'the point of view of Labour and probably . . . the Wee Frees'.[161] None the less he was 'at first sight . . . inclined to . . . favour' it. At the cabinet, although objections to the scheme were not ignored (there would be for example a 'good deal of protest and it would be represented as the beginning of a reconquest of Ireland'), it was thought that the 'present situation' was 'so serious' that 'all the requirements of the Irish executive should be promptly met'.[162] On 21 May the details of the scheme was formally approved: the force would consist of eight garrison battalions (not gendarmerie) to be raised by the war office, with the legal status of 'soldiers under the army act', and administered by the war office with a proportion of officers of thirty-five per battalion.[163]

There would be no martial law, at least not for the moment. Macready opposed it and Greenwood was 'against' its introduction 'at the present'; amongst ministers there were expressions of doubt as to the desirability of placing 'supreme power in the hands of a court-martial'.[164]

There would be other problems, particularly in connection with recruiting the new force: Churchill thought so and considered there would have to be a publicised 'appeal from the PM and Bonar Law', which would run the risk of 'no response'.[165] Lloyd George, having read the draft appeals, did not think 'that you would make any young fellow drop his tools and go over to Ireland', a prospect which Fisher agreed was 'most unappetising'.[166] Although the adjutant-general thought they would 'get the men', Macready, in other parts of the war office, found 'no great alacrity among the officers to go to Ireland', and he warned that 'You do not want the scallywag'.[167] In any case the decision had been taken, and recruitment could be considered again in a week or ten days.[168]

By the end of May 1920, therefore, Lloyd George had resolved to persist with the new Irish bill and to prepare for its implementation by the restoration of order. Neither he nor Law wanted a declaration of war, and both maintained that the 'civilian' element must not be lost sight of. Yet order must be restored. The reorganisation of the Irish administration, police and military combined with the meeting of Macready's demands and the raising of the special force should, or so it was hoped, benefit the preservation of order. At an administrative level the new chief secretary, Greenwood, would have the assistance of two new men, Anderson and Cope, especially recommended by Warren Fisher to provide first-class advice and assistance. Regarding the police and the military, there would also be new blood and fresh organisation. General Tudor would be responsible for co-ordinating both police forces. Macready, therefore, had been given, or at least promised, what he had asked for; and an additional special force was to be raised to assist in the special 'emergency' conditions which existed in Ireland.

Between May and October 1920 there was no deviation in principle from the course settled in May. The Irish bill, which was to become the 'Government of Ireland Act' would be enacted; and in the meantime order would be restored, without which the act would not have a chance. At the same time, however, this course was confused and complicated by the differences amongst the politicians which emerged over Ireland. Despite the May 'plan', attitudes were neither uniform nor unchanging. It is in that context that Lloyd George began to indicate and formulate what he would give, and why he would not give more to the Irish. Yet whereas differences existed as between those who, like Churchill and Birkenhead, advocated 'stronger' measures, or those like Fisher and Churchill, who would offer financial autonomy, or those who advocated from time to time a conference with Sinn Féin, the differences were not divisive, and the lines were never clear. It was not until later on, in October and November 1920, when the measures designed to restore order began to backfire, and when the additional forces became discredited, that the views became more decisive and the differences potentially more divisive. In the meantime, there was neither certainty nor resolution as to what ought or ought not be done.

Among the politicians neither Law nor Lloyd George changed views. Both considered that there should be neither truce nor war, and both continued to urge the restoration of order before the new act could be imposed. Walter Long, who chaired the Irish committee, who conceded that the context of the Irish question had changed on the Unionist side since 1914, i.e., that unionists would now work home rule, did not believe that there would be dominion home rule. Fisher and Montagu, the Liberals, had a professional if not personal interest in the question. Fisher was flattered by Lloyd George's maintaining that he gave 'an intellectual *cachet* to his ministry, like Morley'; and though he had had his differences over, for example, the Ulster administrative area, they were not at all serious. He had at one stage even allowed himself be considered for Irish secretary.[169] Montagu, on the other hand, had his differences with Lloyd George. He insisted he would resign 'if the Turk is kicked out of Constantinople'; and although he had 'no interest' in Ireland (he had refused the chief secretaryship in 1916 for that reason and because he was a Jew) he was nonetheless willing to refer critically to Ireland as part of his rhetoric of discontent.[170] Curzon neither wanted to, nor managed to, make much of what was happening in Ireland, while Chamberlain's interest seems to have frozen with his failure to secure a 'federal' solution to the matter in 1918 although his fears about its grave condition had not. Birkenhead and Churchill had views, mainly in that they advocated strong measures. Balfour's interventions throughout reflected his views that nothing could be done with the Irish, and that there never existed, nor could there ever be, such a thing as Irish unity.

Views were complicated by the attitudes of the Irish advisers, themselves divided. Of these, Tudor, Macready, Anderson and Cope were new but French was not.

Tudor, the new chief of police, had been the second, if not third choice for the job. Macready's nominee, Bulfin, had turned it down.[171] With French, Tudor pressed Lloyd George for martial law. French considered that if the Irish were met 'by a proper military force' the whole agitation could be crushed in a few months and Tudor felt it would be 'impossible to convict' without martial law.[172] By June 1920 Tudor thought the life he led 'wearing' and he drove about 'with a revolver across his knees' never knowing 'when' he might 'be shot at'.[173]

Macready, Anderson, Cope, and Greenwood opposed martial law as affording any solution. In June, Cope urged 'an open and definite undertaking that dominion home rule . . . will be given'; he warned that 'machinery', no matter how good, would not resolve matters, and that 'now' was the time for 'action'.[174] Anderson believed in July that the 'remedy cannot be found entirely in . . . coercion'; for even if the 'immediate purpose' were achieved, none the less 'all hope of a political settlement' would be relegated 'to the distant future'.[175] Firm measures should be accompanied by a 'declaration of policy and an appeal to moderate opinion' to create an atmosphere and prepare 'for an ultimate settlement by consent'.[176] Moreover he warned, by implication, that the forces currently in Ireland would be inadequate to deal with any of the demanding tasks involved in the restoration of order. On his arrival he had found the position of the police critical, and their inspector-general feared there might be 'wholesale resignations' or that his men would run 'amok'.[177] In addition the members of the military were inadequate, the rank and file quite 'raw', and the force 'almost useless' as far as giving support to the 'civil authority in the . . . task of maintaining law and order'.[178] Macready confirmed that the army was not that 'of 1913'; the politicians should realise that below the 'first rate' officer, there were many 'young and untrained'.[179] He feared that if the 'strain were doubled you would get near the danger limit'; and he continued to insist, in any case, that repression would solve nothing.[180] 'No amount of coercion' could alleviate the 'impasse' into which Ireland had been allowed 'to drift' by July 1920. Even if enforced, martial law — beyond possibly cowing the country 'into quiescence' — might not be stood for by either the troops or 'the British public'.[181] The present policy was merely one of 'attrition'; and nothing but the 'bold dramatic political stroke' would 'solve this matter'.[182]

The Irish advisers therefore were divided amongst themselves, with some of them out of sympathy with the government's avowed object of restoring order in the context of the proposed home rule bill. Tudor and French wanted martial law; Macready, Anderson, Cope, and Greenwood did not; while Macready, Anderson, and Cope deprecated coercion and the limitations of the present bill. What was needed, in their view, was a fresh initiative. But whether or not there would be a fresh initiative, they none the less agreed that stronger measures were generally needed; and this view was considered by the cabinet in London on July 23, when Tudor, in addition, pressed for martial law.

The meeting revealed the degree of confusion amongst the politicians, and the differences which existed as to what should or should not be done. Birkenhead and Churchill, for example, supported Tudor and pressed for stronger measures. Birkenhead deprecated the absence of any practical advice from the 'experts' (that is apart from Tudor) beyond their implying that the bill should be scrapped and an offer of dominion home rule made.[183] He thought Tudor's suggestions should be put in force 'at once', that the police should be made 'our first line' and the soldiers 'our second'.[184]

Churchill agreed. He proposed that the 'temperature of the conflict' be raised; that a 'trial of strength' be introduced (in the hope of 'a . . . settlement on wider lines'); and that a special 'Ulster' force of 30,000 men be raised 'by whom the authority of the crown could be vindicated', not only in Ulster 'but throughout' the rest of Ireland.[185] Although Churchill would go further with concessions than the present bill, he would not do so at that stage, when such concessions 'would be claimed as a victory for the Sinn Féiners'.[186]

Curzon disagreed with Churchill. The 'Irish Question could never be settled' on his lines, and the 'arming of Ulster' was 'a most fatal suggestion'.[187] He favoured 'getting in touch with the . . . leaders of Sinn Féin', keeping the present bill before the commons, and then 'remodelling' it 'in the light of a conference with the Sinn Féiners'.[188] H.A.L. Fisher, although he thought 'we ought to keep in unofficial contact, with the Sinn Féin people, and 'let them know that the present bill was not the last word', also thought that 'crime must be put down and criminals punished'. He felt the present bill was 'a very good' measure which had been 'unfairly condemned', and that it should be passed 'as expeditiously as possible'.[189]

But Balfour was not in favour of modification. He thought it 'impossible' to consider bringing another home rule bill in two or three years.[190] There were dangers in leaving 'the door open' (as advocated by Fisher) for the ideal 'at the heart of Sinn Féin' was a 'separate republic', and a meeting with the leaders would give nothing but 'humiliation'.[191] Balfour moreover, had wanted Ulster to remain part of the UK; and his 'worst' opponents had been those who 'hated' the idea of dividing Ireland.[192] He liked it: 'It was a geographical accident that Ireland was surrounded by sea.' This accident should be 'ignored' and 'their inveterate religious and racial prejudices recognised', for, on any other lines 'an Irish settlement was a pure illusion'.[193]

With regard to Curzon's proposals — which involved a conference with Sinn Féin — Law would 'agree', 'if there were people in Ireland who could be relied upon'; whereas Long was 'satisfied' that if the Sinn Féin leaders began to negotiate, they would be 'shot by extremists'.[194]

The meeting, like the views maintained, was inconclusive. Against the Greenwood proposition that 'sooner or later' the government of Ireland must be 'brought into accord with the views of the majority of the Irish people', and Macready's reiteration that 'no amount of coercion could settle the Irish question', the discussions were hypothetical.[195] The differences too were hypothetical. They were about whether or not to introduce martial law; whether or not to modify the bill; whether or not to consider talking to Sinn Féin. Churchill and Birkenhead supported Tudor's line — that the conflict must be heightened — as against Greenwood and Macready who warned against leaning 'too hard' on the forces, and who did not believe that coercion would ultimately resolve anything. Curzon wanted a conference now, Churchill later; Fisher wanted to restore order, but he would go further than the present bill, and would let Sinn Féin know that; Balfour would not leave the door 'open' to further negotiations, because they would be 'illusory'; and nor would Long, because they would be impossible.

Lloyd George, though not in favour of martial law because the 'civilian element' must be maintained, did want stern measures; he had seemed to Scott in early June to be 'entirely occupied with plans for repression'.[196] While holding that the 'civilian' element must be maintained, that, for example, there must be a civilian on the proposed tribunals which were to try cases in Ireland without a jury, for otherwise the people would be 'shocked at the . . . criminal administration being put into the hands of soldiers', he determined to show that his government was resolute.[197] He had decided in June to make a public statement, to indicate how the government was 'strengthening the administration'; and he prepared to make a further declaration in August, to reiterate the nature and basis of the government's Irish policy.[198] His government must 'secure the upper hand' in 'establishing law and order in Ireland'; and he simultaneously determined to resist the increasing number of demands to introduce, instead of the present bill, a broad measure of dominion home rule.[199] Lloyd George resisted these demands then, as he continued to do subsequently.[200] He was, as he claimed to be later, a 'Gladstonian home ruler' (see below p.65). The Irish, or some of them, would want complete independence. What would happen to defence, 'especially control of the harbours'? What of finance, taxation, the war debt?[201] If Ireland had its financial autonomy, if would be the 'only country in Europe with no share of the war debt' and would be able to bribe Ulster 'to give up a position she has fought for'.[202] He did not see 'any difference' between 'coercing Ulster by . . . the sword' and coercing it by 'imposing a penalty upon it'.[203] Lloyd George continued to resist the proposals of the Liberals to grant fiscal autonomy. He may, like Long, have believed that fiscal autonomy meant the rupture of the union.[204] There were practical difficulties. Who in Ireland was in control? Griffith? Mac Néill? Figgis? De Valera?[205] There were election pledges, not least the promise made to the northern unionists that 'within this parliament' the north would not be abandoned. Like Asquith, with whom Lloyd George claimed he agreed on this matter, he held that 'we cannot coerce Ulster'.[206]

On 13 August it was decided at the cabinet that the prime minister would 'make the position of the government clear'.[207] He would publicly reiterate that the pledges to the six counties would not be broken; that the six would not 'be coerced to any form of government which they do not desire'.[208] He would insist that 'we will not have a republic' and that England would keep control of the 'navy, the army, the ports for strategic purposes' as well as 'international affairs' and coinage; though within these limits 'we are willing to pay a great price for peace'.[209] If Ireland did not choose to negotiate within those terms, then there would be no peace 'but unending strife'.[210] The public statement would reflect the private contention that he would keep Ireland in the empire; that he would not endanger the security of Great Britain; that he would control finance and the ports. Local powers were one thing, an independent republic another.

Whereas Fisher and Montagu continued to urge fiscal autonomy (Fisher would give this to both Irish parliaments 'subject to their agreeing to a contribution representing a percentage of their share of the national debt'), Lloyd George continued to resist it.[211] He considered it would be 'a mistake', as he did in October 1920, 'to make any great concession at this stage', that the prospect of 'getting anything in return' was 'so small', and there would be 'nothing . . .

left with which to negotiate if the Irish adopted a conciliatory attitude'. Nor had he any desire to give up customs or income tax.[212] The giving up of customs ('always regarded as a sign of unity') and of income tax was 'not the home rule' on which he had been 'brought up'.[213] If customs had to be conceded in order to obtain peace, it might be considered, but only when it was impossible to get other terms.[214] Sinn Féin would have to come forward and bargain.[215] Lloyd George looked 'forward' to using customs, excise and income tax as a means of reducing Ireland; and if these were given up without 'anything in return', it would be 'the worst piece of business' which the government had 'ever' done.[216] Lloyd George was 'still', or so he claimed, 'a Gladstonian home ruler' and he wished to keep Ireland as an integral part of the UK; and that was why he hoped that the present bill — a 'good and generous one' under which it would be possible to keep the UK 'together in some sort of unity' — should be proceeded with.[217] He would 'stand by' the bill 'until someone with real authority in Ireland appeared with whom it was possible to negotiate'.[218]

Lloyd George did 'stand by' the bill; and he would not, even as late as November 1920 'listen to' Montagu when the latter pressed fiscal autonomy.[219] Like Long, he believed or hoped that 'financial control would meet the case' of preventing 'practical if not legal independence' when Ireland demanded 'complete dominion status', which she would 'sooner or later'.[220] So Lloyd George, unlike Montagu, Fisher, or Churchill, would not concede financial powers. Like Long, Balfour and Law, he would not coerce Ulster, regarding which he would allude to Asquith's promise on the subject, in order to cover himself with the Liberals. His position was more that of Long and Law before 1914; he would not allow, as Long did, that there had been change since, for he knew he could not and would not satisfy that change.

There was no evidence to suggest that the Irish would be content with dominion home rule. All reports from Ireland alluded to the 'deteriorating' position, the 'increased outrage' in the country, and on 23 July Macready and Greenwood had referred to the danger of pushing the troops too hard.[221] On 29 June Brugha had given an account to the Dáil of the state of defence; and he held that 'as a result of the work of the Defence Department and owing to the efficiency of the headquarters staff, the enemy ... had got the worst of the argument' since the last meeting of the Dáil.[222] In most parts of the country the 'so-called enemy police force had been driven out or confined to certain strongholds with the result that British law did not exist in those places'.[223] In consequence his department had been obliged to perform police duties, 'capture criminals and put down crime'. Although the department of defence 'would provide such protection and assistance as was necessary to enforce decisions ... by the courts set up by the Dáil' it was hoped that the work of the Volunteers would be 'as light as possible' so as 'not to take up the time which must be devoted to their military duties'.[224] Reference to the more precise relationship between the Dáil and the Volunteers was not made. Although the formal connection now existed of the Volunteers taking the oath 'to the Irish republic and the Dáil' (a general order had been issued setting out the way in which it should be administered), and although the Dáil allocated various sums of money for defence, the connection remained theoretical.[225] It was given effect in some measure at headquarters level, by the overlapping of Dáil and staff functions.

The most notable example of overlapping was and continued to be Collins, who while minister for finance in Dáil Éireann, also served as adjutant-general and director of organisation and intelligence in the Volunteers. As a result he continued to be involved with schemes for reorganising the Volunteers. He was implicated in the headquarters' orders, instructions and memoranda to the units; and although many of the local attacks in the country would have been the result of local initiative, Collins himself was particularly concerned with intelligence work in Dublin. He also arranged for the buying of arms from, and the planning of operations in, Liverpool, Glasgow, Manchester and Birmingham. As minister for finance in the Dáil, as well as in connection with the national loan announced in April, Collins during the June

1920 session had moved that a department for the collection of income tax he instituted and that all persons who 'pay income tax to that department which otherwise they would pay to the British government' should be indemnified against losses caused by distraint or otherwise.[226] Collins had felt that the creation of this tax department would be an 'easy matter' and would 'strike the imagination of all'. While it was not possible 'to estimate' the resulting revenue, it was 'certain' that a 'very popular feeling in favour of paying to the Dáil' existed: and 'we can get a very considerable revenue amounting to £500,000 annually'.[227]

How far was Collins in control? Or as Lloyd George rhetorically demanded *à propos* the suggestions for a conference: who, in Ireland, exercised control? Griffith? Mac Néill? Figgis? De Valera?[228]

3
October 1920 — July 1921

By October 1920 the 'restoration' of order had begun to backfire on the government, with the reports of indiscipline amongst the new recruits in Ireland, the Black and Tans and the Auxiliaries. In the month of September, the government had become sensitive to what was referred to as 'public opinion' or the 'public mind' during the hunger strike in prison of MacSwiney, the lord mayor of Cork, which led to his death on the 24/25th. Allusions had been made to the effects of MacSwiney's detention, or death, on the 'public', and the 'press' seemed *en bloc* to demand his release, in which context reference had been made to the 'special circumstances' of the case (such as MacSwiney having been described as a 'political prisoner'); to his not being 'amenable to forcible feeding'; to the 'distinct line of demarcation in the public mind between a political and a criminal prisoner'; to MacSwiney having done nothing 'worse' than 'things . . . done by some of the leaders of the Ulster party'.[1] But there had been no release; for 'to give in to hunger striking meant paralysis of the law', with the additional danger that release might 'completely disintegrate and dishearten the police . . . and . . . military' in Ireland.[2] In Lloyd George's view it must be made clear to the public, to 'British public opinion' and 'the foreign public' that MacSwiney's detention was not due to 'cruelty or . . . obstinacy on our part, but to high policy' from which 'we cannot depart . . . without sacrificing the supreme interests of the British empire'.[3]

The sensitivity to 'public opinion', the 'public mind' or the 'foreign public', which had been displayed during the MacSwiney discussions, was to recur subsequently in connection with the Black and Tan reprisals. By 1 October, reports of burning by the forces led to 'complete agreement' at a meeting of ministers that 'reprisals by burning must . . . stop . . . at the earliest . . . moment'.[4] By that stage the Irish executive had already issued 'appropriate orders to the military and the police'.[5] But the reprisals had continued and by mid-October, the matter (in connection with which Greenwood had been instructed to prepare a memorandum on the 'whole question') had become particularly sensitive in view of the impending opening of parliament.[6] Moreover, no request for an inquiry would be conceded, except for one undertaken by the government.[7]

Yet the reprisals did not cease; and it became plain that part of the difficulty in bringing them to a stop lay in their very effectiveness. They were thought to have had 'a visible effect in enabling the executive to obtain information about ambushes and plots' as they were, also, in driving a wedge between moderates and extremists in the Sinn Féin camp.[8] In any case, under the prevailing conditions in Ireland, it was considered 'hard to stop' the 'reprisals in hot blood', as for example one which followed 'within a short time' the 'murder of a police officer or constable'.[9] By early November complaints were still being made that the troops were 'getting out of control, taking the law into their own hands'; and that 'besides clumsy and indiscriminate destruction, actual looting and thieving as well as drunkeness and gross disorders' were occurring.[10] Although court-martials were being held upon soldiers, it nonetheless seemed to be the case that given the 'position of the troops' who were 'always liable to be murdered by the Sinn Féiners', it would not be 'possible to restrain their anger when outrages occur in their neighbourhood'.[11]

Failure to stop the reprisals, or to want to stop them effectively, coincided with the escalation of 'public' disapproval of the government, or lack of government in Ireland, and with expressions of discontent from those who would normally support the coalition.

To C.P. Scott, editor of the *Manchester Guardian* and occasional confidant of Lloyd George, the conditions in Ireland seemed 'almost incredible' and the 'whole position . . . anarchic and indefensible'.[12] Even the moderates, whom the government wanted to 'win' (or claimed to want to win) were repelled by 'the hollowness and immorality of the reprisal government'.[13] From within the government, Fisher had been 'greatly shocked' by Greenwood's recent reports; he had been particularly so by the references to 'violent counter-attacks on property resulting in extensive destruction and damage' which had followed the attacks on the police and the military in various Irish towns and, in connection with which it had not been possible 'definitely to fix responsibility'.[14] Fisher felt that they could not 'allow this state of things to continue'. Not only did 'these acts of lawless violence offend the conscience of English people', but they could not 'help . . . to achieve the object which we have in view' and were unlikely to influence 'the minds of the desperados . . . or of the wild fanatics who murder out of theological conviction'.[15] They would 'exasperate and embitter the temper of Ireland' and would 'give us a bad name in the world'; while the only result of the burnings and lootings would be 'to induce Englishmen to say that if we can only govern Ireland by such means as these', then 'we had better not govern Ireland at all'.[16] Montagu, too, 'strongly condemned' the reprisals in a speech to his constituents in Cambridge; and though he did distinguish the reprisals from 'the act of self-defence', he denied that the government had 'ever ordered or connived at reprisals', on the authority of Greenwood.[17] Outside the government Smuts intervened to suggest that a 'responsible' Irish leader might appeal to the prime ministers' conference, as the court of appeal in the empire 'for an Irish settlement'.[18] Midleton urged the appointment of a 'plenipotentiary' to negotiate with all parties in Ireland.[19] Moreover he felt that the government would not 'last indefinitely'; that Lloyd George settled nothing but put 'a 48 hours plaster on each wound'; that in Ireland 'the loyalists disapprove of the government' as much as Sinn Féin; that an end 'must come to this' and the time would come when people would ask for leaders who could be 'relied on to stand to a policy'.[20]

By 1 December the cabinet had resolved to apply martial law to certain areas in Ireland, the proposal for which had been mooted two months earlier and had since then been suggested as a means of keeping the reprisals under control. On 1 October, at a meeting of ministers chaired by Lloyd George, it had been suggested that under martial law 'appropriate steps' could be taken when assassinations occurred; that these would be in accordance with 'official warnings' issued beforehand; and that 'in this way reprisals could be kept under official control'.[21] On 3 November Churchill, as secretary of state for war, had circulated a memorandum to the effect that 'very strong representations' were being made to him by the military authorities that reprisals, 'within strictly defined limits' should be 'authorised by the government and regulated by . . . responsible officers'.[22] Churchill did not consider that the present attitude on reprisals, which was not 'fair on the troops . . . or the officers' could be maintained 'much longer'. He urged consideration of a 'policy of reprisals within strict limits and under strict control in certain districts' where it would be declared that conditions 'approximating to a state of war' existed.[23] The attorney-general's view was that 'anything in the nature of authorised reprisals' could not be carried out without legislation;[24] and on 1 December, following the attack and killing of British forces near Cork, it was decided to apply martial law to certain areas, subject to the acquiescence of the civil and military authorities in Ireland.[25] Lloyd George, Greenwood and Law considered the Cork attack to have had a different character to previous ones: whereas they had been assassinations, this was a military operation.[26] In 'these circumstances' the proposal had been made that 'something in the nature of martial law' be applied to that 'particular district'.[27] Action, which would depend on the acquiescence of the local authorities in Ireland, would be on the lines of a proclamation 'ordering the surrender of arms and uniforms' and 'naming a date' after which anyone found with either in his possession 'would be treated as a rebel'.[28]

At the cabinet Lloyd George indicated that the government had been 'pressed a good deal by the military authorities to do this'.[29] It is not clear who these 'authorities' were, or what was the nature of their 'pressing'. Macready, for example, was resting in France and he had unequivocally made his reservations about martial law clear in the preceding months. Wilson would not have had martial law for such a restricted area. Rather he would have extended it to the whole of Ireland, as would Jeudwine.[30] Churchill had suggested on 3 November that the military authorities wanted 'authorised reprisals' — presumably in the framework of martial law; but he too did not specify, nor was it recorded, who the authorities were. It is probable that Tudor and French were still pressing for martial law but they could hardly be described as the 'military' authorities, for that was not their capacity in Ireland. Instead, Lloyd George had, by 1 December, come to look upon martial law as worth trying, *manque de mieux*. He made it rational by referring to the 'military' character of the attack on the Cork cadets; and he claimed there was 'a good deal to be said for trying this experiment in this corner'.[31]

The proclamation for martial law was ready on 5 December; and it would take ten days, in Jeudwine's view 'to get ready from the word "go"'.[32] Its 'immediate result' would be the 'localisation of military courts, the speeding up of trials . . . and the imposition of the death penalty at the discretion of the general — for carrying arms, harbouring outlaws or rebels' and for 'any other crime' he may by proclamation set out.[33] Greenwood indicated that success would depend on the 'active co-operation of the navy' and he wondered could the military make martial law effective 'in a reasonable period, say two or three months'?[34]

Simultaneously with these preparations to apply martial law to the south came the interventions of two clergymen for peace: the Australian archbishop, Clune, and the man who had been acting president of Sinn Féin during the period following the German plot arrests in 1918, Fr Michael O'Flanagan.

Clune had acted as chaplain to the Australian forces during the war, and Lloyd George considered he was 'thoroughly loyal'.[35] Clune wanted to see Griffith and Eoin Mac Néill; he was anxious 'to promote peace' and felt it was 'no use discussing any terms of settlement', until the 'present horror has come to an end and the country is in a calmer frame of mind'.[36]

O'Flanagan's intervention was initially by way of a telegram published in the newspapers, to which Lloyd George referred at a cabinet on 8 December.[37] He wrote that 'you state you are willing to make peace at once without waiting for Christmas' that 'Ireland also is willing. What first steps do you propose'?[38]

The messages prompted a discussion not upon what kind of settlement might be made, but rather what measures might be taken to facilitate discussion. Lloyd George claimed that he agreed with Clune's proposition that there was 'no use discussing . . . settlement until the present horror' had come to an end and the country was, as Clune had suggested 'in a calmer frame of mind'.[39] He felt it 'idle' to discuss 'dominion home rule and customs and excise and questions of that character in the present atmosphere'; and he thought 'our first object should be to secure a truce that would put an end to murder'.[40] Once that was 'ensured' the country would not 'go back to the present system of terror'.[41] Lloyd George thought that if Greenwood was 'convinced' after hearing an account of Clune's talk with Griffith and Mac Néill that 'these two . . . really mean to exercise their influence with a view to arranging a truce on honourable terms', then they might be released from prison.[42] The 'terms' of such truce would include an 'undertaking' from the leaders of the republican army 'that no new murders would be committed'.[43]

Lloyd George therefore considered that a truce would be essential before any discussions took place; and that such a truce would involve the cessation of 'murders' by the republican army. He chaired the cabinet which approved the reply to O'Flanagan – which indicated that his government would 'afford facilities for . . . free discussion' to the elected representatives of Irish constituencies and that a 'safe conduct' would be granted to all except those individuals 'gravely implicated in the commission of crime'.[44] But the government would insist that 'effective measures' were taken 'to ensure the cessation of murder and other crimes . . . and the surrender of all arms unlawfully held'.[45] Moreover it adhered 'absolutely' to the conditions laid down by Lloyd George in the house of commons on 16 August 'to which any political settlement must conform'.[46]

By 9 December, therefore, Lloyd George was prepared to consider a truce, on the basis that the murders in Ireland stopped; and with his colleagues was prepared to lift the ban on Sinn Féin – proclaimed in September 1919 – to facilitate a discussion of the Dáil. But certain individuals would not be given a 'safe conduct'; while measures must be taken to stop 'murder and other crimes of violence' and to secure the 'surrender of all arms unlawfully held'. And when that was done any settlement could only be within the context of the offer already made, with possible concessions on tax and customs and excise.

By 20 December Lloyd George may have thought a settlement more likely; although it was 'not an easy one', and might 'take several months', and there might be 'awkward steps', it was well to be 'optimistic'.[47] But he had now resolved, at least temporarily, on a course other than the restoration of order and the imposition of the new bill, for he feared that otherwise he might lose Ireland. With regard to reprisals, he warned that 'we must hold the balance even', that 'we must be sternly just or we will not get Ireland back'.[48] There could be one of two policies: the first of which was to crush the embers and 'take your risk and not welcome negotiations for peace'; the second was to 'crush the murder gang but whenever there is any opening for peace take it and do not be too rough on the purely political lot'.[49] Whereas he had formerly adhered to the first, he now began to vacillate between the two – which he continued to do until June 1921.

Verbal messages had already been sent to the Irish through Clune that the 'so-called reprisals etc. would stop automatically, if murder, arson and outrage ceased', and that no execution would take place without trial by court-martial. But the arms, ammunitions, uniforms, and explosives would have to be surrendered in the proposed martial law area, and elsewhere in Ireland 'handed over to the custody of [the] government'; and Sinn Féin would have to order 'cessation of all violence'.[50]

The 'main obstacle' proved to be 'the handing over of arms', to which Sinn Féin objected, and Michael Collins, 'the organiser of murder' – whom, nevertheless, Clune described as 'the only one with whom effective business could be done' and who 'desired peace'.[51] Although some arms had been and were being surrendered, there was no 'data' available by 24 December as to the proportion involved, but the general view expressed by the politicians was that the surrender could not be suspended.[52] The last date for the surrender of arms in the martial law area was 27 December; there were no definite reports as to the numbers handed in, and as the day passed so too did Lloyd George's interest in taking the 'opening for peace talks'.[53] Would it not 'be wiser to postpone . . . approaches towards Sinn Féin' until after the new act had been 'brought into operation', in view of the 'fact' that Sinn Féin was 'rapidly being discredited in Ireland?[54] Moreover, any decisions would depend on the election. What were the prospects for holding a *bona fide* one? These questions, posed by Lloyd George, reflected his diminishing interest in a December settlement, as well as an assumption about Sinn Féin which derived not from circumstances, but his own wishes.

On 29 December the generals, Macready, Tudor, Strickland, and Boyd, gave their views to the cabinet about conditions in Ireland, with respect to which they were guardedly optimistic. Macready considered the situation 'from the military point of view' to be improving. Everything was 'satisfactory' in the Cork area, and he indicated that he had applied to extend martial law to counties Kilkenny, Clare, Waterford and Wexford.[55] Tudor too recounted that 'from the police point of view' the position had 'improved'; that there were now 'plenty of men to hold the police barracks'; and that unlike the position of six months previously when the police lived 'behind sandbags and wire' they could now 'move about freely, and with the exception of ambushes' were 'practically out of danger'.[56]

Should there be a truce? If there were a chance of one could Strickland and Tudor 'keep their men in hand'? Lloyd George was 'afraid' there had been 'a good deal of drunkenness amongst the Black and Tans' and he hoped Tudor would realise 'the importance of preventing such incidents'![57] But there were two questions of a 'semi-political character' which he wanted to put to Macready and the officers. What was Macready's opinion regarding a truce without the surrender of arms as a condition? Was it 'worthwhile' having a truce of that kind, or could Macready stop lawlessness without a surrender of arms? If the Sinn Féiners were to stop murdering, what could the military do in return? If there were no truce, how long would it be before 'the extremist gang of the Sinn Féiners' was entirely broken?[58]

Macready and the advisers warned what the consequences of such a truce would be. There would have to be a 'cessation . . . of raiding'; and although the truce itself would not have 'any great drawbacks', Macready warned that if the raiding, searching and arresting stopped, then 'the intelligence machinery would go slower and slower'; and if the campaign ever resumed 'the military would find themselves at a disadvantage' for 'the extremists would have had time to put up a new organisation'.[59] General Boyd felt the government 'would certainly be the losers' if the campaign were subsequently resumed. John Anderson believed that a truce would enable Sinn Féin headquarters 'to re-establish their central organisation'.[60] In any case he was 'not at all convinced' that it would be possible to get a truce 'observed by the other side': the attitude of the leaders was that they 'would fight until they dropped' and 'would not admit they were beaten'; they were men 'kept going by despair and the forlorn hope that there would be reactions in this country'.[61] Tudor agreed with Boyd and Anderson that the interval would 'undoubtedly be used by the Sinn Féiners to re-establish their system of communications throughout the country'; and if 'the murderers were still to be arrested, it would not be possible to have a truce'.[62]

The generals and Anderson believed that a truce would be used by Sinn Féin to reorganise, and that the British forces would be the 'losers'. *A propos* the prospects for a general election — about which Lloyd George had also enquired — Macready could not guarantee that there would not be a 'general boycott at the point of a pistol, on the word of Michael Collins'.[63] Although that conclusion prompted Lloyd George to remark that if Collins could stop three million people using their vote, it 'did not say much' for the success of the government's policy, he resolved to proceed

with that policy, *manque de mieux*. In view of the opinions
as to the consequences of a truce and the prospects for an
election, Lloyd George deduced he had no choice but to
persist in the course which he had recently formulated, i.e.,
to 'crush the murder gang' but to 'take' the 'opening for
peace' whenever it presented itself; and 'not be too rough
on the purely political lot'.[64] For proceeding there was
some justification. Macready thought that the 'terror would
be broken' if martial law were 'spread all over the country'.
Strickland looked to 'definite and decisive results in four
months time'. Tudor, too, considered that within four
months 'the terror would be broken if there was no truce'
and suggested that the 'great hope of the extremists' was 'a
change in policy'. Boyd felt that four months was 'not too
optimistic a prophesy, speaking for Dublin, Meath and
Wicklow'. Henry Wilson thought a truce would be 'absolutely fatal', and that there was one party in Ireland which
had not been mentioned 'the decent peasant who was
nearly on the government side'; 'perhaps' if military law
were applied to the whole of Ireland, 80 or 90 per cent of
the people 'would be on the side of the government' in six
months time.[65]

There the matter rested. On 30 December the cabinet
agreed to extend the area of martial law to the four
counties of Clare, Kilkenny, Wexford and Waterford; it
applied already to Cork and Tipperary. The south of Ireland
was now under martial law. Simultaneously, instructions
were given that all preparations should proceed for the
introduction of the new home rule bill, the Government
of Ireland Act, while the chief secretary should make a
'personal appeal for discipline' in his weekly summary to
the police.[66]

But the policy still had its critics. As the year closed
Macready lamented the attitude of the politicians, doubting
whether they realised that 'the real solution lies with them
and not with the military and police'. He observed that 'the
dangers of these armed and practically indisciplined police
levies' were not 'appreciated by the civilians'.[67] What he did
not know, but what Lloyd George 'knew', was that without
the 'indisciplined . . . levies' there could be no solution: for

what was a 'real' solution for Sinn Féin was not 'real' for Lloyd George.

Greenwood's proposition in December 1920 that there was 'no need to hurry' in this settlement seemed to be borne out in early 1921.[68] Lloyd George, having abandoned the opportunity for 'peace' in December, subsequently reverted to the feeling of festering pessimism and indifference which characterised his attitude to the Irish question. Publicly he merely wished to seem to have a policy, and one which was reasonable and just; hence he continued to support the preparations to bring the Government of Ireland Bill into law. He also affected to believe it would be necessary to restore order as a prerequisite to the success of the new act; and whatever his personal sympathy, if not support, for the activities of Tudor's Black and Tans, he officially called for stricter discipline and an end to outrage. But he none the less failed to avert the criticism of those with a 'conscience'; or the malaise amongst supporters or Conservatives; or those who, like Henry Wilson, castigated the government for its failure either to 'govern' Ireland, or to 'come away'. His unspoken attitude throughout early 1921 – though there was still something of the opportunistic desire to 'take' a 'peace' prospect if it came – was reflected more by the position of Greenwood that there was, in fact 'no hurry'.

From late in 1920 Greenwood had developed the blustering optimism which characterised his attitude towards his responsibilities in Ireland. In December he had alluded to the various peace 'movements'; he had warned that 'we must keep the pressure on to secure the murder gang and their accomplices'; and he anticipated that 'we can in due course and on our own . . . terms settle the Irish question for good'.[69] He advised that Lloyd George should not see de Valera for that would make him (Lloyd George) 'suspect by your best supporters'.[70] By 26 January he claimed that 'the tide' had 'turned against Sinn Féin'; and he looked to the implementation of the Government of Ireland Act to supplement the final devastation of the rebels.[71] He did not seem to entertain serious doubts as to its prospects of success; he justified his optimism by referring to the views of

O'Connor, Irish lord chief justice, who thought the 'Sinn Féiners' would work the act 'if fiscal autonomy is promised' once it was in operation.[72] By 7 February he could cite the Lenten pastoral of the Irish bishops, who, while condemning the policy of the government, also united in condemning 'methods of violence' as contrary to the law of the Church.[73] By the 14th he believed that the present activity of the rebels represented 'the maximum of which they are capable'; and he explained away the lack of any discussion on the proposed act amongst non-Sinn Féin politicians as being due to their fear of Sinn Féin.[74] By the end of February he had promised that the 'preliminaries' for putting the act into operation would be completed by late March and that therefore 'any subsequent date' might be settled as the 'appointed day' for its implementation.[75] He believed that the existence of the northern parliament would prove that the act was 'a reality' and the independence of 'Northern Ireland an accomplished fact', while it would also show 'the whole world' and Southern Ireland the 'fullness and importance of the powers . . . delegated by the act'.[76]

Greenwood's reference to the view that fiscal autonomy would bring general acceptance of the act was one which reflected the confusion which Lloyd George had allowed to circulate on this matter. But there had been no decision on the issue. There is no evidence to suggest that he, in any case, had changed his mind, unless by doing so he would win a truly imperial settlement. Law, for example, maintained his objections to fiscal autonomy which were, he claimed, 'as strong as ever even if it were possible to grant it'.[77] Not only would he make no such offer unless he knew 'in advance' that the Irish would accept it, but he considered it 'the height of folly' to make any 'such proposal', as they would simply use it 'as a jumping-off ground for further demands'.[78] Unless there was a 'complete change in the situation' which he could not foresee, there was, he thought, 'nothing for us but to go on and put the act into force'. If the south refused to work it, 'well we would just have to go on with military rule there' for 'there does not seem . . . to be any alternative'.[79] Coercion was the 'only policy': in the past it had been followed by periods of 'quiet for about ten years';

that was 'the most we could hope for' from the present repressions; and he had come to the conclusion 'that the Irish were an inferior race'.[80]

One alternative, if possibly a hypothetical one, presented itself in January, in the form of a letter from de Valera, who, according to Lloyd George, wanted 'to come and see me secretly'.[81] On the one hand he did not automatically dismiss the suggestion; but on the other he did not seem determined to exploit it. He reminded his colleagues that 'we have said repeatedly ... we would see anyone who could deliver the goods'; that it would be in the interests of 'peace with America' (about which a 'most gloomy' account of the situation had been received) and in helping to 'clear up our American debt'. Jeudwine had said the 'present policy' would need twelve months to 'put through', and Lloyd George thought 'we ought to see de Valera and try to get a settlement'.[83] But there were problems such as Law's opposition, and Michael Collins, who was 'quite definitely responsible for the murders', who carried a gun and made it 'impossible to negotiate': for if de Valera said he would 'give up Irish independence' he 'might be shot'.[84] Throughout the spring and early summer this was one of the difficulties to emerge, or at least one of the reasons alluded to in order to explain why negotiations were impossible.

Lloyd George, therefore, was partly restrained from negotiation by his own intuition that Ireland was not 'ripe for conciliation' and that de Valera did not control 'the guns'.[85] His views were consistently reflected and reinforced by those of Greenwood and Law. Jones remarked in February that Law had been 'one of the most persistent opponents of conciliation' and had 'greatly influenced the PM throughout', and Greenwood continued to maintain that Lloyd George should not see de Valera 'not yet at any rate' and that de Valera could not 'stop the murder gang'.[86] There would be no negotiation, at least 'not yet'; preparations would proceed for the new act, and these would be accompanied by measures to restore order and official declamations against the excesses of the troops.

The damage which these excesses might do to the standing of the government continued to be one of the paramount considerations in their suppression. When, for example in January, the publication of the Strickland report on the Cork burnings was raised at the cabinet, it was resolved to suppress publication; though in view of the likelihood of questions in parliament it was thought that some explanation should be offered, but one which would refer to the indiscipline of the troops and their punishment.[87] Lloyd George had been particularly anxious to be able to say at the opening of parliament that indiscipline had been proved and suitable action taken in the case of the men and the colonel in command.[88] He warned Greenwood, however, that he was not 'satisfied with the state of discipline of the RIC and its auxiliary forces' and that the charges of 'drunkeness, looting, and other acts of indiscipline' were in 'too many cases substantially true'.[89] But it was not clear for example to Anderson that Lloyd George was not behind the reprisals. Anderson feared, even in mid-February, that many 'serious breaches of discipline' continued; that whereas Tudor would privately 'agree' that they should be dealt with, 'he took another line when he met his men'; and that 'the PM was the person really responsible for the policy of reprisals'.[90] For whenever Tudor went to see Lloyd George 'he returned very much strengthened in his policy'; and it seemed that 'even if not in words[,] yet by atmosphere and suggestion[,] the PM conveyed his encouragement to Tudor'.[91]

As the reprisals continued, so too did the criticisms, from supporters and opponents of the coalition alike; from backbench MPs; from the 'liberally' minded, whether bishops or newspaper editors, came condemnations not only of the reprisals, but of the government's policy in general.

Derby, for example, had been 'very disturbed' about the reports; and he was 'entirely opposed to indiscriminate reprisals.[92] He had referred dubiously in January to Greenwood's optimism, which although he hoped was justified, 'Heaven only knows' 'what the end of the whole thing will be'.[93] Nor did Warren Fisher, after a six-day visit to Ireland, know what the end would be. He was sceptical of Greenwood's optimism, the basis of which he questioned. The chief secretary lived 'immured in his lodge', his visitors 'restricted to the officers of government' and 'the ascendancy party' who were 'out of direct . . . touch with the ordinary public of Ireland'.[94] His stay had 'coincided with . . . [a] large number of deaths by violence'; and he did not see how the parliament in Southern Ireland could be assembled under the present act, or if it could be, whether it would not transpire to be 'a fiasco at every stage'.[95]

Macready too was dubious. Unlike Greenwood's, his weekly reports throughout January and February had indicated that there was little change. On 1 February he claimed that there was 'no sign' that the IRA was 'losing its grip on the country'; on the 5th he reported an increase in rebel activity, particularly in Dublin city, with an increase in 'outrages' in the martial law area; while the IRA still seemed to be 'well supplied with arms'.[96] By 19 February there was still 'no change' in the 'general situation'.[97] Moreover, Macready objected to Greenwood's optimism, particularly in the 'public speeches and writings', for it did 'an infinity of harm' and encouraged the extremists to keep up their pressure, in order to show that 'Hamar' was 'talking nonsense'.[98] More seriously though, he was not 'very happy'; so many factors seemed to fight against a 'peaceful solution', which, in his view would 'never be attained through coercion'.[99] By March Macready considered a truce imperative in connection with the impending elections. Either Sinn Féin would decide to put up their candidates (in which case anyone standing against them would be intimidated into standing down), or they would boycott the whole thing (in which case they would prevent the elections taking place).[100] Macready maintained that he could not provide soldiers for the elections, and that all his generals agreed with him that 'it would be folly' to hold them 'under present conditions' — unless a truce was arranged.[101]

H.A.L. Fisher, who agreed that the demands of Sinn Féin 'just cannot be met', none the less maintained that 'moderate opinion' had been estranged by British policy in Ireland; that there was 'legitimate grievance' regarding the indiscipline which prevailed in some of the companies; and that unless the British 'public' were satisfied on this, there would be a 'revulsion of feeling' which would affect 'the credit of the government'.[102] But the restoration of discipline would not be enough; and the government should be prepared to consider again the question of a truce.[103] A truce would illustrate the sincerity of the government in its wish to establish a parliamentary constitution; it would make it far more difficult for the 'rebels' to get up again; it would encourage the emergence of the moderates and enable 'avenues of compromise' to be explored.[104]

Montagu was also 'anxious' for a truce before the election which would, in addition, serve 'the purpose of negotiation'; and it would be 'far better' if the Sinn Féin candidates standing could say they had 'reached an arrangement' with Lloyd George, which enabled them to recommend the act 'as something worth working'.[105] Addison too urged a truce, to rally the right influences towards a 'lasting settlement'.[106]

From outside the government came further exhortations, not merely for a truce, but for the postponement of the elections. Midleton, who spoke for the southern Irish Unionists, warned that an attempt to hold them would have 'the gravest effect', not merely in defeating the bill 'but in aggravating existing disorders'.[107] And on 6 April, a letter from the bishops and church leaders of England was published in *The Times*. They deplored the 'practice of indiscriminate and unauthorised reprisals' by the 'irregular' forces of the crown; they claimed to be dissatisfied with the present act and they urged a truce, with a view to a 'deliberate' effort at an agreed solution.[108]

These observations and recommendations were made throughout March and April 1921, that is during the two-month period immediately preceding the elections. Whether Lloyd George intended to heed them remained unclear, but he seemed to affect to do so. On 8 March Midleton was present at the cabinet when his proposal urging postponement was considered.[109] At that stage Lloyd George inquired how long the elections should be put off.[110] Again on 22 March the matter was raised at the cabinet, but referred to the home affairs committee, in consultation with Greenwood, Macready, Tudor, and Anderson.[111] Although the committee did meet, Lloyd George had reached his own decision by 24 March, after consulting Greenwood: the elections would proceed, and in order to take advantage of a privy council meeting that day, he had determined that 19 April be the 'appointed day' and 14 May the day on which both northern and southern parliaments be summoned.[112] The cabinet confirmed the decision but the matter was by no means dropped; as late as 26 April, for example, Midleton was under the impression that Lloyd George was still 'considering the possibility of postpoining the . . . elections'.[113]

The timetable was not, in fact, adhered to, but the decision to proceed was, and on 27 April Lloyd George indicated his position. He claimed that whereas he had previously been 'in favour of postponement' he was now, on the whole, against.[114] He rejected Montagu's proposal of making an offer, for Sinn Féin 'would use it as a base for further demands'.[115] His position seemed to be, as it had been since January, one of waiting; he claimed that Ireland was 'not ripe for conciliation', and he warned that 'in our anxiety to put an end to a disagreeable business . . . we may pay a price which this country will regret later'.[116] He was for the elections now; for 'you cannot guarantee things will be better' later; and with 'an act like that on the statute book . . . the commonsense of Ireland will reassert itself'.[117] He also opposed a truce. They 'are gradually being beaten' and a truce 'would give them a breathing space'.[118] 'I am against an offer. It is bad tactics.'[119] Although nothing was settled then, when the proposal of a truce was considered on 12 May, it was finally rejected. Greenwood, Winter, Macready and Anderson were against, as were Balfour, Chamberlain, Horne, Fitzalan, Shortt, Curzon, Worthington-Evans and Denis Henry; Fisher, Addison, Montagu, Munro and Churchill were in favour.[120] Lloyd George reiterated that the government would 'restore order . . . in the end'; that truce and negotiations would lead to impossible Irish demands; that the home rule act was 'generous'; and that anything beyond would 'contain germs of trouble'.[121]

When the nominations closed for the Southern Irish parliament, it became evident that Sinn Féin had a 'walk over', with, according to Macready, 50 per cent of the individuals nominated belonging to IRA headquarters staff in the provinces. The 'moderate element' had disappeared completely.[122] The elections were unnecessary, since the candidates in every constituency were unopposed. Of the 128 new members, 124 were Sinn Féin, and four were Unionists (from Trinity College, Dublin). The Sinn Féin group included twenty-three in prison, thirty internees, three escapees from prison, thirty-six who were 'on the run' and four for whom internment orders had been made.[123] The result posed, according to Macready, the question of 'whether Southern Ireland' was 'to have a republic or not?'[124]

But as far as the British government was concerned, the south would not have a republic; and on 24 May when the cabinet discussed the arrangements for the state opening of the northern parliament on 26 June it also considered its alternative policy for the south. If the Sinn Féin members refused the summons to the southern parliament (the last date for accepting would be 12 July), there would be martial law and crown colony government. Macready and Wilson had advised that if the government was prepared to impose martial law 'throughout the country' (except the six counties), and to place all possible troops at Macready's disposal, then he would institute a general policy 'to show the flag' and would make every effort 'to stamp out' the extremists.[125] But neither he nor Wilson could 'promise any definite result' or guarantee that this object 'will be attained'.[126] Despite the implied reservations of the military that even with the additional forces and the extension of martial law, there could be no certainty of ultimate success, the cabinet had resolved to proceed with such a course.[127] Reinforcements 'to the extent that the war office can spare them' were to be sent to Ireland 'as soon as possible'; and 'every preparation' made for the establishment of martial law and crown colony government.[128] In the meantime the Irish situation committee should meet to consider the extent to which martial law should be imposed in Southern Ireland, after 12 July.[129]

Throughout early June the practical arrangements proceeded for the imposition of martial law.[130] By 10 June four battalions had left for Ireland; two more were due to leave on the 23rd; a further two on the 25th, and thereafter there would be 'a continuous flow out'.[131] On 15 June Austen Chamberlain chaired a meeting of the committee, with Macready, Greenwood and Anderson present, to consider Macready's draft statement on martial law. This would be used as the basis for the proclamation. It included proposals for the proclamation of Dáil Éireann, the IRA, the IRB; and it indicated that membership of those organisations could mean the death penalty, as could illegal possession of firearms.[132]

It was then that the resolution to proceed with martial law began to crack. Was Dáil Éireann 'a treasonable organisation'? Chamberlain wondered whether, if its members were apprehended and refused to resign, they would be shot.[133] Balfour, while agreeing with the substance of the announcement, disparaged its 'unnecessarily terrifying form' and he wanted transportation, not hanging, as punishment. Anderson opposed treating Dáil Éireann as a treasonable body; only 'active membership' was illegal. Chamberlain urged that the government's aim should be to separate the 'extremists from the moderates'. Shortt felt that time might be given to members to resign.[134] Although Macready defended his draft on the grounds that 'it must be "all out" or some quite different policy', that after fourteen months experience he believed the government could not carry out a policy of coercion, 'unless they went "all out" . . . it was a case of "all or nothing"', the meeting was inconclusive.[135] Whereas Macready's object had been to make it plain that coercion if it was 'to succeed at all' could only do so 'by being applied with the utmost thoroughness', he had not concealed his personal view, shared by Anderson, that coercion would not succeed, but would, instead 'land this country deeper in the mire'.[136] Lloyd George had not been present. Chamberlain in the chair had appeared 'nervous right through as to the parliamentary reactions of the policy'; he indicated that the cabinet would have to have a full discussion, and that the policy, if adopted, would have to be announced by Lloyd George in the Commons and debated there; and Macready would require his instructions 'no later than 5 July'. Would the cabinet 'go through with it'? Or would they, as Macready wondered, 'begin to howl when they hear of our shooting one hundred men in one week'?[137] The implications of the question were not military. They were political.

Lloyd George, who before the May elections, had maintained that Ireland was not 'ripe for conciliation', that order would be restored 'in the end', that these people would 'come round sooner or later', that the government of which he was head would 'never give way upon the fundamental question of secession', and who afterwards had supported the preparations for full martial law and crown colony rule, now resolved to investigate, as he had done the previous December, the opportunity for peace which presented itself in the form of an intervention by Smuts.[138] Smuts regarded the Irish question in the context of the 'empire as a whole', and considered the present situation to be an 'unmeasured calamity' and a 'negation of all the principles of government which we have professed as the basis of empire'; he considered that the time had come, with the establishment of the northern parliament (which would eliminate 'definitely . . . the coercion of Ulster'), to deal with the rest of Ireland; he proposed that the king should, during his speech on the opening of the northern parliament, 'foreshadow the grant of dominion status to Ireland, and point out that the removal of all possibility of coercing Ulster now renders such a solution possible'. The king in turn recommended Lloyd George consider it, in the context of its being incorporated in the speech.[139] By 17 June, Lloyd George, influenced by the cost involved in quelling rebellion by force, by the unease amongst his ministers at the prospect of draconian martial law, by the refusal of the generals to guarantee a successful conclusion, by the ambiguous attitude of de Valera (see below p.90ff.), and encouraged by Smuts and the king, told his ministers that the 'time for a gesture' had come. The northern parliament was opened; the king again urged Lloyd George 'to take action' and not to let the psychological moment 'pass'; the exhortation was heeded. On the same day the cabinet approved two letters which Lloyd George hoped to send to de Valera and Craig respectively, inviting each to a conference in London, to settle the differences.[140]

What, by June 1921, was the Irish attitude, or that of
de Valera, to settlement? How did it contrast, if it did, with
the reactions of the Irish to the proposals for truce of the
previous December? Had de Valera's return from the United
States made any impact on the prospect of peace? What
attitude had he adopted throughout the period of preparation
for the 'Ireland' act and the simultaneous suggestions that
peace should be arranged?

De Valera had been in the United States the previous
December when the so-called 'feelers' had been put out, and
both Collins and Griffith had been responsible for dealing
with them. Although the official attitude to the O'Flanagan
telegram, and another by the Galway county council (which
was desirous of peace) had been to insist that the first was sent
without 'authorisation' and the second was both 'untimely'
and an exhibition 'of cowardice', that is not to say the
'feelers' were ignored.[141] Griffith had already been interested
in another move by a man called Moylett, though Collins's
view of the latter was that he was 'a bit of a Big Blower';
both he and Collins saw Archbishop Clune, while he also
saw Henderson of the English Labour party in connection
with an independent intervention of the latter for peace.[142]
In late November Griffith had been arrested by the military,
without the sanction of Lloyd George, and to the latter's
apparent fury (he berated the military for making such an
'important' arrest without political sanction); but the discussions had continued between Griffith and Clune in jail.[143]

What Griffith maintained was that though not asking for
a truce 'we are not rejecting one if offered'; that the 'final
terms' must rest with the Dáil, though before that body
could meet 'a truce would be necessary'; that far from, as
had been suggested, abandoning the 'republican demand',
he had insisted that neither he nor his colleagues would do
so, for 'we had a mandate for it from the people and only the
people could revoke it'.[144] But while willing to talk and to
discuss proposals, which must ultimately rest with the Dáil,
he would under no circumstances agree to the surrender of
arms as a prerequisite to a truce: for that would not be a
truce 'but a surrender, and there would be no surrender no
matter what frightfulness was used'.[145]

Griffith therefore was firm. He would not surrender arms –
one of the points on which Lloyd George insisted – and he
did not abandon the 'republican demand', for only the
Dáil could do that. He communicated with Collins by letter
about developments, and warned, for example, that it would
be 'indiscreet' to see Clune.[146] Collins did see Clune, but
having tentatively interested himself, as it were, hypothetic-
ally, in the discusssions, he quickly came to see the moves as
a trap designed to separate the Irish people from their leaders.
He was, he claimed, 'profoundly distrustful . . . of all these
people'; and he looked on the 'whole thing . . . as being an
effort to put us in the wrong' with the world and 'particularly
with our own people'.[147] He did not, in fact, see the 'faintest
hope' of a truce 'materialising': for it took 'two' to make a
truce, and the 'enemy' by his 'daily rounds of butchery and
burnings' did not show 'that his mentality is truce inclined'.[148]
On 7 December he wrote to the *Irish Independent* (the letter
was not published). He referred to others rushing in to talk
of truce, while the leaders of the Irish people, de Valera and
Griffith, were away: 'Let us drop talking and get on with
our work', he urged, and, until the English politicians fulfilled
the 'promise' of their 'peace talk . . . carry on as before'.[149]
By 10 December he considered that 'peace' was no longer
'in the air' and that 'we have come well out of this danger'.[150]

Both Griffith and Collins had been, therefore, wary of the
peace talk and proposals. Griffith would not agree to a surrender of arms, on which Lloyd George continued to insist
as a preliminary to truce (which both parties considered
essential to the success of any proposals). Lloyd George
maintained that he could not talk to Collins, and the Dáil
ministry insisted that he must let Griffith out of jail.[151]
Collins had been initially prepared to see Clune, though it
is not clear on what basis he might have been prepared to
discuss; he quickly lost interest in the matter, seeing it as
a 'danger' and an attempt by the enemy to 'do by propagand-
ist jugglery' what he could not do 'by force', and to 'put us
in the wrong with the world and particularly with our own
people'.[152]

And that was where matters stood when de Valera returned
to Dublin on 23 December after an absence of almost eighteen
months.

De Valera resumed his duties as president or first minister of the Dáil and the ministry. His attitude towards settlement throughout the spring and early summer of 1921 remained grand and enigmatic. He did not commit himself, as Griffith had done, to specific demands or conditions; nor did he, as Collins had done, abandon all interest in negotiations as a 'danger' and urge his people 'to get on with the work'. Although it is not clear whether he did in fact write to Lloyd George in January 1921, it is not impossible that he might have done (or that the letter might have been subsequently removed, when the files were put in 'order', under one of his subsequent administrations). Indeed de Valera's actions and statements throughout the period February to May suggested that he was not averse to a settlement, though he was to its being arranged through someone else. He continued to make his terms public, and while these stressed the independence of his country, they were, none the less, vague and philisophical. Until April 1921 he continued to receive peace 'feelers' which he did not reciprocate; and his policy was one of simultaneously discrediting and denying the claim of the British to govern Ireland while remaining conscious of the possibility of settlement, which he did not wish to damage.

In January 1921, for example, apart from the letter which he did or did not write to Lloyd George, he was anxious to publish a statement which would 'deal with the peace negotiations', though in what perspective was not clear. He was also anxious to include a statement of the 'atrocities committed against the people of Ireland' since his own departure to the United States.[153] In February he received O'Flanagan's account of his interviews which he directed his secretary to acknowledge without comment; in March, when approached by an intermediary, he was prepared to arrange an appointment with a British representative, though ostensibly only to prevent certain executions planned.[154] On 17 March he met Art O'Brien, Sinn Féin's London representative, with Johnson of the Irish Labour party; they had seen Shortt and had been apprised of the dissatisfaction of certain Liberals with 'present conditions in Ireland'. This seemed to confirm de Valera in his view that 'feelers are being thrown out in all directions just now'.[155]

But although, as in the O'Flanagan case, he would make 'no comment' on the feelers, he was none the less careful not to damage their prospect. When the Dáil, on 11 March, finally resolved that the president should draw up a statement regarding 'the acceptance of a state of war by the Dáil' to be issued at his discretion, it was initially considered that publication of that decision should be deferred.[156] For the present it was thought inopportune to issue any statement by which the Dáil undertook 'full responsibility for the Army'. This may have been due to de Valera's wishing to keep the 'gun business' apparently distinct from the political institution of the Dáil, of which he was president, in view of the 'feelers . . .'.[157]

Throughout April and May he became increasingly preoccupied with the 'feelers', and while he maintained that his position had been laid down in a statement published in the *Irish Independent* on 1 April, that statement had been somewhat ambiguous. It referred to the basis of 'right and justice' upon which Lloyd George could have peace; it claimed that if England could show 'any right with which Ireland's right as a nation would clash' then 'we are willing that these be adjusted by negotiation and treaty'; and it insisted that settlement could only be reached 'as . . . between two moral equals', that Ireland must negotiate 'on the basis of right and equality, or not at all'.[158] He continued to receive the potential peace makers: the Irish businessmen's committee led by the whisky distiller, Jameson; MacNeill; Bishop Fogarty; Fr O'Flanagan; Lord Derby. He did so to support his claim that he was not averse to settlement, but he rejected their methods, or displayed disdain or incredulity at the prospect of any proposals being taken seriously by Lloyd George. He told the businessmen that their committee's efforts would 'prove futile' and reported to his colleagues that at his meeting with the 'influential Englishman' [Derby] 'nothing of real importance transpired'.[159] It was 'a mere contact meeting', in the course of which he conversed 'as with a press man'.[160]

De Valera's real objections were to what he called the 'hole and corner methods' employed. He was determined to ignore, or appear to ignore, such feelers as did not adequately recognise his status as leader of the Irish people: it was neither by such methods 'nor by unofficial intermediaries to the nth degree removed' that questions 'affecting the fate of our nation should be dealt with'.[161] De Valera had, since returning from the United States, been particularly concerned with those details which impinged on his status and bearing as president and leader of the Irish nation. Whether this concern may have partly derived (as has been claimed by some since), from the impact on him of the grandness of his reception in the United States as president of the Irish republic, is not clear. But he most likely had been affected by the rallies and the receptions, by the enthusiasms and emotions — as he must also have been by the criticism and the splits. On his return to Ireland he may also have considered it essential to re-establish his claim as leader of the Irish people, from whom he had been absent for eighteen months, and who had managed their campaign quite effectively without him. But he did not join the fighting men, for his links with them had been tenuous, at least since 1917. Instead he resumed his position as president and presented himself as the grandest and most enigmatic of patriots. He had been in command in 1916; he had been incarcerated in Lewes and Dartmoor and had returned to Ireland as the heroic and sole surviving leader of 1916; he had taken one of the first seats for Sinn Féin in 1917, in east Clare; he had replaced Arthur Griffith as president in the re-organised Sinn Féin organisation; and he had, in January 1919, assumed the presidency of Dáil Éireann, the government of the Irish republic. His spectacles and cloak, his bibliophilism and learning, his cultivation of the Irish language, his stature and his asceticism all tended to suggest that he was quite distinct from his peers; and he fostered this impression by the combination of formality and secretiveness with which he ran the ministry. In February, for example, he directed that all notes from ministers must come through his secretary's office; and that only matters requiring his 'personal attention' should be passed on to him.[162] He signed letters (invariable addressed to 'president') not with his name but with a hieroglyph resembling the mathematical 'delta', or a large figure '8'. His notepaper was of the highest quality, with the harp embossed heading, around which the words '*Saorstát Éireann, Republica Hibernica*' worked themselves, and under which was 'Saorstát Éireann, Office of the President'. Despite being 'on the run' the typescript produced by his typists was faultless (indeed the attention to presentation resembled that of de Gaulle when in exile as leader of the Free French). He was personally concerned with detail, as is reflected by his request in early 1921 for a 'good leather attaché case . . . of the very best'.[163] And he determined that in public he would tolerate no 'hole and corner methods' of approach to him as president.

He refused to commit himself to a categorical reply to the question posed by Derby as to whether Lloyd George might say in the house of commons that 'those controlling the Irish movement' would not 'meet him or any representative' of his government 'unless the principle of complete independence is first conceded'; he turned the question so as to inquire whether Lloyd George would not meet him, unless such a principle was 'first surrendered by us'.[164] Although unwilling to surrender the principle of complete independence as a condition of negotiation, he was unwilling to damage the prospect of negotiation by not doing so. His insistence that 'England is the aggressor'; that 'once the aggression is removed, there can be peace', whereas if maintained 'it will be resisted', did leave an opening, which he was determined to leave.[165] In early May he revealed that he thought 'we ought' to let those 'groping for some way out . . . see a glimmer of light in the direction of an independent friendly state with . . . a guarantee of neutrality from U.S.'.[166] He was 'keen personally' to adopt an attitude which would 'lead on those Britishers who are anxious to come to terms'. He had referred in an interview to the first article of the Platt amendment, which in his view involved the helpful position whereby those 'Britishers' were led 'to accept the republic as a fact from which all . . . compromise must proceed'.[167] What he *seemed* to be saying was that compromise could follow from beginning with the republic, rather than as happened at present, whereby compromise began 'by positing the destruction of the republic – hence all the home rule schemes'. But it was all very vague, sufficiently so to satisfy both the extreme Volunteers, IRB men and Sinn Féin, on the one hand, and Lloyd George on the other, that he might be the man to negotiate.

He met Craig on 5 May, though it does not seem to have passed off very successfully from his point of view, as Craig presumably did not appreciate his view of Irish history. He prepared to meet the South African leader Smuts, who was keen to end the conflict, and who would be in England shortly in connection with a dominion conference. But he wanted Smuts to 'come openly', and what he really wanted was Lloyd George to send 'an accredited envoy with written terms of settlement'.[168] By mid-June he considered that Smuts was being sent to see whether 'we would accept' terms which included 'fiscal autonomy, free trade . . . no reserved services, and the Belfast parliament to retain its present powers, unless by mutual agreement with the rest of Ireland'.[169] But, in de Valera's view, this was the 'wrong track'; not necessarily because these provisions would be ultimately rejected, but because it was 'the wrong track' on which to start, rather than on which to finish. The 'right way' would be to propose a treaty with Ireland as an independent state, after which 'Irish representatives would . . . be willing to consider . . . concessions to England's fears and England's interests'.[170] Moreover, the 'campaign of terror' had 'created a very bad atmosphere' for any Irishman wishing 'to plead for . . . concessions to England'.[171]

Was de Valera such a man?

De Valera's reactions to the peace proposals throughout the period March–June 1921 had shown that he was not averse to settlement. They must begin, however, on the basis of the Irish republic, or, more recently, Ireland 'as an independent state'; but, as he had implied, concessions might be made from there. Without insisting on that point to start with, de Valera might not bring the extremists with him. And the question uppermost for de Valera, no less than for Lloyd George, after receiving the latter's invitation to a conference in London with Craig 'to explore to the utmost the possibility of settlement' was whether de Valera could 'control the murder gang'.[172]

It is difficult to say precisely who controlled the men with the guns, whose numbers and strength had increased quite dramatically since the summer of 1920. By March 1921 there were 100 Volunteer units, by comparison with 45 nine months previously; and supervision was to some degree vested in Diarmaid O'Hegarty, now acting as staff director of organisation.[173] O'Hegarty was also secretary to the Dáil ministry and a member of the IRB.

The case has often been put that the IRA was run, at least from the top, by the secret revolutionary society, the Irish Republican Brotherhood, whose leaders included not only O'Hegarty but Collins and O'Sullivan, all of whom were on the IRA staff in 1921. De Valera, who had only allowed himself to be sworn into the IRB with reluctance before 1916, subsequently refused to concede that secret societies were necessary, and would have no further part in it, or so his biographers imply.[174] In any case, if Collins, O'Hegarty and O'Sullivan wished to exercise IRB influence on IRA matters, they would have been in a position to do so, that is in so far as any measure of central control could be exercised on the local units. Secret societies leave few records; but from the fragmentary correspondence, for example, between Collins and his Liverpool correspondent (responsible for purchasing arms), it seems that the IRB or 'organisation' came before the army, or had a special function within it: members of the organisation belonged to the Volunteers, not as Volunteers, but as IRB men, and had 'no business interesting themselves' in IRA matters.[175] Funds should be kept separately and 'organisation money' should be used, as Collins instructed 'for our own purposes only', while it was thought important for a member of the organisation executive to be influential on Volunteer company staffs.[176] These details do suggest that there was some degree of IRB infiltration of, or attempt to infiltrate the Volunteers, but they do not justify the view that were it not for the IRB, the developments in Ireland during 1921 and 1922 would have been very different.

What is the case is that Collins was in a position to influence the IRA; that he was also a confidant of de Valera; that his co-operation would be essential to 'control' the men with the guns; and that much might depend on how he interpreted the position and prospects of those men, in the spring and early summer of 1921.

Collins had regarded the peace moves of December 1920 as a 'danger' and a trap from which he had been pleased, or so he claimed subsequently, to have escaped. Although there is little or no surviving contemporary documentary evidence which directly alludes to his assessment of the position of the Volunteers during the first half of 1921, there is some indirect evidence, none of which is conclusive in itself. At the time, of course, none of the leaders would have made any statement in public or in writing which might undermine the morale of the Volunteers or which might be used by the 'enemy'. In March 1921 the Volunteers were reorganised into fourteen divisions, though the strengths or fervour throughout the country were by no means uniform.[177] In April, de Valera reported to O'Brien in London that 'MC [Collins] and all the boys are . . . in good form'.[178] In May, the commander of the Belfast brigade could report with some optimism on 'the increase of activities', and the increase in the strength of the brigade, which was up by twenty-eight since the previous month; and from Dublin came the dramatic report of the raid on the Custom House, the burning of which was seen as 'a wonderful success'.[179]

On the other hand, it may be that Collins was more interested in arranging a truce in December 1920 than he officially conceded, for his allusion, in a letter to Griffith in January, to 'the rushing in' which 'torpedoed the efforts', suggests that he may have resented the 'rushing in'.[180] By March 1921 it had become 'impossible' to collect the income tax under 'present circumstances' and after a raid on the Dáil propaganda department de Valera, according to Collins, had been 'nervous' lest the name of the minister on documents had been found. He felt it would now be 'very dangerous' for him 'to visit any office where . . . general work was being done'.[181] It was also 'very unsafe' for 'persons of importance' to travel and for that reason there had been a 'very big difficulty' in getting anybody to attend the funerals of the mayor and ex-mayor of Limerick.[182] On the military side the reports were not entirely optimistic. The officer commanding in mid-Clare indicated in March that civil life had not been 'disrupted', though it was 'seriously inconvenienced' and by April communications between the second northern division and headquarters had broken down. The officer there had only received one communication from Dublin since January and was 'working here practically in the dark without any orders from GHQ'.[183] There were problems too with the first northern, about which the adjutant-general was disappointed, while communications with Belfast seemed 'to have collapsed'.[184] In Dublin, despite the 'wonderful success' which the attack on the Custom House was held to be, of the 120 Volunteers involved, five had died, three were wounded, and between fifty and sixty imprisoned.[185]

By early May Collins was writing that, with regard to 'Myself: Things have been very hard. In fact too hard'. On 15 June he discovered about the proposed impositions of martial law, which was to be of the 'most rigorous', and was to put the civil courts 'entirely out of commission'; and which would be supported by 'three times the present military strength', while the order for the dissolution of the southern parliament was already in print.[186]

This news, which Collins communicated to de Valera on 16 June, may have strengthened de Valera's desire to show those 'Britishers' who wanted 'a way out' a 'glimmer'.[187] When de Valera did receive Lloyd George's invitation of 24 June to a conference in London, he first summoned a meeting of unionists in Dublin, his 'political minority', before committing himself either way.[188] Although Craig would not attend de Valera's meeting, the southern unionists did; Midleton, one of their number, crossed to London on 4 July, in order to impress upon Lloyd George the need to arrange a truce.[189] The Dáil ministry had met on 1 July and considered the present proposal; it had approved the action taken so far, and decided that the terms for a truce, suggested the previous December by their side, might be accepted.[190] In London Midleton claimed that de Valera recognised the 'necessity of stopping all fighting', on which matter his unionist colleagues felt so strongly that he considered it would be 'useless' for him to return to Dublin, without 'written assurances' from Lloyd George on a cessation.[191] Lloyd George agreed. On 8 July de Valera wrote to Lloyd George that he was 'ready to meet and discuss' the basis upon which the proposed conference 'can reasonably hope to achieve the object desired'.[192]

But if de Valera had been willing to agree to a truce, and if his colleagues had settled upon the 'Christmas' basis, it was Collins who made the practical arrangements: Macready, Boyd, Tudor and Cope met in conference; and their suggestions were countered by Collins's.[193] The general understanding was that operations by both sides should cease, but beyond that there was no agreement as to detail either then or later.[194] The understanding continued to be that operations would cease; but disagreements persisted as to what constituted operations and it was only throughout the course of the next four months that the details were settled. The truce could begin on Monday 11 July at noon. The British agreed to stop all raids and searches, limit military action to aid the 'civil power', and lift curfew.[195] The Irish, according to the order circulated by Mulcahy as IRA chief-of-staff, would cease 'attacks on crown forces and civilians . . . provocative displays of forces armed or unarmed', and 'interference with government or private property'.[196] The more simple order to suspend 'active operations' was published in the *Irish Bulletin* on 9 July, with a message from de Valera warning against 'undue confidence' in the outcome of the negotiations, and urging his 'fellow citizens' to be ready 'should force be resumed against our nation'.[197]

4
July — October 1921

The fighting did stop on 11 July at noon. Three days later de Valera was in London to confer with Lloyd George. But although he had agreed to come to discuss 'the basis' upon which the proposed conference might take place, it was neither clear then, nor did it become clear over the next three months, that he and Lloyd George would agree on that 'basis'.

Agreement was complicated by the many and sometimes indefinite views on the Irish side. It was also complicated by the number and nature of the views pressed on Lloyd George, which in turn were affected by considerations such as the extent to which the Irish desired peace; the influence of the 'moderates'; and the desirability of terminating (or not terminating) the truce.

There is the additional difficulty for the historian of discovering, particularly with regard to the Irish, precisely what their leaders thought, at the time, about the peace proposals and settlements. The problem has arisen not only out of the shortage of contemporary written evidence, but out of the many and contradictory accounts adopted subsequently by protagonists and antagonists of the treaty. But what seems to have been the case is that, initially at any rate, there were no serious differences between Collins and de Valera and that the mutual co-operation which had manifested itself before the truce continued subsequently.

From the outset de Valera was determined to appear to make no compromise, while simultaneously he would make no move which might prejudice or arrest the negotiations. On the one hand he had warned Lloyd George that he could see 'no avenue' by which peace could be reached, if the latter denied 'Ireland's essential unity' and set aside 'the principle of national self-determination'; and when he saw Smuts on 5 July he was reported to have spoken 'like a visionary' of the 'generations of oppression'; and he seemed 'to live in a world of dreams, visions and shadows'.[1] He had not included Collins, who had been 'out of touch', in the meetings with Smuts (though he had Griffith, Duggan and Barton), possibly in order to imply that any settlement would have to satisfy the extremists.[2] But at the same time he would do nothing to endanger the negotiations, rejecting Collins's plan to extend the 'propaganda war' to the effect that no English connection should be tolerated. He crossed to London for his first meeting with Lloyd George alone on 14 July, with some cryptic tactical advice as to protracting the discussions.[3]

The idea which de Valera brought to London seems to have been to pose questions about the practical implications for Ireland about the kind of settlement proposed; to treat the British proposal as 'theirs' (i.e., made by them) which 'we will be free' to consider 'without prejudice'; and to concentrate more on the Ulster difficulty than on the republican status desired for the country.[4] In this way there would be no rupture resulting from insistence on impossibilities and de Valera could return to Dublin with proposals. This was a course with which Collins seems to have agreed 'exactly' and one which was borne out by Lloyd George's reports.[5]

Although Lloyd George thought the first meeting passed off 'reasonably well', and although he had allowed 'no question of an Irish republic or of a separate Irish nation' outside the empire, he became more puzzled as the discussions proceeded. By 20 July he found it difficult to say 'exactly where the Irish leader stood'.[6] What seemed to be the case was that both de Valera and Craig (whom he had also seen), wanted a settlement, but were 'afraid of their supporters' and as the conversations progressed, it became 'increasingly clear' that Ulster was the real difficulty.[7] Craig had insisted that 'in no circumstances' would Northern Ireland agree to a single parliament for all Ireland on the basis of its representatives being in proportion to its population; de Valera, for his part, had criticised the prime minister's proposals, saying that 'while conceding something, they took much away'.[8] These proposals, according to Lloyd George's own account to the cabinet on the 20th, made it clear that there could be no republic, or no Ireland outside the empire.[9] Beyond that he had been less definite. He had not been categorical on fiscal autonomy.[10] He had warned with regard to Ulster that the outcome of de Valera's insisting on the north coming under a southern parliament might be 'civil war', but he did not necessarily exclude settlement on Ulster.[11]

Lloyd George, therefore, had tried to make it seem to de Valera that a settlement would not be impossible, provided it did not exclude the empire. He had conveyed to his colleagues the sense that although Ulster was 'the difficulty' it was not an insoluble one, for when he remonstrated with de Valera about forcing Ulster into a position which might lead to civil war, de Valera had insisted that he would not want to do that. On this point, de Valera, who had 'an agreeable personality', claimed that Southern Ireland would 'never allow itself' to be implicated 'in a civil war' over the north, and would rather 'let Northern Ireland alone'.[12] On the empire, he had come to the point of asking questions about entry, about swearing alliegance, about the form of the oath, and the name of the new state.[13]

If de Valera had seemed conciliatory before 20 July, his manner changed on the 21st after reading the statement of proposals drawn up by Lloyd George, Chamberlain and Balfour, and sent to him the evening before.[14] He rejected these and demanded instead that Ireland should have dominion status *'sans phrase'*, that such matters as the royal navy be left for subsequent arrangements between the British and Irish governments, and that Ulster become part of the Irish dominion.[15] Failing that he demanded as his only alternative 'complete independence in southern Ireland'.[16] But Lloyd George would not consider the alternatives. He had already given de Valera 'a very serious warning': if disorder broke out again, the struggle would bear 'an entirely different character, and the forces which were now becoming available (in view of commitments being reduced in different parts of the world) would be sent to Ireland 'where a military concentration' would suppress the 'rebellion' and restore order.[17] He now rejected de Valera's alternatives and he indicated that if they represented his last word 'the only question remaining . . . was the date and hour at which the truce would terminate'. According to his own account, this had made a 'deep impression' on de Valera, as had his indication that he intended to publish the proposals.[18] De Valera asked him not to do so, as this would increase his difficulties; and he proposed, instead, to return to Ireland and send counter-proposals.[19]

An exchange of letters between de Valera and Lloyd George subsequently occurred, lasting until late September, not concerning the ultimate terms of settlement but the basis upon which a conference could be held. During this period Lloyd George prepared to afford every facility, and extend a measure of unparalleled patience, in order to secure negotiation. But that negotiation must be on the basis that the union would not be broken, and that Ireland would remain within the empire. Beyond that he was indeed prepared to 'explore to the utmost' the possibility of settlement, including some concession on the 'principle' of unity, if not the practice, possibly maintaining the present status of Ulster, but granting some of the reserved powers to the south. What was, and remained, essential was not the fate of Ulster but the constitutional status of Ireland; if the Irish persisted with their demands for a 'republic' or 'complete independence', then he would break and revert to war. There is no evidence that Lloyd George was bluffing, or that his colleagues — even those Unionists who would sooner go to war than press Ulster to co-operate — thought him to be bluffing. His attitude reflected not only the desire amongst his colleagues to reach a settlement but also their absolute rigidity from Fisher to Law that such a settlement could only be within the context of the union. And if ultimately it would be necessary to revert to war for this reason, then that was that. Indeed it might be better to revert to war sooner on this issue rather than later — for the Irish might try to break on Ulster, and Lloyd George would only break on crown and empire, and not on Fermanagh and Tyrone.

Lloyd George's willingness to make concessions which

might facilitate the convening of a conference was shared by his colleagues. He consented to the release of various Irish leaders such as Constance Markievicz and Joseph McGrath (despite the reservations of the military),[20] as he did to the more controversial liberation of the Co. Longford IRA leader, MacEoin, the recommendation for which was made in his absence. Shortt, Fisher, Churchill and Baldwin had all 'specifically agreed' to that release, as had Horne who thought 'so much' depended on it 'in relation to . . . peace' and Curzon on account of its potential impact on making the difference 'between success and failure of [the] negotiations'.[21] In addition there was some feeling against going back to war. Montagu did not feel initially that if de Valera rejected the conference 'we should be justified in embarking' upon the alternative policy.[22] Chamberlain warned Lloyd George on 21 July against the 'dangers' involved in the termination of the truce.[23] The cabinet had asked Lloyd George on 20 July to avoid a 'sudden rupture' which would put British troops at a disadvantage; and on 5 August it postponed consideration of a memorandum on breakdown, on the grounds that it would be 'premature'.[24]

But this attitude, whether of making whatever concessions which could be made to promote negotiations, or of displaying reluctance to break the truce prematurely, had its limits and the feeling persisted from the outset that no matter what happened now 'we shall have public opinion on our side'.[25] Lloyd George was 'absolutely confident' of this.[26] So was the king who hoped that if negotiations broke down, the prime minister would publish the terms refused, by the generosity of which he had been struck. He felt that such a move would win for the government 'the support of every right-thinking country in the world' and 'of a considerable number of the . . . Sinn Féiners themselves'.[27]

In addition to the feeling that he would have 'public opinion' on his side in the event of a break, Lloyd George was impressed with the difficulties of reaching a settlement by his consultation with Law, Balfour and Chamberlain.[28] He had implicated Balfour in drawing up the proposals for de Valera as 'the most extreme exponent' of his policy. Law, who had left the cabinet in March, and who was potentially more dangerous to Lloyd George outside than inside it, continued to maintain (from outside) that though 'very anxious for peace in Ireland' and willing 'to give the South almost anything' including fiscal autonomy, he would not 'quarrel with Ulster even to make peace with the South'.[29] Chamberlain, who had succeeded Law, had also shown a degree of irreconcilability. He was reluctant to overlook any 'slips' or concessions to the Irish and he simultaneously tended to interpret the ambiguous nature of de Valera's communications as evidence that there would be a break.

De Valera's counter-proposals reached London on 11 August. Lloyd George was in Paris, and Chamberlain, who received the document, considered it amounted to a 'definite rejection of our proposals'.[30] Its basis had been agreed upon by de Valera's colleagues to be 'external association', though its 'general line' had been left to him. The result, which had been approved at a Dáil ministry, had been 'a less definite offer of association'.[31] Although not on the face of it a demand for a republic, the letter seemed to Chamberlain to go 'out of its way to add that dominion status would not satisfy them'.[32] Chamberlain had summoned a cabinet for 2.30 p.m. and he failed to conceal from his colleagues the 'gravity of the situation created by this reply'.[33] His 'nervous manner conveyed a feeling of mild panic to his colleagues' for whose benefit he provided a 'palpitating summary' of the document.[34] Worthington-Evans became anxious about the troops and Greenwood about the police 'as though Michael Collins was about to break the truce in ten minutes or a quarter of an hour'.[35] Chamberlain's opinion was that it constituted a 'refusal of our terms', though he would not sanction the concentration of troops, awaiting instead Lloyd George's return: for the reply could only be properly weighed by Lloyd George in the light of his talks with de Valera.[36]

On his return Lloyd George, though ostensibly anxious to avoid a return to war, nonetheless seemed to prepare for the prospect. He had already instructed that the Irish be told they would receive the 'final' reply by the 14th. Despite the case being put to the cabinet on the 13th that the Irish document had not been a rejection, and Lloyd George maintaining he wished to do 'everything possible' to prevent the 'renewal of strife', he began to contemplate the measures necessary for resumption.[37]

On the 15th the cabinet met. It resolved not to denounce the truce yet, but acknowledged it must end if the rebels once again began 'their campaign of outrage'.[38] Moreover, it was thought that a parliamentary debate on the subject might help to secure a 'consensus' that 'the government had gone as far as possible'. This, in fact, was not forthcoming, and the proposed debate was abandoned.[39] (Asquith had been prepared to be 'helpful', but Clynes of the Labour party had not.[40]) On the 17th it was decided to set up a committee – whose members would include Lloyd George and Chamberlain – to consider the civil and military policy and action in the event of the Dáil rejecting the government's proposals.[41] Lloyd George wanted the report, which should deal with a plan of campaign and military measures, within three days.[42] The committee resolved to recruit as many men as were needed 'to raise to full establishment the forces now in Ireland', should hostilities be resumed, and a statement would be issued according 'belligerent treatment' to those rebels who observed the rules of war, as laid down in the Hague Conventions.[43] On the 18th Lloyd George told the cabinet of the committee's conclusions: if, as 'seemed probable', the government's offer to Sinn Féin were rejected, and the truce came to an end, a new policy involving both military and civil measures 'of the greatest' importance would be adopted; and parliament, which might have to be summoned at short notice 'if affairs in Ireland' necessitated it, should be adjourned, not prorogued.[44]

Lloyd George, therefore, had by 18 August made the necessary preparations to resume the campaign, should Sinn Féin reject his terms. He had treated de Valera's communication with gravity; he had returned from Paris 'immediately' and had done nothing to dispel the anxiety arising from Chamberlain's panic. His committee had made the necessary recommendations for finding the forces and for dealing with the rebels after hostilities resumed. Parliament would be adjourned, ready to be summoned should 'affairs in Ireland' require it. Lloyd George was ready; he had convinced himself and his colleagues of this; he would wage the 'terrible' war to which he had alluded for some six months, and for which, he was 'absolutely confident', he would have the support of 'world' and 'public opinion'.

But the doubts of his advisers held him back. On the one hand the military seemed increasingly dubious about the military prospects, given that winter was approaching and that the various drafts due for service elsewhere were being withdrawn. On 18 August Wilson emphasised that the position was now 'very different' to the intensive campaign against the rebels envisaged in June, 'based on the supposition that we still had some three months of fine weather' and that the drafts due to be sent east would not be withdrawn.[45] Already there had been serious depletions; by the end of the year over 13,500 men would have been withdrawn; and though there would be replacements, the 'net result' would none the less be that the infantry battalions would only average 495 ration strength.[46] A recruitment of 40,000 already trained to arms and ready to engage in active hostilities was needed. This would be the only means by which it would be possible to undertake a 'successful campaign' during the winter months.[47] In addition to the problem of logistics and that of the weather, there was another: Macready, though willing to administer martial law in the twenty-six county area, objected to the new proposal that its administration be separated from the command of the troops.[48] He would not consent to a divided command and would sooner 'hand over his duties', rather than serve as 'a figurehead with practically nothing to do'.[49]

On the other hand, the advice from Ireland indicated that there might be no need to encounter these difficulties, for the Irish would settle. From the outset Greenwood had suggested that the truce created a 'new world . . . in Ireland' where 'public, press and priests are . . . all out for peace, conference and settlement', and where the Sinn Féin cabinet was 'devoutly glad the "war" is over and the whole republic busted'.[50] In August when the Dáil met, Cope anticipated 'fiery speeches', but urged patience.[51] Fitzalan, the new viceroy, reported that out of the whole Dáil, only six members 'held out against acceptance', of whom three carried 'weight' — 'Mulcahy, Childers and a name something like Burgess' — and he believed a settlement could be got, without Lloyd George 'giving way an inch'.[52] By 23 August he claimed that 'de Valera himself' was 'beginning to see that however important' it was 'for him to hold his wild men by keeping a bold front against England', he could not continue this attitude 'with impunity'.[53] 'No matter what they ask for or what is refused them, it seems taken for granted that they will climb down' somehow.[54]

Lloyd George remained undecided. Despite the military reservations, or the promises of the advisers that the Irish would settle, he had made his preparations to resume; and that course would be necessary, if not desirable, sooner rather than later, on the crown rather than on Ulster. By the end of August he was resolved to bring the correspondence, if not the truce, to an end and he seemed to be supported in this course by his colleagues, whose initial confusions as to what precisely the ambiguous letters from de Valera meant were giving way to irritation and impatience. Whereas as late as 25 August, there were those who, despite being 'perplexed as to the real meaning' of de Valera's letter of the 13th, 'fastened on' its last paragraph and argued that the reply was not an 'absolute refusal', the reactions began to change.[55] On the 26th Lloyd George told the Irish messengers Barton and O'Brien, that he was leaving for Scotland: if Mr de Valera wished to see him, he must come to Gairloch or Inverness. Otherwise he could negotiate with Chamberlain in London.[56] In reply to a question about the truce he indicated that a week's notice would be given; and he warned that if a 'flagrant breach' occurred, it would be necessary to give notice 'at once'.[57]

By then he was assured of that support for a campaign which had been denied him in June. Derby, for example, wrote on 29 August that Lloyd George would, if the truce ended, 'get the men' for recruiting; and that 'quite apart' from the unemployment motive, people would be 'exasperated

by the refusal of . . . too generous terms' and would 'willingly
support the government in suppressing avowed rebellion'.[58]
The king considered Lloyd George's letter (of 26 August) to
de Valera to be an 'excellent answer' to the 'extravagant and
defiant demands of Dáil Éireann' which would have the
'approval of all reasonable opinion throughout the civilised
world'.[59] At a special cabinet on 7 September in Inverness,
the ministers were at one in their exasperation and the
readiness to break became more evident. Fisher had already
written about the 'insolent' and 'defiant' opening of
de Valera's most recent letter, with its 'apparently irrevoc-
able rejection' of the offer.[60] Hewart felt that 'to act' in the
teeth of the letter as a whole 'would be . . . to carry patience
and conciliatoriness [*sic*] to a point which nobody is
entitled to expect'. Derby thought that the reply meant that
the door, 'to use Winston's language', had been 'banged,
bolted and barred'.[61] Churchill told the cabinet on the 7th
that it should 'not assume it is going to be a terrible war'.[62]
Although Lloyd George disagreed and maintained it would
be 'a considerable operation', he nonetheless felt it would
be better to break now on crown and empire than later at
a conference over Ulster: 'men will die for . . . throne and . . .
empire' but 'I do not know who will die for Tyrone and
Fermanagh'.[63]

   Yet there would be no break for the moment and the
majority of those present seemed to oppose insistence on a
conditional conference, possibly influenced by Cope's
advice that the mass of people would 'follow de Valera
and not Lloyd George'.[64] It was then that Lloyd George
resolved to deal with all subsequent communications
himself and to insist that the Irish leaders must come to a
conference on the proposals of the government, without
which it could not be held.[65] He publicly repudiated de
Valera's claim to an Irish sovereign state in which he
received the support of Fisher and Chamberlain; and by
19 September he seemed to Law to be 'working for a
break'.[66]

   But he had not yet decided, and in view of de Valera's
less intransigent communications of 16 and 19 September,
which had 'taken the edge off British feeling against him', he

remained undecided.[67] He consulted some of his colleagues 'close at hand', i.e., in Scotland, as a result of which two considerations seemed paramount: first, there should be no compromise on 'allegiance to the crown and the integrity of the empire' in attempts to secure a conference; second, that it was of the utmost importance to carry 'the opinion of the empire and of this country in particular', that the country expected a conference and would not be 'quite satisfied that everything has been done to prevent rupture' unless a conference were held.[68] On 21 September he accordingly circulated the terms of a fresh draft, which invited delegates to a conference to ascertain 'how the association of Ireland with . . . the British empire can best be reconciled with Irish national aspirations'.[69]

That was the draft which, having been partly revised in the light of advice from Fitzalan, de Valera accepted on 30 September.[70]

De Valera's attitude since 21 July had been complicated by his apparently contradictory positions, of rejecting Lloyd George's proposals and appearing to countenance reversion to war on the one hand, and of not dramatically breaking off negotiations on the other.

He had rejected Lloyd George's proposals for the first time on 21 July and his counter-proposals of 10 August had appeared to Chamberlain to be a definite rejection of the government's terms, while they also failed to satisfy Lloyd George. On 23 August the Dáil had unanimously opposed the proposals and favoured instead a basis of 'government by the consent of the governed', and de Valera had officially informed Lloyd George of that rejection.[71] Simultaneously he gave instructions for the Sinn Féin organisation to be reorganised and on 7 September he instructed that a note be sent to each of his ministers to be prepared 'in the event of the truce coming to an end' for 'the resumption of office activities under war conditions'.[72] Between 10 and 13 August he had visited the first southern division and had met the divisional officers and on 15 September his ministry had met to discuss the setting up of a 'new army'.[73] He had from the beginning of the truce alerted the army to remain ready, and throughout the period July—September he did not seem to abandon the position of anticipating that there would be reason for that readiness. Whatever he privately may have felt, his position publicly seemed to be as that of Collins and O'Sullivan, who anticipated that the truce would end abruptly.

Collins had continued to hold this opinion. By 19 September he was warning his IRB contact in Liverpool that they must 'be prepared for absolutely all eventualities' and urging that ammunition was 'very very important' as 'one of our present wants'.[74] Simultaneously O'Sullivan, as adjutant-general of the IRA, believed that the truce period was 'coming definitely to end' and was arranging that an 'on guard' message would be conveyed to all units.[75] On 23 Setpember *An tÓglach* warned that the situation from the army point of view remained 'uncertain' and it was still a matter of doubt 'whether our troops will be recalled to active service or not'.[76]

Yet, for all that there had been the persistently paradoxical attitude of de Valera, whose communications to Lloyd George had at no stage constituted an outright refusal to negotiate. On 21 July, after Lloyd George had made his position clear, and had threatened to revert to war, de Valera instead had offered to consult his colleagues and despatch counter proposals, which he had duly done on the basis of 'external association'. His subsequent communications had not been categorical and their confusing complexion seemed to suggest that there was still a chance of settlement; that, as Cope and Fitzalan reiterated, he would settle and that words did not mean what they said.

By 26 August he had begun to consider sending representatives to London. At a private meeting of the Dáil on the 26th, he had emphasised that plenipotentiaries should be given a 'perfectly free hand' in the negotiations; that members of a 'commission' should 'go and do their best' while remembering 'that everything they did' would be referred to the Dáil, which would have 'to say . . . whether it approved . . . or not'.[77] When the ministry made its recommentation that such plenipotentiaries should be given a free hand, it must be remembered that 'if the house voted that down, that would be a vote of no confidence'.[78] On the 27th the Dáil ministry decided that the plenipotentiaries, 'if appointed', should be ratified by the Dáil, and that this decision 'should be submitted to the Dáil' that same day.[79] On 9 September the Dáil ministry chose its representatives to a conference, subject to approval by the Dáil. Griffith, Collins, Duggan, Barton and Gavan Duffy were appointed; Childers would act as general secretary; de Valera would not take part in the conference.[80]

De Valera, therefore, would not go to London. Perhaps his interviews and his correspondence with Lloyd George had convinced him that he could not bring back what he wanted; that the constitutional limits of a settlement were already fixed; that even if he were willing to accept such a position, he could not hope to bring the extremists, or the ideologues, or the IRA men with him. For that, Collins would be necessary; and Collins would drive the hardest bargain with Lloyd George. Griffith would go as a man of experience, as a popular name, as the father of Sinn Féin. Barton, the Protestant landowner from Co. Wicklow, had been educated at Rugby and Christ Church; he was a Sinn Féiner now, but had served with the British army during the war; he had been in the Dáil cabinet, had acted as de Valera's messenger during the summer, had in de Valera's words been present 'at all our discussions' and 'knew our views thoroughly'.[81] Duggan was a solicitor, who had had a 'reputation' with the British for extremist views, and he had since the truce acted as the chief liaison officer between the IRA and the British army. Gavan Duffy had been active in anti-Redmondite politics since the war; he was a lawyer, and had been the Dáil minister for foreign affairs; he had a good name, being the descendant of the 1848 patriot. With Griffith, Collins, Duggan, Duffy and Barton would go Erskine Childers as secretary. Childers was Barton's cousin, who like Barton had served in the British army. He had done so twice — in the Boer War and in the Great War; in the intervening period he had become a home ruler, had run arms to Ireland in 1914, had joined de Valera, and had become increasingly extreme in his views.

But de Valera would not go to London. Yet there was no reason then, in late September 1921, to anticipate that he would be dissatisfied with the terms brought home, and no reason to believe that, given his interviews with Lloyd George, he did not know what these terms would be. Nor was there any reason to expect he would dissociate himself from those terms. Throughout September, October and November he may have hoped that, come what would, Collins would control the 'men with the guns' and that he, de Valera, would accept the terms and remain president of some 'externally associated' Ireland. But he may have underestimated the passionate republicanism of Brugha, who remained behind with him in Dublin, and he made his first slip — for that is what it would initially have constituted — when he dis-associated himself from the terms which the delegates brought home in December.

But all this was in the future. On 30 September he had accepted Lloyd George's invitation to a conference, which would begin in London on 11 October.

5
October — December 1921

1. The Conference on Ireland and the Regulation of the IRA

The conference on Ireland opened in London on 11 October. The British representatives were Lloyd George, Greenwood, Worthington-Evans, Churchill, and the attorney-general, Hewart, who attended constitutional discussions. The Irish were Collins, Griffith, Barton, Duggan and Gavan Duffy. The general issues of the settlement were considered in a series of plenary sessions, and the particular ones in a series of sub-committees, ranging from those concerned with finance and trade to that on constitutional matters.

Although there were, therefore, a number of issues for settlement, the conference came to hinge on the attitude of the Irish to the crown, the empire and the ports — in regard to which the question of Ulster was crucial. But a more particular issue had as important a bearing on the Irish delegates, and revealed the way in which their new responsibilities conflicted with those of the IRA men at home. This involved the truce and the behaviour of the Volunteers.

When the conference opened, the decision had already been taken by the British politicians, prompted by Macready, that the activities of the IRA must be regulated by agreement with the Irish delegates. Throughout the summer complaints had been made by Macready that the IRA had continued to drill and form fours; to set up training camps; to parade in uniform, with arms; and to behave generally in a manner which seemed to Macready both provocative and aggressive. The question had been all the more serious for Macready, in view of the claims of the IRA that the truce involved a recognition of its status as an army — claims which Macready and his subordinates continued to deny, but to which they remained sensitive in view of the complications which would result, particularly if hostilities were to be resumed. In any case, on 27 September, Macready had urged that the truce should be placed 'on a satisfactory and simple basis' once the conference opened, a proposition which had been supported by Worthington-Evans and Fitzalan.[1] On 6 October the cabinet had agreed that a truce committee be appointed at the outset of the conference.

During the summer, Lloyd George had seemed to ignore Macready's complaints about IRA activities, presumably in order to avoid antagonising de Valera, but after the conference began in October, he became more determined to intervene. Now that the Sinn Féin representatives were in London, he could of course afford to do so. But he was also influenced by the questions tabled in the house as to the circumstances of the truce, and by the grumblings of the Conservatives, many of whom would be meeting in Liverpool in mid-November. Unless he could satisfy potential critics on the 'truce', he could not carry them on the more important aspects of the settlement, however they might work out. Midleton, for example, believed that the government would be given a 'very warm time' at Liverpool, not only over the conference itself, but over the way in which the truce had been 'broken in all directions'.[2] Throughout the period 12 to 25 October, the British determined to resolve what they saw as the more offensive IRA activities by securing Irish agreement on drilling, parades, arms importation, camps, republican courts, and levies. They had decided by 10 October that such activities could not be tolerated.[3] But although the Irish were to be warned that the government might otherwise be forced to take steps which might prove prejudicial to the results of the conference, at the same time it was privately decided that the importance of not 'interrupting the conference' must be borne in mind.[4]

The 'Committee on the Observance of the Truce', as it was officially called, first met on 12 October, with Collins, Barton and Duggan on the Irish side and Worthington-Evans and Greenwood on the British. Anderson, Macready, Tudor and Cope also attended. Agreement was reached instantly on certain matters, facilitated by the finding of formulae, rather than by precise undertakings given by the Irish, who did not 'countenance' either levies or the commandeering of premises by the IRA, and who undertook generally, in regard to funerals and Church parades of IRA men, that though the numbers would not be limited, neither arms nor uniforms would be displayed.[5] The British, for their part, agreed to notify local liaison officers of troop movements, and to permit the joint inspection of prisons.[6] Both sides resolved to improve liaison arrangements, and both agreed that seventy-two hours notice of the termination of the truce should be given — an arrangement which would be recorded in writing.[7]

The outstanding issues — drilling, IRA camps, courts, coroners' inquests, and the withdrawal of the Irish republican police — were referred to the conference and when Lloyd George presided over a meeting of the British representatives next day, it was decided to tell the Irish that these 'violations of the truce' would not be tolerated.[8] Unless the Sinn Féin representatives could put a stop to them 'they' i.e., the British, 'would have no option but to use force to prevent them'.[9]

Lloyd George had been particularly irritated by the publicity surrounding the opening of the Irish courts 'in the name of the Irish republic', reports of which had appeared in the *Star* on the 12th, as he had also been of the photographs of 'ostentatious' drilling which had appeared in the *Illustrated London News*.[10] Sensitive to potential criticism among Conservatives of his handling of these matters, he determined to stop them and he held that during the conference the status quo must be maintained, and the precedent of Vereeniging followed — which would permit only that activity which had been possible before the truce.[11]

On the 13th the Irish representatives agreed to prepare a formula in respect of the courts, drilling, and the camps.[12] Regarding the courts they suggested that none should be held 'otherwise than as before the truce', while in respect of the displays of drilling, they promised that 'causes of complaint have been or are being removed'.[13] By the 17th the formulae proposed had been approved in Dublin.[14] By the 20th agreement had been reached on what had been, for the British, the most contentious matters: levies, church parades, funerals, comandeering of premises, drilling camps and courts; the Irish had, in turn been mollified by certain British concessions.[15] Notice would be given of the movement of crown forces, and joint prison inspections would begin.[16] Both sides would try to improve liaison arrangements, and both undertook to give seventy-two hours notice of termination of the truce.[17] By the 24th arms importation by the Irish had been prohibited by mutual agreement, following the announcement — of which much was made by Lloyd George — of the discovery in Hamburg of a shipment of arms, destined for Ireland.[18] Although the Irish denied that arms importation breached the truce, they none the less recommended to de Valera in Dublin that in view of the objections of the British and in order to give evidence of 'bona fides . . . we shall refrain from importing arms and munitions' during the truce.[19] The proposal was duly accepted in Dublin.[20]

By 25 October the outstanding implications of the truce had been, as it were, 'officially' settled between the parties, and a white paper, 'Arrangements governing the cessation of Active Operations in Ireland', was published on the 26th for presentation to parliament.[21] Lloyd George intended to refer to this paper when replying to parliamentary questions on the subject, and the matter would, in a sense, be both legitimised, and dropped.[22]

Irish agreement to British requests to regulate the IRA had been secured for a number of reasons. The Irish were reluctant to break off negotiations on a matter which seemed to them to be removed from the real business of the conference, the constitutional position of Ireland and the unity of the country. The possibility existed that, if they refused to co-operate, there might be a break. Collins, for example, after the discussion on the 13th about camps and drilling, wrote to the IRA adjutant-general O'Sullivan, in Dublin, that 'at one time today [it] looked like a break', and to de Valera that 'things looked very serious at one time'.[23] Childers, the secretary to the delegation, who subsequently became an opponent of the signing of the agreement, partly because it did not represent England's last word, at that stage urged de Valera on 13 October to approve 'by return' the formulae governing the courts, 'else we shall have to break off the negotiations, which on a matter like this would be absurd'.[24] Moreover, the delegation felt that certain activities (like the importing of munitions under the circumstances as reported) could not 'be defended' at the conference, not because they breached the truce, but in view of British objections, and in order to give evidence of 'our bona fides'.[25] In addition, Collins, recognising the political difficulties arising out of ostentatious IRA activity for Lloyd George, explained to O'Sullivan that the objections to the camps were 'again . . . a question of publicity'.[26] Collins had also been irritated and embarrassed by the publicity which some of the IRA men had lent themselves to. He had 'never felt so ashamed' as when the British produced photographs of armed men and 'joked about the actions of men with a machine gun covering their faces with handkerchiefs'.[27] He resented the IRA 'performance' and claimed that 'if the unostenticity part of it had been maintained we would not have been let down like we have been. It is . . . a dam [*sic*] shame . . . and cheap bravado at that'.[28]

Nor was it felt that the regulations would have any real effect on the IRA or the courts. Childers considered that the courts could be 'efficiently carried on without this display', and Collins that if the publicity surrounding the camps and drilling were removed, so too would the 'real grievance'.[29] In the case of the levy, the Irish leaders – both those in London and in Dublin – had already concerned themselves with its replacement by a voluntary collection, and notices had been issued to that effect.[30]

In general the new regulations were passed on to the IRA from Collins in London, through O'Sullivan, or Mulcahy (IRA chief-of-staff) or de Valera – to whom the various formulae were also submitted for official approval. De Valera tended not to withhold his sanction, and any hesitation which he did entertain arose from his determination that the 'civil' ministry must not be undermined. He insisted, for example, that 'we cannot give way an inch on this question of the civil functioning' but conceded that it was 'certainly too bad that the other side should have got the opportunity which [the] blaze of publicity gave them'.[31]

De Valera readily fell in with the prohibition on levies. Indeed he wanted the voluntary collections to be stopped altogether and a central payment substituted.[32] The position at that stage — October 1921 — was that each IRA brigade was or should have been financed by its local area, as suggested by the IRA staff general order of December 1920.[33] That general order did not sanction the use of force by the Volunteers to get their money, but rather emphasised the moral duty of the population to contribute to a collection.[34] By the summer of 1921, however, the collections had assumed something of the character of a levy, due to the intimidations which accompanied them from time to time, and which according to Mulcahy were 'not in . . . the spirit of the general order'.[35] As a result, even before the conference in London had begun, headquarters had prohibited the levy. O'Hegarty, the IRA director of organisation, laid down the principle to which both Brugha and Mulcahy agreed. The collections might be made, provided there was no resort 'to force or threats'.[36] Privately O'Hegarty sympathised with the local IRA officer who claimed that the people who wanted a republic were 'not prepared to pay' for it.[37] Although headquarters had decided to pay a token five pound note to three officers in each division, this had made little impression on local finances: administrative expenses had to be 'borne by the divisional area itself', and since the truce began the expense of running the army had risen, in the view of some local officers, fourfold.[38] By October, Mulcahy estimated that even for training and administration the cost would be over £200,000 for a twelve-month period — and that was a 'skimpy' estimate.[39]

De Valera's proposal, therefore, to pay the IRA from central funds, seemed a reasonable proposition, if an expensive one. Central payment would remove the irregularities which still accompanied the collections, and it would also 'react very favourably on the subscription to the bonds', i.e., the Dáil loans.[40] Moreover, such a move would increase de Valera's effective control over the Volunteers, just as his ultimate veto over the spending of Sinn Féin funds had done with that organisation. For the funds involved would be the Sinn Féin funds, from which no money could be issued 'except on the requisition of the president', and against which no orders were to be issued which did not have his 'approval'.[41]

De Valera's attempt to introduce central payment of, if not presidential control over, the Volunteers failed. From London, Collins, his minister for finance, warned that the treasury couldn't afford it, and that in any case even the enemy admitted that 'we had a right to our collections'.[42]

But de Valera's interest in army matters did not stop there. With Brugha and Stack – ministers for defence and home affairs respectively – he intervened in matters connected with the army which had hitherto not concerned the cabinet, for example in allocating £1,000 to the first western division for an arms factory.[43] With Brugha and Stack he approved the new regulations from London. Instructions were issued by Mulcahy to the units prohibiting, for example, comandeering or arms importation, while Brugha put his name to the instructions on levies and collections.[44] But de Valera's most dramatic intervention was that suggesting a new army, proposals for which he had announced on 15 September, but had then apparently abandoned until after the delegation had left for London.[45]

De Valera's plans for a 'new' or re-commissioned army emphasised the supremacy of the cabinet and government over the army, at the head of which stood the minister for defence as the cabinet's own representative.[46] Commissions to staff and officers would be issued by the government[47] and the irregular nature of the composition and control of the local IRA units would be undermined. The staff meetings would henceforth be attended by Stack and Brugha – a proviso which may have been directed towards counteracting the staff officer and IRB tendencies in the army with his own men.[48]

There the matter had rested until November, when the ministry, prompted by Mulcahy, decided to summon the delegation from London, for the ceremonial passing of the old army, and the 'formation of the new'.[49] Collins treated the affair lightly – it reminded him 'of Napoleon' – and at the 25 November cabinet the civil supremacy of the government over the army was recorded, as was the procedure for granting fresh commissions.[50] The minister for defence, a civilian, would be 'administrative head of the army', with the duty of sanctioning all appointments, and the power of veto.[51] Mulcahy remained as chief-of-staff, with O'Duffy and Stack as deputy chiefs-of-staff; O'Sullivan continued as adjutant-general; Collins as director of information, rather than intelligence; O'Connor remained director of engineering, though his other 'job' as O/C Britain was not recorded; O'Hegarty alone was dropped from the staff, his post as director of organisation being filled by Eamon Price.[52]

De Valera's interventions in the affairs of the army had little immediate impact. He had been discouraged from proceeding with attempts to pay the army centrally; his 'new' army was little more than the old one with fresh commissions; and it was unlikely that the principle of 'civil' control would bear any immediate effect on the local Volunteers, who had not yet experienced its implications, and to whom Mulcahy explained there was neither a 'new army' nor serious change.[53] None the less, de Valera persisted in publicly associating himself with the army — probably to impress, not only upon the Volunteers, but on Lloyd George, that he too was prepared for war, should the negotiations break down.

In November he prepared to visit local units, the second southern and first western divisions, on a grand tour of inspection, from Limerick to Galway, accompanied by his minister for defence and chief-of-staff. Although the specific object was to inspect the army, he would meet the people (chosen beforehand as leading local figures), and receive the addresses of the local councils as well as the Freedom of Limerick. The local commanding officer would arrange all details on the basis of suggestions submitted by the president's department beforehand, and the Sinn Féin cumainn would assist where possible.[54] The president would inspect the units and meet brigade staffs. He would be accompanied by a 'film man' who would take the pictures. The photographs of Mr de Valera inspecting rows of uniformed men would serve to establish the president as head of the army, ready to resume the war, if need there should be.[55]

Although the president would meet local people, he would spend the nights with the bishops, and his standing in the community would be enhanced by the status of his hosts, as it also would be by the ceremony granting him the 'Freedom of Limerick'. He would be entertained by the local children who would sing and dance at organised evenings of Irish entertainment.[56] He would be further honoured by the ceremony installing him as chancellor of the National University.[57]

Yet neither de Valera's visits to the divisions nor the new instructions or commissions made any great impact on the IRA. The headquarters staff continued to be anxious about discipline, and the local officers complained of insubordination. The commanding officer of the first southern division, Liam Lynch, for example, remarked that 'the sooner all our officers realise they are nothing more than the ordinary fighting man, the better for the army as a whole'.[58] Mulcahy sympathised with him — particularly over Barry's threatened resignation as liaison officer — and suggested that the latter's trouble was vanity, as well as his being 'petulant and childish in some statements'.[59] Regarding the resignations of the martial law liaison officers, proffered by Barry, he warned that 'this thing must stop. We have either truce or war, and whoever by any want of discipline reopens the war prematurely, will have to be held accountable for it'.[60]

But the indiscipline in the IRA — as far as the staff and politicians went — could be more serious than swollen heads. Looting, drinking and unseemly local squabbles between the units provoked headquarters investigations, general orders and presidential concern. After a meeting of the Dáil ministry, which considered Volunteer drinking habits, de Valera requested that the officers be ordered to use stern disciplinary methods to have 'this thing stamped out' and a general order was drafted threatening reduction in the ranks for a first offence, and dismissal for a second.[61] O'Duffy recommended similar penalties — from reduction in the ranks to dismissal from the army — to deal with the rivalry and resentments within the 'mid' and 'city' Limerick brigades, where disagreements were exacerbated by the differences between the city and country men, and the desire to control arms, cash and appointments.[62] Mulcahy prohibited the Volunteers from intervening in civil affairs, following the attempts of two IRA men in Clare to secure a teaching job for one of their number and a hospital appointment for a sympathetic doctor. Mulcahy warned that 'we cannot afford that public representatives would feel . . . the army were interfering . . . with their special functions'.[63]

Meanwhile, despite the new regulation of the activities of the IRA, much of which was initiated in London, little change occurred. On the whole, the feeling in the units was that the truce was a preparation for war. Headquarters' representatives continued to visit the training camps and the divisions, and rumours of a break continued to be circulated. Some army men believed in nothing but a break followed by the resumption of hostilities. Others were willing to be influenced by the presidential precautions and the systematic warnings from the leaders that a break was possible, if not probable. The adjutant-general had preparations made to circulate the units when the truce snapped and de Valera, whether to keep the Volunteers ready or to strengthen his own position, did not discourage the increased activities. He warned, for example, in late November, that the Dáil departments should prepare for an immediate breakdown.[64]

There was also the view, which Fitzalan conveyed, that the drilling afforded a means of keeping the men together,[65] for 'once they let their men go and there is no conference, they wont [sic] be able to get them back again'. In any case, the Volunteers were ready, and it seemed they had no other plans for the long term but to be ready — unhindered by either the restrictions coming from London or the instructions issued in Dublin.

Arms continued to be imported. A report in December 1921 showed a big increase in the proportion brought in since the truce: the imports for the July-December period exceeded those for the previous eleven months.[66] IRA numbers increased dramatically and systematically: 30,000 in July; 50,000 in October; 75,000 in December; though the figures may have been nearer an impression than a count, based in some cases on the numbers at a parade.[67] Oblivious

to what happened in Dublin and the ministry, and even more
so of events in London (except perhaps in respect of tighter
regulations) the Volunteers continued as hitherto, indifferent
to politics, and with renewed self-confidence. Although levies
were prohibited, the degree of force employed in a collection
remained, as it were, 'a matter for God and the local O/C'.
Volunteer drinking or, as it was called, 'indulging in excesses'
may have diminished – though there is little evidence either
way. Nor is there evidence that the Kerry men stopped
drinking either after hours or with the 'enemy' police.[68]

As before the truce, the IRA remained insensitive to
politics and indifferent to central control. Not that they
resented de Valera's visits or the uniformed parades for the
'film' man, for these provided a sense of occasion. Nor did
they refuse fresh commissions, for those were for the
'officers', and brought little change. On the whole they were
not concerned with the constitutional dialectics of de Valera,
or the odd, if not slightly ridiculous, sobriety of Brugha.
The Volunteers were a-political rather than anti-political,
though within, it must be said in many cases, an ideological
context; and it was only when the treaty was signed that this
context became relevant to the men with the guns.

2. Ulster: A negotiable quantity?

*I am quite certain however that if you attempted an
all-Ireland parliament, without the willing assent of
Ulster, at all events in this part of the world, there
would be a tremendous rally to Ulster's side.* (Derby
to Lloyd George, 18 November 1921.[69])

When the conference on Ireland opened in London on
11 October, although Lloyd George indicated to the Irish
that he did not wish to 'hurry the proceedings', he also made
it clear that there were 'forces at work in this country' which
thought that the government 'had gone too far already'.[70]
Despite the apparent tactical nature of this warning, Lloyd
George, for his own part, was not oblivious to these 'forces'.
Although he seemed initially in no hurry to settle, he became

increasingly determined to do so, particularly from the end of October, by when it was clear to him that a settlement could only be won through a satisfactory resolution of the problem of Ulster.

On 4 October Griffith put forward the Irish case. He suggested that if the British government were to stand aside, then the south would reach agreement with Ulster, but that Ulster would adopt a *non possumus* attitude 'so long as they feel the British government [is] behind them'.[71] He denied the legitimacy of the Government of Ireland Act's delineation of Northern Ireland: in the historic nine-county province of Ulster, there were 850,000 Protestants and 750,000 Catholics, whereas in the six-county area there were 800,000 Protestants and 400,000 Catholics.[72] The present division was 'unnatural'; Tyrone and Fermanagh should not have been included, while Armagh and Derry would have voted against partition.[73] The 'Ulster question', in Griffith's view, amounted merely to a 'Belfast city question'.[74]

Although in discussion with the Irish, Lloyd George referred to the way in which Ulster had 'defeated' Gladstone and 'would have defeated us' — i.e., between 1911 and 1913 during Asquith's attempts to proceed with home rule — although he told them they had 'got to accept facts' and 'the first axiom is ... we could not coerce Ulster', none the less he became increasingly worried that Tyrone and Fermanagh would 'wreck' the settlement.[75] He warned the Irish of the 'growing sentiment in a powerful section' of Chamberlain's party, particularly those who viewed 'with grave disfavour our attempts to produce a settlement'.[76] He insisted that 'Northern Ireland' was not his government's 'definition' of the problem, but rather 'our compromise', to 'get out of a problem which wrecks every bill'.[77] On 21 October — the day upon which he announced the discovery of the arms ship in Hamburg destined for Ireland — he insisted 'we must know where we are'; he asked that the Irish submit a document which would give their 'definite attitude' on the matters of allegiance to the crown, inclusion in the empire, and on the British claim to coastal facilities. He subsequently determined, on the basis of that document, to see what could be done so that Ulster would not 'wreck' the settlement.[78]

When the Irish document was received on the 24th, although it provided no definite answer on allegiance to the crown, Lloyd George determined to concentrate 'on the ground of agreement reached'.[79] After a meeting between Chamberlain and Lloyd George for the British side and Collins and Griffith for the Irish, Lloyd George reported to his colleagues that he felt they would accept the crown 'all else being arranged'.[80] He had secured an undertaking from Griffith that although he could not accept the crown himself, as a representative of the 'republic', he would 'recommend it', 'all else being satisfactory'.[81] The Irish had claimed that 'the only way to reconcile Ireland to the crown' would be to secure Irish unity; and the British representatives resolved to set up another committee 'to explore the Ulster question' with Chamberlain and Hewart as the British members.[82]

On the 25th, after a meeting with Griffith and Collins who promised that they would give Ulster all her 'existing powers and possibly more', on condition that 'she accepted [the] position of a provincial legislature and came into the central Dublin parliament', Chamberlain reported that they had put what could not be 'a more difficult question'.[83] Having disputed the present 'boundary' of Ulster, they asked why the British would 'not allow county option'.[84]

The position for the British was 'impossible': even before the negotiations, Lloyd George had referred to the problem in terms of men who would die for king and empire, but not for Fermanagh and Tyrone.[85] Now, Churchill referred to the difficulty: they simply could not 'give way on [the] six counties; we are not free agents', though they could 'do' their 'best' to include the six in a larger parliament plus autonomy, and to press Ulster to hold autonomy for the six 'from them instead of from us'.[86] Birkenhead agreed that 'our position re six counties is an impossible one if these men want to settle as they do'.[87] As far as Churchill and Birkenhead were concerned, the British could not break on the county issue nor could they 'give way' over the six; at most they could press Craig to extricate them from this 'impossible' situation. It was this course which Lloyd George chose.

Lloyd George determined to resume the discussion with

the Irish, but not on Ulster. Instead, he would ask them to state their position 'on vital things', indicating simultaneously that he would be willing to discuss the Ulster 'area', and to consider 'any machinery by which [the] unity of Ireland should be reorganised or strengthened'.[88] If they accepted 'all subject to unity', then he would be 'in a position to go to Craig', but if they did not accept 'all', then the break would not be on Ulster.[89]

By 25 October, therefore, Lloyd George had resolved that he would try to settle the Irish question by obtaining Irish assurances on what mattered — allegiance and the empire — in return for Irish unity, and on that basis press Craig. At best, he assumed that with these assurances he could secure a solution and that so 'armed' he might manage, somehow, to arrange a settlement. But without 'unequivocal answers' on the main issues from the Irish, he thought it would prove 'very difficult for my Unionist colleagues who . . . have been fighting this business for the last thirty years'.[90] He was preparing to make a statement in parliament on 31 October by which time the Irish 'answers' would be known to him.

Griffith and Collins were the Irish representatives on the Ulster sub-committee. Privately, Griffith felt that the British believed that 'on the crown they must fight', it being the only link with the empire they possessed,[91] and on 24 October Griffith had, as Lloyd George later reported to his colleagues, indicated that whereas they could not accept the crown, as representatives of the republic, if all else were satisfactory, he would undertake to 'recommend it'.[92] They had made it clear that the only way to reconcile Ireland to the crown was to secure 'Irish unity'.[93]

Griffith, therefore, by 24 October was willing to accept the essential demands of the British in return for Irish unity. But it was not certain that the Irish at home would accept such a bargain. Collins, by that stage, felt the conference was entering its 'final' stage.[94] Uncertain of its outcome, he warned O'Sullivan in Dublin that the IRA training camps should be struck up 'quickly and quietly but effectively and fairly rapidly'.[95] He did concede that, as yet, this was precautionary and there was 'no need at all to be excited', for the British would not 'return to war with any haste'.[96] On the 25th, when he and Griffith discussed the matter with Chamberlain and Hewart, they denied the legitimacy of the existing unit; it was after that that Lloyd George determined to obtain their attitude to the essentials in writing, and on that basis (if it were satisfactory) to go to Craig.[97] On the 28th Duggan sought an assurance that Lloyd George would not reveal the contents of the Irish reply during his parliamentary speech on Monday the 31st, for if favourable in tone, their supporters, who had not been prepared for concessions, would be disturbed.[98] Lloyd George agreed, though if the reply was a refusal, then he might be bound to do so.[99]

The document arrived on Saturday the 29th and was sent to Lloyd George who was at Chequers. In London Greenwood and Chamberlain read it. Greenwood described it as containing 'substantive' statements which 'make a great advance, and assuming good will and sincerity mean that the republic is dead': Ireland, like Canada, would be 'a "free partner" in the British Commonwealth' swearing 'allegiance to the same king'; and although there was also 'qualifying' statements, the 'substantive' ones were, according to Greenwood 'the keys to the document'.[100] Chamberlain was less happy. He hoped the document could be withdrawn, and felt that the Irish were 'just playing with us, just fooling us'.[101]

In the evening, Jones, the cabinet secretary, who continued, throughout the conference, to intervene unofficially with all the participants in order to promote a settlement, met Cope and Duggan. Jones suggested that in addition to the document a further one might be submitted, drafted perhaps by Hewart and Griffith, or that a private letter might be written, acknowledging allegiance, common citizenship and imperial defence, which would serve to 'arm' Lloyd George in his forthcoming speech.[102] Duggan proposed, instead, a private meeting between Griffith and Lloyd George, with or without Collins.[103]

On Sunday evening, 30 October, Lloyd George returned to London. He felt the Irish reply left him in a 'very insecure position; that it was essential . . . to carry Birkenhead with him . . .' for 'he would control most of the Unionists, as they regarded Chamberlain as a Liberal Unionist'.[104] Lloyd George would be dining with Churchill and Birkenhead that night at Churchill's house, and he wanted Griffith and Collins to come there.[105] He intended in his speech the next day to talk 'to the country', and not to the diehards ('these worms') and would make clear what the alternative to breakdown would be.[106]

Lloyd George first saw Griffith alone, Griffith and Collins having decided on that course rather than on seeing Lloyd George together.[107] The prime minister again reiterated that there were three 'vital' matters: the crown, the empire and the navy.[108] He said that he could carry a six-county parliament subordinate to a national parliament, or, referring to another plan, he mentioned the prospect of a new boundary on a vote on inclusion or exclusion of the whole of Ulster as a unit.[109] Afterwards, Lloyd George, Churchill and Birkenhead assured Griffith and Collins, that, if certain 'of our good will' as Griffith later put it, then they would 'go strongly' against a 'diehard attack'.[110] Collins felt that matters were now getting down to 'dead level'; that the position might be reduced to a 'united Ireland' provided the Irish constitution recognised the crown, as 'the centre of the British Commonwealth of Nations'; and provided that 'certain safeguards' would be accorded to the north-east and the southern unionists, and that in turn an assurance would be given that 'we won't have our freedom impaired by any association against the British Commonwealth of Nations'.[111]

Lloyd George's position by 1 November was that, having spoken on the Irish matter the previous day in the commons (the voting was 439 to 43) and been pleased with the reception of his speech, he had decided to resume negotiations the next morning with Griffith and Collins.[112] His attitude, in which he was supported by Birkenhead (whom he considered to be vital as far as the Unionist party went) and Churchill, was that provided the Irish would settle on essentials, he would oppose the diehards over Ulster. But it was an attitude of hope, rather than of firm intention, and one which tormented him over the weekend of 28-30 October, when preparing his speech for the 31st. On the 30th, it looked to him as if the 'Sinn Féiners' would settle on the king, the empire and naval facilities, in return for Tyrone,

Fermanagh and customs, with excise and the post office to be controlled by one parliament instead of two — northern and southern.[113] But 'the Ulster people' would 'never agree' and then the question would arise 'whether the English people are prepared to fight in order to support them'.[114] Yet although the doubt as to how far he could deal with Ulster remained, he was simultaneously determined not to continue the Irish war if a settlement were possible on those lines.[115] He would resign.[116] He told C.P. Scott on the 28th that he was determined, if possible, 'to put the negotiation through and secure peace' even if as a result a general election were necessary to 'ask the people if they wanted peace or not'.[117] Although he would resume the war with Sinn Féin if they did not settle on the essentials, he would fight the Tories if they refused to accept the 'minimum concessions'.[118] He was tired and disenchanted; having had 'fourteen years of office' his life was not 'a bed of roses'; instead of a holiday in Gairloch, for example, he had had as much work as in London — and blood poisoning to boot — and he was now under medical orders to rest each day.[119]

Whether Lloyd George was serious about resigning or about fighting the Tories is unclear, but it was also unclear to himself. He may have hoped that the suggestion would bring the majority of Conservatives to his support, and cut off the diehards, and that it would, as it were, force the Irish to settle, rather than leave their fortunes to an unknown but probably reactionary government.

What is clear is that Lloyd George was particularly dis-appointed with Law. Although he had been careful to bring Birkenhead into the negotiations and secure his co-operation throughout, because it would be Birkenhead, not Chamberlain, who would be the more influential with the Unionists (and particularly the thirty or so in the Liverpool area), he had not anticipated the intervention of Law. Law had resigned, on grounds of ill-health, the previous March. Lloyd George had not thought he would recover 'so soon', or that when he did 'he would want to return to active political life'.[120] But Law had recovered; and he had come back; and though 'reasonable and moderate up to a point . . . at heart he was an Orangeman and the Orange fanaticism was there', which he had brought with him from Canada.[121] He and Carson had breakfasted recently with Lloyd George, who felt that Law might 'at any time, in defence of what he regarded as an attack on Ulster, lead a Tory revolt'.[122] Lloyd George did not know whether Law was 'solely actuated by a conscientious desire to champion the cause of Ulster', or whether 'he thinks he sees his opportunity to become prime minister'.[123] Although he could scarcely bring himself 'to believe that he would desire to supplant me', there were, as he repeated 'no friendships at the top'.[124]

None the less, Lloyd George, after the division in the house on the 31st, resolved to try to bring the negotiations through. On 2 November he secured from Griffith what he considered to be the essential document with which to confront Craig and the diehards.[125] Griffith referred to his undertaking to give an 'assurance' in relation to the commonwealth, the crown and naval defence, provided 'the essential unity of Ireland' was recognised.[126] 'As to the north-east of Ireland' Griffith, while reserving for further discussion the question of area, would agree 'to any necessary safeguards (and to the maintenance of existing parliamentary powers) . . .'[127] Griffith sent de Valera a copy of this letter, and explained that he believed that the British would be 'satisfied' to face "Ulster" on it, adding that they 'assure me . . . if "Ulster" proves unreasonable they are prepared to resign rather than use force against us'.[128]

On 7 November Lloyd George saw Craig, who would not 'budge an inch'. This would mean, therefore, a break and he asked Jones to see Griffith and Collins and prepare them for it.[129] But he would not be a party to coercing the south, and he resolved to 'go out'.[130] He could not, he claimed, 'rely on' Churchill, though Birkenhead and Chamberlain might go with him.[131] He feared 'we are in for five or six years' reaction', which he did not want to lead.[132] The only 'possible way out' might be if the twenty-six counties took their own dominion parliament and had a boundary commission, leaving Ulster with her present powers plus representation in the imperial parliament, plus the 'burdens of taxation which we bear': he 'might be able to put that through', if Sinn Féin would take it.[133]

On the 8th, Griffith and Collins were warned of the impending break. They did not want a boundary commission. Griffith would prefer a plebiscite, and Collins did not like the suggestion 'at all' because 'it sacrificed unity'.[134] Lloyd George, meanwhile, had resolved, or so he claimed, 'to go'.[135] He would not 'be a party to firing another shot in the south of Ireland'.[136] He had told the king; and although his colleagues claimed they would 'stand by' him, he felt they would all — Curzon, Worthington-Evans and Baldwin — 'go over to Bonar' if the opportunity came.[137]

On the 9th, however, Griffith indicated that if Lloyd George wanted to press ahead with the boundary commission, they 'would not turn him down on it'.[138] 'It is not our proposal ... We cannot give him a pledge but ... We are not going to queer his pitch'. Although the Irish would prefer a plebiscite 'in essentials a boundary commission is very much the same' but it would have to be for the six counties, rather than for Tyrone and Fermanagh only.[139]

By then, 9 November, Lloyd George had recovered his confidence in his own position, and was more certain of the support of Birkenhead and Chamberlain, who, he felt, would 'go straight through even at the risk of wrecking his political career'; and he resolved to say a few solemn words of warning 'about Ulster' during his speech at the Guildhall that night.[140] He may have had second thoughts about resigning. On the one hand he may have been heartened by Birkenhead and Chamberlain, and on the other discouraged from resigning by Churchill. Churchill warned him that day of the consequences which would follow resignation: the criticism would be made that the government 'in resigning have abdicated their responsibility'; and that if, in particular, the reason given was that they were 'debarred by honour from coercing the north, and by conviction from coercing the south', then it would be said that despite knowing what should be done and with an 'overwhelming parliamentary majority', they had simply laid down their commission and 'declared themselves incapable of action in any direction'.[141] As a result, Law would form a government, and the Conservative party would rally to the Conservative leader, forming 'a Conservative government ... to fill the gap created by the suicide of the coalition'.[142]

Such a warning may have helped to convince Lloyd George that he should make a final attempt to settle; he would try again with Craig; and if that failed, he would revert to the boundary commission. Otherwise, his resignation might mean the end of the coalition; for, as Churchill reminded him, the Conservatives, instead of rallying to him at the prospect of resignation, would follow a Conservative leader, and that would mean the end not only for now but for ever of his period as prime minister.

On the same day, the 9th, Griffith apprised de Valera by letter of the new situation: Lloyd George would be meeting the whole cabinet next day for the first time since the negotiations began. If he got the support of the whole cabinet, then he would be in a 'strong position to fight Craig and his backers'.[143] He referred to the proposals for a parliament in the twenty-six counties and for a boundary commission to delimit area.

At the cabinet on the 10th emphasis was placed on the need to exercise 'patience' with the north.[144] Lloyd George had prepared a letter for Craig, in which he had wanted, with regard to finance, to warn Ulster of the disadvantages of staying out of the all-Ireland parliament. But during a morning discussion beforehand — with the British 'seven' — it became clear that such tactics 'disturbed' his colleagues, particularly Chamberlain and Worthington-Evans.[145] At the cabinet Lloyd George gave a resumé of the negotiations, concluding that 'We' had not come 'to a break but to a point which is serious'.[146] The discussion turned on the question of coercion. Lloyd George insisted that force could not be used against the Irish once it became known 'they are willing to remain in the empire', and the distinction was drawn, *vis-à-vis* Ulster, between coercion and exerting moral pressure.[147]

Lloyd George wrote to Craig after the cabinet that the time had come 'when formal consultation' between them was necessary for the 'future progress' of the Irish negotiations. He indicated that the settlement towards which his government was working would involve Irish allegiance to the throne, partnership in the empire, provision for those naval securities 'indispensable for Great Britain and her overseas communications', retention by Northern Ireland of 'all the powers conferred . . . by the Government of Ireland Act' and recognition of 'the unity of Ireland' by the establishment of an all-Ireland parliament, upon which would be devolved further powers.[148] Lloyd George added that these proposals were only the 'broad outline' and he invited the ministers of Northern Ireland to meet his government in a conference to approach the details.[149]

Craig rejected both the 'broad outline' and the prospect of discussing details.[150] An all-Ireland parliament could not 'under existing circumstances be accepted by Northern Ireland'; such a parliament was what 'Ulster has resisted for many years'.[151] Northern Ireland, he went on, had accepted the Government of Ireland Act 'as a final settlement and supreme sacrifice' and no government representing 'the loyal population' of Northern Ireland could enter into a conference where an all-Ireland parliament was 'open to discussion'.[152]

Lloyd George did not give up, encouraged most likely by Chamberlain's first reactions to the Craig letter, which he felt had been written 'for a *Morning Post* audience'.[153] Chamberlain believed that Craig's statement to the effect that Ulster would 'prefer exclusion from the imperial parliament, to inclusion with equal taxation' (a claim which had 'never yet' been stated) would 'most seriously prejudice her in the eyes of the British public'.[154] Chamberlain now recommended two courses. First, Lloyd George should see Griffith, bearing in mind that he and Collins had anticipated the prospect of Ulster refusing a united parliament, in which case 'they expected us to allow a vote by constituencies or poor law areas', a vote which would, they felt 'give them more than two counties and would leave "Ulster" economically paralysed'.[155] Second, Chamberlain advised that 'We should . . . discuss how far we can put pressure on Craig in this matter of boundaries'.[156] Moreover, Chamberlain reminded Lloyd George that when talking to Griffith the presumption should be that Sinn Féin would accept dominion home rule for the south, and a 'boundary commission or new delimitation by some other machinery', on condition that 'we do not give new powers to Ulster'.[157]

Lloyd George, therefore, seemed to have the support of Chamberlain who, while urging patience, warned that if Ulster 'goes out she cannot have her present boundaries'.[158] He had the support of Law for a similar course – to allow the south have a dominion parliament, the north to remain in the UK, the establishment of a boundary commission, and the north to have representation in Westminster and share UK taxation.[159] Chamberlain referred to the chance to 'put pressure on Craig in this matter of boundaries', which might result in his deciding to acquiesce in an all-Ireland parliament.[160] Even Law and Carson recognised 'the weakness of his [Craig's] case there' and all Carson's talk pointed to 'agreement on a boundary commission'.[161]

Agreement on the boundary commission was essential in view of the opinion of the Irish, as recorded by Chamberlain, that a vote by constituencies or poor law areas would give the south 'more than two counties and would leave "Ulster" economically paralysed'.[162] If Craig would not agree to the proposals on unity, it did not matter: for Law, Carson, and Chamberlain did; and the Irish had indicated that there were grounds for their doing so as well.

By 12 November Lloyd George had every reason to suppose he had sufficient means for dealing with Craig's objections. He had the support of Law, not only important as an influential Unionist, but all the more so as far as Lloyd George was concerned, in view of his position outside of the government. He had the support of Chamberlain, who was then impressing on party officials, like the chairman, Hope, that he need not resign 'on the mere rumour that the Unionist members of the government are going to break their word'.[163] He had the acquiescence, albeit reluctant, of the Irish to the alternative of a constituency vote which would bring them more than two counties and 'paralyse' the rest of the north economically; and he had that weapon – the possible outcome of a boundary commission or some new frontier delineation (endorsed by Law and Curzon) – with which to convince Craig that he would lose most by remaining outside.

Although Lloyd George determined to press his advantage with Craig, he was deflected from doing so immediately, in view of the impending conference of the 'Conservative Association' at Liverpool on 17 November. Craig's request to Lloyd George to publish their recent correspondence had been rejected, partly because it was seen as an attempt to 'prepare the pitch for the Liverpool meeting'. The feeling existed that if Liverpool were 'adamant' then Craig would be 'impossible', whereas if Liverpool wanted peace, then Craig, on the day afterwards 'would be more placable'.[164]

In the meantime he wrote to Craig that his counter-proposals to make the north and south into two separate dominions were 'indefensible', and he hoped that he would come to a conference and not persist in his 'many preliminary conditions'.[165] But he also thought it would be easier to deal with Sinn Féin before Liverpool, and he set to work on the draft of the treaty with Sinn Féin, which he discussed with the legal adviser, Liddell, on the 15th, with Collins and Griffith, and again with Birkenhead and Liddell on the 16th.

On the 16th he left for Bournemouth, just as the Conservatives and Unionists were gathering in Liverpool. By late afternoon the news from Liverpool was that the die-hards were withdrawing their resolutions, except a mild one proposed by Gretton.[166] The dominant influences at the conference would be Salvidge and Derby. Salvidge 'the nearest to a Tammany boss that we have in this country' and with something of Law's Orange 'fanaticism', had already been approached by Birkenhead, with what must have been, at least as far as his views at the conference went, success.[167] Salvidge, Derby, Birkenhead, Chamberlain, and Worthington-Evans had all urged the conference to support the continuation of negotiations with the Irish[168] and Gretton's resolution was defeated by 1,730 to 70.

In the meantime Craig had written to Lloyd George agreeing to meet him, having made 'our position . . . clear'.[169] Lloyd George, who returned from Bournemouth on the 17th, was now in no hurry to see Craig, the Liverpool vote having 'altered the situation'.[170] He may have been impressed by Derby's warning, after the Liverpool conference, that Liverpool went well only 'on the surface'; that although the result gave 'full authority to continue negotiations', there was 'a good bit of disquiet under the surface' and 'a distinct feeling against coalition'; and that if Lloyd George attempted an all-Ireland parliament 'without the willing assent of Ulster... in this part of the world, there would be a tremendous rally to Ulster's side'.[171] After Liverpool, Lloyd George did not feel it imperative, given Conservative support, to gain Craig's immediate and explicit co-operation, neither, as yet, did he wish to risk Craig's objections.

On the 18th he wrote to Craig, noting that the latter had 'influenza' and deferring a lengthy answer until Craig was better and 'we can have a talk'.[172] On the 20th Craig wrote that when in London, he would be glad to meet him for an informal talk, on Wednesday 23 November.[173] Having thus written to Craig, postponing any talk until the latter recovered from influenza, Lloyd George concentrated on the Sinn Féin representatives. On the 18th he saw Griffith and Collins to discuss the draft treaty, and throughout the course of the next few days discussions and consultations proceeded.

What had the Irish attitude being during the run-up to the Liverpool conference? Griffith and Collins had accepted, albeit reluctantly, Lloyd George's scheme to confront the diehards and, if all else failed, to try to bring about a settlement through the boundary commission. Although not their own, it might reduce the area of Northern Ireland by more than two counties and paralyse it economically.[174] On the 9th Griffith had written to de Valera of this proposal (p.132). On the 11th Collins had left for Dublin, and on the 13th he had attended the Dáil cabinet.[175] Although there is no record of Collins's conversations with de Valera, he must have apprised him of the course the negotiations were taking. At the cabinet in Dublin, de Valera gave it as his opinion that whilst the 'utmost co-operation should exist between Dublin and London, the plenipotentiaries should have a perfectly free hand but [they] should follow original instructions regarding important decisions'.[176] But the problem, of course, lay in the nature of the original instructions and the delegates' interpretation of them. Griffith, for example, had considered the wording of his letter to Lloyd George of 2 November to have been consistent with 'external association' and 'external recognition'.[177] Moreover, de Valera indicated that he did not exclude the possibility of break. At the cabinet on the

13th, he indicated that it was his opinion that concrete proposals should be reached as soon as possible, and if break were 'inevitable' then Ulster would be the best question on which to break — presumably 'better' in de Valera's opinion than the crown or empire.[178] Therefore the problem for the historian may well have existed for the delegates at the time: how far did de Valera privately encourage the delegates — by manner, hints, omission, by the very vagueness of his appreciations — to continue the negotiations along the lines as recorded by Griffith and Collins? How far did he acquiesce in their plans and proposals? How far was the record of the cabinet on 13 November a fair indication of his attitude that although Ulster would be the best question on which to break (if a break were 'inevitable') he was neither clear that a break must take place nor on what issue to break. De Valera referred on the one hand to the plenipotentiaries maintaining a 'perfectly free hand' and on the other to following 'original instructions'. Griffith seems to have assumed that he was following original instructions. Thus in his letter of the 3rd, for example, he pointedly referred to 'external association'.[179]

Collins returned to London after the cabinet of the 13th and on the 15th he and Griffith discussed the draft treaty with Lloyd George.[180] The next day, on which Lloyd George left for Bournemouth, and the Unionists were convening in Liverpool for their meeting, the Irish were sent the draft treaty.[181] The negotiations between Lloyd George and the Irish continued in the days which followed Liverpool. In Dublin the Dáil cabinet had a 'general lengthy discussion' of the peace negotiations on 20 November; two days later in London, the Irish delegates submitted their reply to the draft treaty. From this it seemed that Ireland would be associated with the crown as the symbol and accepted head of the association.[182]

Lloyd George's first reaction to the reply was that it would not do; the Irish were 'back on their independent state again'; they made no mention of the Ulster safeguards; and they must make it clear whether they would be 'in the empire or . . . out'. 'If they are not coming into the empire, then we will make them'.[183] Lloyd George wanted the Irish to be told his views and warned that if their document were not with-drawn, then he would break off negotiations at once.[184] Lloyd George did not break. Griffith indicated that he had not gone back upon his previous position, but the Irish were reluctant to put down all they were prepared to concede, as that would be 'tantamount to giving the PM a blank cheque' and that Craig would yield nothing.[185] Chamberlain simul-taneously advised that though 'we cannot make peace on these terms [i.e., those of the reply] we must not break over this document'.[186] He felt that some words must be found to put into the pact a guarantee for the Irish that the crown would be no more in Ireland than it was in Canada.[187] On the 23rd Lloyd George saw Collins, Griffith and Barton, and 'certain misunderstandings were removed'.[188] A con-ference with the law officers was arranged for the 24th, although its proceedings prompted Lloyd George to think there might be a break.[189]

On the evening of 24 November the Irish delegates crossed to Dublin for the ceremony which marked the 'passing of the old army'.[190] On the 25th the Dáil cabinet discussed the negotiations and unanimously passed a formula regarding the the British crown: 'That Ireland shall recognise the British crown for the purposes of the association as symbol and accepted head of the combination of associated states'.[191] The delegates returned to London and the discussions which ensued concentrated on the form of the oath of allegiance. By 30 November the articles of agreement were ready for submission to the Irish before they crossed again to Ireland on 1 December.[192]

The Irish did not leave for Dublin until the 2nd. On the 1st Griffith met Lloyd George, in order to discuss matters sub-sidiary to the main issues of the treaty, such as the prospect of the north raising an army, the collection of revenue by Ulster, and the proposal that the south would have to pay pensions to British ex-servicemen(!).[193] On the 2nd Griffith and Collins discussed the financial articles with Horne and Curtis, and subsequently saw Lloyd George: certain amend-ments had been made in the draft and allegiance was now to the crown 'as head of the state and the empire'.[194]

In Dublin the Dáil cabinet and delegation met on 3

December to consider the draft treaty, with a further meeting of the cabinet without the delegation which Collins and Griffith attended. At each meeting those present made their positions clear. Griffith was in favour of the treaty; he refused to break on the crown and 'thereby hand to Ulster' the position from which she had been driven.[195] He would not take the responsibility for breaking on the crown; when as many concessions as possible had been conceded and when accepted by Craig, he would go before the Dáil, which was the body to decide 'for or against war'.[196] Although he did not 'like' the document, he did not think it dishonourable. It would practically recognise the republic and the first allegiance would be to Ireland.[197] If it were rejected, the people would be entitled to know what the alternatives were.[198] The country would not fight on allegiance and there would be a split.[199]

Duggan agreed with Griffith, and Collins was in 'substantial agreement' with them. The oath of allegiance would not come into force for twelve months, and it might be worth while taking twelve months and seeing how it would work; he would recommend that the Dáil would go to the country on the treaty, but would also recommend non-acceptance of the oath.[201] The sacrifice to north-east Ulster had been made for essential unity and was justified; and non-acceptance of the treaty was a gamble, as England could arrange for war in Ireland within a week.[202]

Neither Barton nor Gavan Duffy, the two other delegates, agreed. Barton considered that England's last word had not been reached, and that she would not declare war on the question of allegiance. Gavan Duffy agreed with Barton that England was bluffing.[203] De Valera's position was that though the treaty could not be accepted in its 'then form', and that he personally could not subscribe to the oath of allegiance, nor sign any document which would give north-east Ulster power to vote itself out of the Irish state, none the less 'with modification, however, it might be accepted'.[204] He would like to see the plenipotentiaries 'go back and secure peace if possible'; he believed that the delegates had 'done their utmost' and it now remained to them to show that if the document were not amended that 'they were prepared to face the consequences, war or no war'.[205] Brugha agreed with de Valera, except that he would not go so far in recognising the king as head of the associated states.[206] De Valera proposed an alternative form of oath of allegiance 'to the constitution of the Irish Free State, and to the treaty of association and to recognise the king of Great Britain as the head of the associated states'.[207]

The meetings on 3 December, therefore, were somewhat inconclusive. Griffith, Duggan and Collins gave it as their view that the treaty should be signed, and that it represented England's last word. Griffith considered it was for the Dáil to accept or reject it, knowing the alternatives. Collins felt that the Dáil should go to the country – on the treaty – recommending at the same time non-acceptance of the oath. Their view was, therefore, that the document should be signed, and that the Dáil should be responsible for accepting or rejecting the arrangement.

Against signing were Barton and Gavan Duffy – on the grounds that it was not Britain's last word, and that she would not go to war on the oath. Cathal Brugha, filled with bitterness against Griffith and Collins, seemed in accord with de Valera's general lines, but rejected any question of recognising the king as head of the associated states.

But where *was* de Valera?

At the first meeting de Valera expressed 'entire confidence in and satisfaction with' the work of the delegation; at the next cabinet meeting he gave it as his 'opinion' that the treaty could not be accepted in its then form, adding that 'personally' he could not subscribe to the oath of allegiance, nor could he sign any document which would give north-east Ulster power to vote itself out of the Irish state. Was this an 'opinion' rather than an 'instruction'? Were his reservations 'personal' rather than 'official'? He thought the treaty might be accepted 'honourably', 'with modifications' and would like to see the plenipotentiaries 'go back and secure peace if possible', believing that they had done their 'utmost'. From what he said he seemed to suggest that if the document were amended, then it might be accepted.[208] He proposed an alternative form of oath. The delegates were instructed to inform the British that the existing oath would not be accepted by the cabinet, and that if it were not amended, they must face the consequences. Griffith was to inform Lloyd George that the document could not be signed and to state that it was now 'a matter for the Dáil and to try and put the blame on Ulster'.[209]

The delegation, therefore, was despatched with instructions not to sign, unless the oath was altered, but to 'put the blame on Ulster'.[210] There were no more definite instructions, the president and the cabinet having expressed full confidence in the work of the plenipotentiaries, and de Valera having at his most explicit proposed an alternative form of oath, and at his least suggested that he could not sign the document, though that seemed more personal than official. Nor would he join the delegation in London.

Possibly he realised that he could get no more than they could; and he neither wanted 'personally' to sign the kind of document which they would get nor be publicly associated with it. Possibly he wished to remain in Dublin as the arbitrator whom Lloyd George would ultimately have to satisfy, thereby strengthening the position of the delegates. Possibly — and probably — he was, as he seemed, removed from the immediacy of the negotiations, prepared to offer, as he had done with the proposals of 20 July, countless counter-proposals, while simultaneously realising that he could do no better than the plenipotentiaries; that his best course was for the moment to dissociate himself from what Brugha and the extremists would categorise as the dishonourable settlement; and that if and when the time came for a decision, he would only make his mind up then, and not sooner. He had, after all, determined to be away from Dublin from late November until 6 December, though that plan had been interrupted by the return of the delegates on 3 December.[211] Most likely de Valera expected the negotiations to continue as indefinitely as they had already done since 24 June. He hoped that the apparent willingness of the delegates to take the consequences of refusing the treaty, unless the oath were altered, 'war or no war', would deter Lloyd George from making his ultimatum; and if there was to be a break, as de Valera thought there might be, on the form of the oath, it was not to be thought to be on the oath, but rather to be placed on Ulster. All of these were de Valerian considerations, none of which, by 3 December, was necessarily paramount. The course of the negotiations subsequently might or might not have been considered by him, but if it had, it was something to which he neither owned publicly nor admitted privately. The delegates returned to London with the instruction to alter the oath, or otherwise to face the consequences of break.

What happened in London on the delegates' return between 4 and 6 December has become so much a part of the case made against the treaty subsequently that it has tended to put the negotiations themselves up to 4 December, the position of de Valera *vis-à-vis* those negotiations, and that of Lloyd George in respect of them and of his own political position, out of context. The accounts of all sides do not contradict each other. Initially, an impasse seemed to have been reached when the Irish returned and refused to accept the agreement as it stood on the 4th. There was talk of war and break on both sides. Griffith and Collins tried to get Lloyd George to extract from Craig a personal letter saying he would recognise 'unity if the south accepts the commonwealth'.[212] Without something 'on these lines' to offer the Dáil, Griffith and Collins did not feel they could carry more than half of them.[213] Collins saw Lloyd George on the morning of 5 December for a 'heart to heart talk' and the full conference met at 3 p.m. and again at 11.30.[214]

At the afternoon conference a revised form of the oath was discussed, following revision by Collins and Birkenhead, and further discussion took place on the naval and trade clauses.[215] But the outstanding issue continued to be Ulster. The Irish insisted that they should have Craig's decision on accepting the unity of Ireland before they signed any document; Lloyd George claimed they were deliberately trying to break on Ulster, because of their refusal to come within the empire and that Griffith, who had written to him on the subject, was now going back on his word. The prime minister then produced what has become one of the most notorious 'letters' in the course of Irish history, a memorandum in which Griffith had indicated that if Ulster did not accept the principle of a parliament of all Ireland, she could vote to remain subject to the imperial parliament; this course would make it necessary to revise the Northern Ireland boundary. Lloyd George refused to accept that the Irish should have Craig's promise before signing. He dramatically brought out two more documents: one a letter to Craig — which would be sent by destroyer, even now waiting in the docks to leave for Belfast — giving details of the agreement which the Irish delegates had decided to recommend for acceptance to the Dáil; the other letter was a statement that no agreement had been reached. Which would it be? He did not fail to warn the Irish of the consequences of reaching no agreement. And he must, he insisted, have his answer by ten o'clock that night.[216]

Lloyd George's behaviour on this final day has often been treated out of the context of the conference as a whole. His ultimatum to sign or expect the consequences; his timely production of Griffith's memorandum accepting the boundary commission if the north refused unity; his alleged chicanery in giving the impression that, in any case, there would be a revision of the northern boundaries: these have been used as if they alone explained the making of the settlement and the unmaking of modern Ireland.

This of course is far from the case. Lloyd George's 'bargain' over Ulster had developed in the period from 24 October to 17 November. His changing attitudes were influenced by the views of the Conservatives on the settlement he was making, and the prospect that they might withdraw their support from the coalition and set up a Conservative government. At first he had intended to force Craig to acknowledge the unity of Ireland, and was prepared to resign if he did not gain Conservative support. On that basis he secured the co-operation of the Irish on the matter of the crown and the empire. During that time he first determined to press Craig. But his attitude began to change. The Conservative meeting at Liverpool on 17 November had voiced its support for the negotiations, but Lloyd George was warned that the support was superficial, and that he could not count on it if he forced Ulster. By then, in any case, he had begun to have doubts about resigning, and had started to envisage that his settlement could be achieved without Craig, by resorting to the boundary commission. The alternative of a commission had been raised in early November. Griffith had not liked it, but under the circumstances, had, with Collins, co-operated, on the understanding that a vote would probably give the south more than Tyrone and Fermanagh, and thereby render the north-east economically 'paralysed'. The document produced by Lloyd George on 5 December contained nothing new.

What had changed since 17 November was that Lloyd George realised that Craig would not concede under any circumstances, and that therefore the Irish demand for a statement from Belfast on unity before they signed meant that they would not sign at all. This was the worst possible outcome for Lloyd George because not only would the negotiations have failed but the break would have been on Ulster. From the start Lloyd George did not want to break on Ulster: men would fight for king and empire, but not for Fermanagh and Tyrone. His only escape was to force the Irish to sign without reference to Craig and to suggest that even if the north did not vote itself in within the allotted period, there might be a revision of the boundaries favourable to the south. This had already been in the air during the conference. Griffith had indeed written the document which Lloyd George conveniently produced, and he had on 3 November apprised de Valera of these 'personal assurances' — pointing out that his wording was consistent with 'external association and external recognition' — and on the 9th of the boundary commission. Whatever doubts Lloyd George may have had about the efficacy of such a commission, he kept them to himself, as he did any definite assurance regarding the boundary.[217]

Whether Lloyd George would, in fact, have gone to war is something to which he may have given thought, but which he had not yet seriously considered. Like de Valera, he made it clear publicly that war would be the alternative to a satisfactory settlement; unlike de Valera he became implicated in the negotiations, and a break would be a personal and a political failure 'at home and in Washington'.[218] He did of course refer to *making* the Irish settle, and to the military means he would take if a break occurred; but had he forced Ulster, he would have forfeited the support of the Conservative party; and had he broken with the Irish, he would be in the position he had been before. In both cases the alternative might be war, but it might have been war under Bonar Law, rather than under Lloyd George.

6
December 1921 — June 1922

De Valera was shocked as much by the suddeness of the signing of the treaty and its finality as he was by the terms. Not only had he anticipated that he would be consulted before the signing, but he had been physically and mentally removed from the immediacy of the negotiations. As late as 3 December he had indicated to his colleagues that even at that stage he would submit counter-proposals or would propose an alternative, somewhat vaguer, formula for the oath. He had interrupted his visit to the south and west for the cabinet on the 3rd, and had subsequently resumed it, anticipating most likely that the negotiations would be spun out indefinitely.[1] He returned to Dublin shocked by the news, which had reached him in the country, that an agreement had been signed; more shocked that simultaneous publication had been agreed upon before he had seen the terms; and most shocked when he saw them.

De Valera's biographers, Longford and O'Neill, have misinterpreted their subject's reaction to the treaty. In one form or another, their account reflects a commonly held view, whether by supporters or opponents of de Valera. The suggestion has been that de Valera was moved by the document into a condition of deep despondency and that while determined to act fairly he was rent by the fiasco in which the country now found itself.[2] But what should be stressed is that de Valera was as much bemused by the turn which events had taken as he was by the treaty itself. He had not admitted to himself previously that such a document could be signed but neither had he consciously contemplated that the alternative would be either a break or reversion to war, or indeed both. At most he had envisaged that affairs would continue as they had done for the past six months. If 'put to it' he may have hoped that his plenipotentiaries might win the right kind of settlement; or that Lloyd George, once the Irish indicated they might break off negotiations, would persevere rather than revert to war. But he had been certain of nothing. In one sense his strength had been that he admitted to no certainties, alluding instead to the abstract principles of moral right and justice which must settle the fate of the Irish people.

His reaction to the certainty of the treaty was almost one of panic. He summoned those ministers who had remained in Dublin to a cabinet and issued a public statement that he had despatched an 'urgent summons' to those in London 'to report at once' so that a 'full cabinet decision may be taken' at a meeting to be held on Thursday 8 December.[3] A meeting of the full Dáil would be summoned later.[4] De Valera, therefore, slipped into the course from which he subsequently failed to extricate himself: he did not take a decision himself, but probably hoped that the cabinet and the Dáil would share his feelings: the cabinet rejecting the document, and the Dáil following suit.

The reverse occurred. On 8 December, five members of the cabinet declared themselves in favour of 'recommending' the treaty to the Dáil. These were Griffith, Collins, Barton, Cosgrave, and O'Higgins — though the latter had no vote.[5] Three members — de Valera, Brugha and Stack — were against. Griffith would recommend the document on the basis on its 'merits', whereas the others would do so on the basis of its 'signature'.[6] This meant that a majority of the Dáil cabinet favoured recommending the treaty to the Dáil; that they did not (with the exception of Griffith) like it on 'merit', but that now that it was signed, they wanted to put it through. They may have been influenced by Griffith's position, as they also most likely were by Collins's account of the treaty as a 'beginning'.

It was then that de Valera began the process whereby he determined publicly to separate himself from the signatories and the document itself. He would issue a statement to the 'press defining his position' and that of Brugha and Stack; a public session of the Dáil would be summoned for

Wednesday 14 December; ministers, meanwhile, would remain in charge of their departments.[7]

When the Dáil met on the 14th, it was not clear that de Valera had formulated an alternative plan. He still seemed somewhat bemused, referring for example to the failure of the delegates to obey their instructions and submit the final draft of the document to Dublin before signing.[8] The Dáil then went into private session until 17 December and de Valera introduced his alternative to the treaty, which quickly became known as document number two, and in which his policy of 'external association' with the British commonwealth meant that the 'internal republic would not be affected'.[9] But its distinctions were confused. On the one hand it was undermined by its opponents as being a face-saving document for those who needed a means of going 'sideways into the British empire' or 'dodging around a corner when no one is looking'. On the other hand, it was seen as being sufficiently radical to provoke a war with the British over its differences with the treaty.[10] On 19 December Griffith proposed a resolution that the Dáil approve the treaty and the debate continued until 7 January, interrupted by the Christmas recess from 22 December to 3 January.

The publicity given to the treaty and de Valera's setting himself aside from its terms encouraged members of the IRA — who had hitherto stood aloof from politics and the negotiations — to involve themselves in the issues, which seemed, as yet, unresolved. In the Cork first southern divisional area, the staff officers and brigade commandants met on 10 December, and unanimously agreed that the treaty was 'not acceptable to us as representatives of the army'.[11] They urged its 'rejection by the government', submitting their resolution to the chief-of-staff together with a list of those details in the draft which they found particularly repugnant.[12] They subsequently informed the local TDs of their demand that the treaty should be rejected, reminding them of their 'duty' to support this demand: 'to act otherwise would be treason to the republic, to which we have all sworn allegiance'.[13] Though Mulcahy as chief-of-staff objected to this 'most irregular interference' by the Cork men, they were not deterred from insisting that it was 'vital' that TDs should be made to 'realise that their duty was to the republic'. The treaty involved 'the upsetting of the constitution and the betrayal of the republic' and 'who better' than those who had 'fought to maintain' the republic, had the 'right in this crisis to uphold' it?[14]

But the politicians, whatever their views on the treaty, would not, at least not at the outset, tolerate IRA interference in political matters. De Valera had himself publicly referred to the 'constitutional' way of settling 'our grievances' (although that may have served to encourage some to think there was another). Brugha reacted to the Cork correspondence by suggesting that the officer in question needed 'enlightening as to the scope of his duties', that sending reminders to public representatives was 'not one of them' and that it was 'intolerable that military men ... should interfere in matters of this kind'.[15]

But the military interference, on either side, did not stop. Nor did the resolutions throughout the country. De Valera subsequently alleged that attempts to influence reactions to the treaty were made by Collins through the IRB. Some corroboration exists from the time. From Ennis, for example, one IRA officer wrote that he had been ordered by his divisional officer to second a resolution, at the Clare county council, recommending ratification of the treaty, and that orders had been issued by the supreme council of the IRB and by headquarters, IRA.[16] The officer had done as he had been ordered, despite it being 'contrary' to his 'principles': 'I am a republican'.[17] For the moment Brugha continued to insist that there should be no interference by the military men.[18] If Collins none the less instructed that headquarters should intervene or that the IRB should exercise its influence, the rumour was more rife than its evidence, but should not be discounted for that reason.

In any case, as the Dáil continued its talking the country took sides for and against the treaty. Not only the army or the IRB were involved by the time the Dáil temporarily stopped talking, during the Christmas recess: the county councils, farmers, labourers, civic bodies, all passed resolutions *ad infinitum*. From west Limerick the labourers and farmers held a Christmas Day meeting 'approving the treaty' and called on the area's TDs to attend the Dáil and ratify it.[19] They also took it upon themselves to condemn as 'hysterical factionists', those who were now referring to Collins as a 'traitor'.[20] There were other meetings and resolutions. The first southern division persisted in its protestations of loyalty to the republic, warning Mulcahy about taking disciplinary action against those involved. Liam Lynch, the commander of the Cork No.2 brigade, claimed that the 'government, GHQ staff . . . army in the rest of Ireland' outside the southern divisions and the Dublin brigade had 'outrageously' let the latter 'down'; and when the Free State came into existence, 'GHQ can be responsible for discipline which I have great fears will be hard to maintain'.[21] Lynch, for one could not carry out 'any order against IRA principles' when 'such principles stand the danger of being given away by our unthankful government'.[22]

While the country was 'beginning to glow' the Dáil was in recess, but the debate resumed on 3 January and on the 7th the treaty was approved by sixty-four votes to fifty-seven.[23] De Valera then resigned as president and was not re-elected. Collins proposed Griffith as president of the Dáil, whereupon de Valera left the chamber with a body of supporters. Griffith was duly elected.[24]

Historians of the period have rightly pointed out that the delay between 6 December, when the treaty was signed in London, and 7 January, when it was ratified by the Dáil in Dublin, helped to exacerbate the divisions inside and outside the Dáil about the treaty. But what has not been made sufficiently clear is that once the Dáil voted for the treaty, and once de Valera resigned and Griffith became president in his place, the divisions in the country which continued – ostensibly about the treaty – were complicated by the unease within the army as to the fate of the Volunteers; and this unease, though often expressed in terms of ideological loyalty to the republic, was as much about continued employment, local rivalries over occupying the barracks to be vacated by the British, financial problems and a shortage of money, as it was about the treaty versus the republic. Nor has it been made sufficiently clear how far de Valera, during the first six months of 1922, was distinct and quite separate from these Volunteers, as indeed he had been previously. It was only after he had failed to have himself included in the government that he finally resolved upon the unconstitutional way of settling his grievances.

Since the signing of the treaty de Valera had been confused and bemused. His attempts to counteract events had emerged hastily and seemed ill-planned. There had been the public statement on 8 December; the summoning of the cabinet and Dáil; document number two; the speeches throughout the debate, which were both personal and urgent, but which failed to win all the representatives of the Irish people; there had been the recriminations against the disobedience of the delegation; the mistake, if such it may have seemed in retrospect, of not dismissing from the cabinet those in favour of the treaty; there had been the threat in the Dáil (even before the vote on the treaty) to resign; and there had been the dramatic withdrawal as a 'protest' during the subsequent election of Griffith.

De Valera's leaving the Dáil has acquired, in retrospect, some symbolic value as representing his rejection of 'constitutional' methods. That was not the case. De Valera was disappointed. He may have hoped that he would, notwithstanding the defeat on the treaty, be re-elected as president – as he nearly had been. He may have simply lost his head and indulged in 'handwashing' himself of the actions of the assembly. But whatever, he had simply added another 'slip' to the series accumulated since 7 December and he was now without a plan, without power, and, in the eyes of many who had heard him propose document number two, without his principles intact. He had removed himself unwittingly from a position of authority, to one in which his opponents subsequently suggested he had 'nothing to do but to talk'.

Throughout the next six months he attempted to recover something of his position. By examining these attempts as well as the way in which events themselves helped, or were used, to strengthen de Valera's position it becomes possible to clarify what in retrospect has become the confusion of identity as between de Valera's party and the Volunteers. De Valera fostered this confusion between January and June 1922.

In London, despite the initial euphoric reaction to the signing of the treaty and of the 'warm congratulations' all round to Lloyd George, the victory had quickly lost, or seemed to lose, some of its substance.[25] From the outset there had been doubts expressed with regard to releasing the internees before the treaty was 'passed by Dáil Éireann'.[26] In addition there had been the early reports from Dublin that the leadership was 'split in twain', reports which were, of course, forcefully borne out during the remainder of December.[27] From Belfast came Craig's protests against the proposed boundary commission, and his accusations that the provisions of the treaty 'violated' the 1920 Government of Ireland Act, as well as the promises given by the prime minister that the 'rights of Ulster will in no way be sacrificed'.[28] In London Carson took up the attack in the Lords, and reversed what had previously been his favourable attitude to the boundary commission. He was 'disgruntled at the position into which the prime minister had manoeuvered Ulster', while Chamberlain, as leader of the Unionist party, continued to receive the oral and written complaints of Craig against the provision made for the 'automatic' inclusion of Ulster in the Free State and the proposed boundary commission.[29]

Lloyd George privately and publicly determined to do his utmost to help the Irish get the treaty through on their end. His speech, for example, in the House of Commons on 13 December, was '*for* Ireland' rather than for the UK and he 'gladly' complied with Griffith's request to put into writing the verbal explanation of certain provisions given at the conference.[30] He determined to make it clear that once the treaty was ratified 'we propose to withdraw the forces of the crown in Southern Ireland'.[31]

On the whole, however, Lloyd George, while determined to assist in the implementation of the treaty, lost interest in Ireland once it had been signed and he handed over responsibility for the country to a committee chaired by Churchill and including Greenwood, Worthington-Evans, Hewart and Fitzalan. The committee met for the first time on 21 December and discussed the immediate withdrawal of 'non-permanent' troops from Ireland and the concentration of remaining troops in Dublin and the Curragh – that is, their withdrawal from the 'outlying areas'. It was on this basis that the removal of British forces from the twenty-six counties proceeded over the course of the next six months.[32] What should be pointed out here is that although events in Ireland subsequently served to delay certain evacuations, these delays were welcomed neither by the civil or military authorities in Britain. On the one hand it was feared, particularly by Wilson and Macready, that delay meant danger for the troops; on the other, the politicians, like Greenwood for example, looked forward to the troops marching out 'with all arms and equipment and with bands playing' a 'dramatic event' which would help 'your policy'.[33] This determination to evacuate the troops was obscured at the time, and has been subsequently, by the character of Churchill's pronouncements on the subject – he tended to suggest that the troops might have to remain in order to recapture Ireland for the empire – and by the way in which developments in Ireland over the course of the next six months seemed increasingly to undermine the settlement.

Events in Ireland may have meant that Lloyd George could not immediately claim the treaty as a glorious political success. Furthermore, the opposition of some of the 'diehards' to the settlement, particularly on account of the Ulster terms, may have deprived him of Conservative backbench support. But for all that, two points must be made about the treaty. The first is that it removed Ireland from the position it had occupied in British politics since Gladstone's time; as Greenwood put it, Lloyd George had 'localised the Irish question', which could 'never again be the skeleton in the imperial cupboard'.[34] Ireland moved from being a political issue simply to an administrative one, and the transformation would depend on the full implementation of the treaty. The second point is that within the context of 'concluding' the Irish question, the coalition was determined to see the agreement through. What remained imperative was that the treaty must be implemented, that Collins and Griffith must stand by their document, and that they would receive as much assistance as they needed from the British to do so provided the latter were certain of their *bona fides*. If need be the British might, as Macready had anticipated, be forced to re-intervene; but unless and until that happened, Ireland became the responsibility of the colonial office and Lloyd George's coalition concerned itself with other issues, and with its differences over policy in the near east as between the Turks and the Greeks.

It is, therefore, against the quickly diminishing importance of the Irish question in early 1922 in British domestic politics, that the interventions and attitudes of British politicians must be seen. Their anxiety towards what they saw as the growing disorder and the ambiguous position of the treaty may have partly derived from the effect which failure (when seen in conjunction with other deficiencies) might have on the fortunes of the coalition, particularly in view of the prospect of losing its position to a Conservative administration.[35] But such anxiety as existed also derived from a belief in the treaty as the last, and only, means of pacifying the Irish, and from the ebullient, if extravagant reactions and over-reactions of Churchill to Irish developments and the complications caused by relations between north and south.

On 11 January, four days after the Dáil had approved the treaty, the new Dáil cabinet met. Griffith was now president, and the vacancies caused by the resignations of Brugha and Stack were filled.[36] Two days later the Dáil cabinet approved a provisional government, whose business it would be to transfer power from British to Irish institutions, and to implement the treaty.[37] There were, therefore, two 'governments' in Dublin after the treaty: the Dáil ministry and the provisional government. The existence of the latter served to promote the allegations of de Valera's party that the Dáil ministry was not, in practice, the real government of the country, and that authority lay in the hands of the provisional government.[38] The observation, if true, was irrelevant, for membership of both governments overlapped. The distinction did not matter to those involved: it is clear, for example, that minutes seem to have been taken of government meetings without any consideration as to exactly which government was meeting.[39] What was not irrelevant, and what the opponents of the treaty were implying, was that the provisional government was usurping the functions of the Dáil ministry, that it derived its powers, not from the Dáil — the government of the republic — but from the treaty which disestablished that republic, and thus from the British government. In any case Collins, Cosgrave,[40] Duggan,[41] Hogan,[42] McGrath,[43] and O'Higgins[44] belonged to *both* ministries, while Mulcahy and Gavan Duffy[45] were members only of the Dáil cabinet; all supported the treaty; and Collins, Cosgrave, Hogan and O'Higgins quickly came to the point of disconcertingly agreeing with the allegations of the opposition that they neither bore responsibility to the Dáil for 'things [done] in another capacity', nor would they be accountable [to it] for actions taken as members of the provisional government.[46]

From 28 February — when the Dáil met for the first time since 10 January — de Valera's party continued to exploit the existence of the two 'governments' to make what Griffith called 'propaganda' against the treaty, and to establish its identity as a more 'national' party than that which supported the treaty.[47] Not only was de Valera's party opposed to the treaty which disestablished the republic, but it also was to the way in which it had led to the undermining of the 'sovereign assembly of the nation', Dáil Éireann, by the provisional government.[48] By contrast with the period from 14 December to 7 January, when de Valera's objections to the treaty had confused the issue rather than its outcome, the issue was now clear. Once he had resigned as president, the complications about the treaty, document number two and external recognition dissolved, and de Valera's name had become synonymous with 'the republic'. This development may have begun in the Sinn Féin organisation, where the cumainn had very quickly started to divide on the issue of the republic; in addition, rumour was rife that the cumainn membership had been rigged in order to make for an anti-treaty majority at the ard fheis, and that the Volunteers were being brought in to secure this end.

From Dun Maon Muighe a report was despatched on 17 January that there was a move 'on foot' to undermine the cumainn and 'flood' them with new members, who would then select the delegates to the ard fheis on the basis that they would give an 'adverse' vote.[49] From Clonakilty, Co. Cork, came reports that the Volunteers were being 'canvassed and ordered to be present' at the cumainn meetings; that the IRA officers were using their 'authority to compel . . . members to do against their will what they would not otherwise do'; and that, despite the fact that 'all the county are still solid for the treaty' they were 'afraid', and a 'successful effort' had been made 'to rig all the clubs in south Cork'.[50] Collins observed that those methods had been employed 'elsewhere throughout Ireland' and that little could be done to get 'the opposition' to agree to 'the suppression of these unfair actions'.[51] But at the standing committee of Sinn Féin, he ensured that members enrolled after 31 December would not be 'entitled to vote' for the selection of delegates, and that voting at the ard fheis would be by secret ballot.[52] What was notable about these proposals was not that the standing committee accepted them, but that Stack consistently opposed them. It was not clear whether he did so because he hated Collins or because he feared that if they were passed, they would reduce the chances of the treaty being rejected at the ard fheis.[53]

But the rumours of rigging and of unfair methods to secure the election of 'republican' delegates to the ard fheis were balanced to some extent by the reports of republican fervour, in many cases synonymous with devotion to de Valera. From west Wicklow, Mr Ó Tuathail vowed in late January to 'stand by de Valera and the republic, first, last, and all the time' as would his cumann; he, for one, would not 'renege' [*sic*] on 'our president' in order to support 'Griffith and his treaty'.[54] From Ballinbarney, another Wicklow cumann was 'unanimous for a republic', as was that of the Glen of Imaal which had resolved 'unanimously in favour of President de Valera'.[55] The ladies of Cumann na mBan — the 'independent body of Irish women pledged to work for the Irish republic' — were instructed to use their persuasive powers with the Sinn Féin members to keep Sinn Féin 'faithful' to the republic and to send republican delegates to the ard fheis.[56]

How widespread the sentiment on either side among members of Sinn Féin, at that stage or later, is impossible to say. The ard fheis, which might have given some clue even if 'rigged', was postponed until 21 February on account of a rail strike. When it did meet the delegates accepted the proposals of their leaders to 'stand adjourned' for three months. A vote was averted at the meeting on the assumption that there would be no parliamentary elections for the moment, and that when they were held, the constitution of the new state and the treaty would be simultaneously submitted to the electorate.[57]

The three-month suspension may have averted an open division within Sinn Féin but it became increasingly clear that the most serious divisions were within the Volunteers and that these divisions were more complicated than being simply about republic versus Free State. There was, of course, the issue of republican allegiance and the oath the Volunteers had been taking to the republic since 1920. But although their consequent discontent with the treaty tended to make them appear to identify with de Valera's opposition and that of the republican Sinn Féiners, there were other factors: problems of local discipline and local rivalries, manifested often in the scramble to take over the barracks which the British were evacuating and in the raids on property or for arms; the question of who should control the army, and the demand by a group of officers throughout the spring of 1922 that Volunteer control should revert back to an elected executive rather than be vested in the government; there was also the matter of money or lack of it. Many of the IRA men were not in any settled jobs, and since the levy had been abolished in late 1921 and the winter had set in, there were many cases of hardship and poverty. This situation exacerbated the desire to be assured of a position such as 'taking over' a barracks, or the demands that recruiting to the 'rival' force, the civic guard, be stopped.

With regard to the evacuation of the barracks, the uncertain loyalty of the country had its effect on Churchill who, as early as 9 January, had considered that 'all orders' for withdrawal 'must be held up' as it 'now appeared most likely that there would be rows in Ireland'. Although within days he conceded that evacuation should proceed, anticipating 'peace under Collins', he none the less felt that the troops might yet be needed 'to bolster' Collins.[58] In Ireland itself the government had cause to doubt the loyalty of the units either to it or to the treaty. At the outset Lynch had warned that he could not impose discipline on his men, or that he would not if it involved treachery to the republic. On 11 January he was one of eleven officers, representing commands throughout the country and headquarters' men, who wrote formally to Mulcahy demanding that a Volunteer convention be summoned.[59] The purpose of the convention would be to consider a resolution which reaffirmed the army's 'allegiance to the republic', and reiterated that it would be maintained as 'the army of the Irish republic' under the control of its own executive, appointed by the convention.[60]

Although the request for a convention was not necessarily out of order – provision for such a demand existed in the Volunteer constitution – the proposal to remove the army from the control of the government most definitely was, particularly in view of the unrest since the treaty was signed.[61] The cabinet rejected the request as being outside its 'constitutional powers' and Mulcahy accordingly wrote to each of the signatories that the Dáil 'as a whole' was the 'elected government of the Irish republic', that 'supreme control of the army' was vested in it, and that the proposal to change the supreme control of the army lay outside the powers of the cabinet.[62] He would in any case be making arrangements to discuss the matter with them.[63]

Mulcahy and his colleagues, therefore, intervened in order to postpone the convention which might divide the army from the government on the issue of the republic, and which might be used to set up an independent executive. But the officers reacted by indicating that, in view of the government's refusal to call a convention, they would call one themselves.[64] Mulcahy managed to avert such a development by holding a meeting of all the divisional and brigade commandants on 18 January, and suggesting there would be a convention in two months time. In the meantime a 'watching' council (consisting of two signatories, O'Malley and Traynor, and two others) would meet under the chief-of-staff to 'guarantee that the republican aim' (of the army) would 'not be prejudiced'; if, at any stage, two members considered that a staff proposal was 'inimical to the republic' then the proposal would be 'dropped'.[65] The council would meet the headquarters staff 'every Tuesday' at two p.m.[66]

This proposal only partly served to mollify the signatories who had claimed that 'the action . . . of the Dáil in supporting the treaty. . . was a subversion of the republic' and therefore 'relieved the army from its allegiance to An Dáil', necessitating a convention to consider the resolution.[67] But it did not serve to eliminate the tensions between and amongst the men and their officers throughout the country, or between the local units on the one hand and GHQ on the other. Lynch, for example, still did not know what to do with the 'thousands of men who had sacrificed everything during the war'.[68] O'Malley had difficulties controlling his division, the second southern, where indiscipline was exacerbated by a shortage of money. In Limerick there were subsequent clashes between members of the mid-Limerick brigade and outside troops brought in by GHQ to take over the barracks. In Templemore the local men refused to allow outsiders in. From north Cork Sean Moylan explained that the raids on post offices and the forcible collection of dog licence payments had been made to alleviate the poverty of the soldiers, and were therefore 'for the republic'. These matters will be examined below: they revealed that as far as the government was concerned in the spring of 1922, it was the Volunteers, not Mr de Valera's party, who undermined the prospects of the treaty; and the Volunteers did so not merely because of their allegiance to the republic, but because of their demand for a separate executive, and by the complications of local ambition, financial difficulties, indiscipline and rivalry.

O'Malley's control over his division was slipping in early 1922. Although nominated to the 'watching council', he failed to attend its first or second meeting or to obey a summons to GHQ to provide an explanation.[69] In the meantime, reports of 'disorders' throughout certain areas, some of which fell within his command, had reached headquarters: Tipperary, Kilkenny, east Limerick and Wexford.[70] O'Malley seemed reluctant to implement an 'undertaking' reached at the first meeting and he also permitted a vote at one of his divisional meetings, 'at which it was decided not to . . . recognise GHQ'.[71] In addition a local newspaper, the *Clonmel Nationalist*, had been suppressed by some Volunteers, and complaints had been made that within the area motor cars, money and arms had been seized.[72]

Although he subsequently admitted that his own views were anomalous, that he had agreed to the first meeting with Mulcahy 'under protest and . . . for the sake of unity', it emerged that O'Malley's position had been confused by his failure to control his division. O'Malley had voted at his staff meeting 'not to recognise GHQ' in the hope that 'it would bring about unity in his division . . . effective control and discipline'.[73] Subsequently the staff conceded that they would 'recognise' GHQ, but only to the extent of 'conveying orders to the brigades', without insisting that they be obeyed'.[74] In private O'Malley confessed his 'absolute failure to control his division' owing to 'lack of co-operation from the . . . brigades' and 'absolutely no' financial assistance from them. His staff, therfore, was 'dependent upon the charity of the people for their maintenance' and it transpired that the complaints against the seizures of property and motor cars were due to the uproarious behaviour of the third Tipperary brigade, regarding which two divisional officers confessed 'complete inability to preserve control'.[75] Seizures had been made and defended there on the grounds that they were in lieu of a levy, for the order of late 1921 prohibiting the levy had lapsed, or so the Tipperary men claimed, upon the retirement of Brugha. The arms, or so it was explained, had to be got from 'somewhere' in view of 'the failure of the QMG to supply' them.[76]

In general, although O'Malley had signed the demand for the convention which would reaffirm the army's allegiance to the republic, his attitude may have partly derived from his failure to control his division. He had, for example, allowed the vote against GHQ to be taken in the hope that it might bring unity and lead to more effective control. Moreover, the activities of certain units like the third Tipperary brigade seemed to lie outside the confines of either discipline or ideology, for they would not 'accept orders either from the division or from GHQ', while the overall question of divisional discipline was undermined by the shortage of money amongst the staff and the failure of the brigades to contribute.

Although this is neither a 'social' nor an 'economic' study, reference must be made to the financial plight of the Volunteers, whose activities during the spring and early summer of 1922 were partly the consequence of their poverty. Whereas before the truce in July 1921 the Volunteers had been permitted to impose some kind of levy, in the autumn Brugha, prompted by the conference in London, had prohibited it. The Volunteers, therefore, no longer had authority to impose a levy on the locals for their support and although that did not necessarily deter them all, it certainly must have made matters harder, particularly once winter set in. Moreover, after the truce there had been a great increase in the numbers of Volunteers; more men had given up, or were not engaged in regular employment, while the summer and autumn seasonal opportunities would have passed before the treaty was signed. By 6 December the army was at its largest ever, financial support was indefinite, and the weather and conditions generally were causing hardship. There was as yet no promise of regular employment under the treaty, though presumably it would appear to many of the Volunteers that if they could get hold of their local barracks, they would then be given uniforms and pay.

With regard to expenditure, reference should be made here to the amount of money which had been given to the Volunteers from central funds before the treaty. For the five weeks ending 31 December, for example, only five officers on each divisional staff were paid; though an exception was made with regard to the Belfast brigade, whose commanding officer received a payment of £85.[77] This would suggest that apart from a specific payment for individual officers (which for the period mentioned amounted in respect of all the officers and all the divisions to the sum of £3,433) no contribution had been made to the expenses or the upkeep of the men prior to the end of December.[78] After the treaty was signed the question of making specific payments to Volunteers, particularly unemployed ones, was raised by Collins. On 17 February, for example, he referred to 'the advisability' of doing so, and although Mulcahy indicated that Volunteers would be given the chance to join the regular army or the police force, the matter was deferred on the assumption that it would be raised again.[79] It is not clear what exactly happened to the proposal, though there is no doubt that the hardship of the Volunteers did not disappear. From the north — where matters were definitely worse than in most other parts of the country — there were reports that there was neither money nor employment. The officers of the 4th battalion, 1st brigade, 3rd northern division had been out of work for over a year 'and received only 7s. 6d. per week from White Cross' (relief).[80] In the rest of the country, there was probably less relief, or none at all.

Shortage of money led to many of the raids carried out by the north Cork Volunteers in early 1922. In the Dáil Sean Moylan explained how they had been organising, since the truce, 'to carry on the fight for the republic'.[81] But they now found themselves 'out of employment, without a smoke, ill-shod, badly clad and . . . in want of a drink too' and although they had been 'guaranteed payment . . . for . . . maintenance' they did not get it.[82] The fault, or so Moylan claimed, lay with the men 'who told us that the truce was a breathing space'. In order to alleviate the position of his men, he had set about raiding post offices and collecting the dog tax. He had found that just as 'during the war' his word 'went in North Cork', so 'my word goes there yet'.[83] He was not, as he announced in the Dáil, ashamed of his robbery, for 'in doing things like this, I am standing up for and defending the republic'.[84]

The uncertainty amongst the Volunteers about the future, and the 'race' for the barracks culminated and was reflected in the Limerick 'episode' of early March, as a result of which Griffith and his colleagues took fright, and prohibited the postponed convention. In doing so they involuntarily linked the demand for a convention and allegiance to the republic with the activities, dissent, rivalries and complaints of the units throughout the country which had been escalating since 6 December.

With regard to the Limerick episode, on 18 February the

commandant of the mid-Limerick brigade repudiated GHQ publicly. The officer commanding the first western division was instructed by headquarters to occupy the barracks in Limerick city, due to be evacuated by the British on 23 February, until such time as a sufficient number of loyal men in Limerick could be found to occupy them.[85] The mid-Limerick men claimed that the decision to hand over the barracks to outsiders had led to the repudiation, whereas Mulcahy insisted that the decision to do so had been made as a result of the repudiation.[86] In any case troops from Galway and Clare were brought in to take the barracks; but the Limerick men retaliated by bringing in their own 'outside reinforcements' and by 6 March there were 'troops all over the place'.[87] By 8 March the officer who was holding the barracks for GHQ, Brennan, anticipated that the Limerick men would deliver their 'ultimatum today, giving us twenty-four hours to clear out'.[88] His task had been rendered more difficult by his shortage of men and munitions, and by the uncertain loyalties of his own men. He considered it vital to get '100 good men from McKeown' – i.e., MacEoin, whose reputation for toughness was well known – for some of his own men had 'too many odd [*sic:* old] associations with the mutineers to be properly reliable'.[89]

Limerick, therefore, involved a repudiation of the authority of headquarters by the O/C mid-Limerick brigade, though whether before or after headquarters decided to bring in reliable outside troops is unclear. It involved rivalry between city men and outside troops as to who should 'get' the barracks, and the massing in the city of large numbers of troops from outside as well as inside Limerick. It involved clashes in the city and the uncertain loyalties of both sides. Although the Volunteer oath to the republic may have encouraged the formal repudiation of GHQ, local feelings and rivalries and the need to take over the barracks also mattered. Moreover, the reports throughout January and February of the repudiations and counter-repudiations which were becoming fashionable may have also encouraged the Limerick men, particularly as some of them came from nearby areas. In any case, once Brennan's men were brought in to occupy the barracks, feelings rose as the 'jobs' went to the outside Volunteers, and the position deteriorated with the arrival of supporting troops for both sides.

On top of that came the incidents in Templemore and Cork, directed against GHQ, the treaty party, or Michael Collins. During his first visit to Cork under the new regime, for example, shots were fired at a public meeting, a house which was used by the treaty party was raided, and Collins and MacEoin were prevented by armed men from visiting the republican plot in the cemetery.[90] In Templemore, the mid-Tipperary brigade refused to allow troops sent from GHQ to occupy the barracks, and only agreed to do so on condition of 'their leaving by order of GHQ at the earliest moment'.[91]

But it was Limerick which frightened Griffith, and acquired a significance beyond the developments themselves. Griffith, O'Sullivan and Mulcahy were in the town at the time to attend a memorial service and they may have reacted more strongly to the events than they would have done had they been in Dublin receiving reports. Mulcahy refused to consider any accommodation with the mutineers – as Brennan had called them first – and Griffith insisted that the barracks would continue to be occupied by the troops, until the mutineers withdrew: 'there could be no evacuation at the demand of a mutinous section of the army.'[92] On 15 March it was decided, at the Dáil cabinet, that the Volunteer convention would be prohibited on the grounds that the Dáil was the 'sole body in supreme control of the army' and that any attempt to 'set up another body' would be 'tantamount' to setting up a 'military dictatorship'.[93] The decision was unanimous.[94] A convention would be forbidden 'during the lifetime of the Dáil'.[95] The order – signed Griffith, and circulated by Mulcahy on 16 March – made it clear that the convention, due to be held on 26 March, was absolutely prohibited and any member of the army who attended it, would automatically 'sever his connection with the IRA'.[96]

The convention, therefore, which had been deferred for at least two months on 18 January, had been definitely prohibited by 16 March. In the intervening two months the incidents involving various units of the army had suggested that the unrest amongst certain Volunteers was as much the result of local rivalry, dissatisfaction with the provisions made by headquarters for the welfare of the men, anxiety about the future, physical and financial distress, indiscipline amongst certain brigades, as it was about allegiance to the republic. But amongst some of the signatories to the demand for the convention, allegiance to the republic, the need to reaffirm the army's allegiance and to maintain it as the army of the republic under an elected executive, were paramount considerations. Rory O'Connor had led the signatories to the demand. He was director of engineering at headquarters, an ideological republican with a warmth of manner and a capacity for reflection which did not emerge from his fiery public statements. Mellows too was a republican. O'Connor was an engineering graduate and a member of the republican army, who before the truce had also been O/C Britain, a position which may have encouraged the zealot in him. Mellows had been 'out in 1916': he was a Galway man, a member of the Dáil as well as belonging to headquarters, an Irish speaking, quiet but fanatic westerner who nursed a terrible bitterness against those who supported the treaty, and for whom the republic was a 'living tangible thing' for which 'men gave their lives . . . were hanged . . . and . . . are still prepared to give their lives'.[97] Of the other signatories, Liam Lynch was a Cork man and a republican who led the largest IRA division. Although he and his subordinates had promptly insisted that they would remain loyal to the republic after 6 December, the constant negotiations and discussions with headquarters, particularly from April 1922 onwards, suggest that the Lynch republicanism and that of the Corkmen was reinforced by feelings of southern 'separatism': the largest of the pre-treaty divisions, now 'badly hit, was unwilling to accept the orders of the Dublin headquarters staff, particularly if these resulted in a violation of the republic. O'Malley, commander of the second southern, was also a republican, but one with disciplinary problems with his brigades. He had been a 'fighter' before the truce, an adventurer, with a highly developed sense of the dramatic and the dangerous; he now sought to 'unify' his division, where his control was slipping, in the context of that republic.

After 18 January, O'Connor particularly had continued to look to the summoning of the convention to resolve the issue of the republican allegiance of the army. On 31 January, for example, at one of the joint council/headquarters meetings, he referred to drafting of troops 'from one division to another' - a practice which might interfere with the convention, presumably in respect of representation.[98] Lynch too had continued to look to the convention, though Mulcahy had hoped that even if held, it would postpone electing an executive.[99] Lynch maintained that a convention would insist 'right away on an executive controlling the army' and even when Griffith prohibited its taking place, demanded that it should merely be postponed. He also demanded that, as part of a bargain with Mulcahy, 'recruiting for the civic guard' be discontinued. Mulcahy would not concede these terms.[100]

Of the signatories to the demand for a convention, O'Connor and Lynch had continued to look to it. Lynch had expected it immediately to elect its own executive averted. O'Connor anticipated it would reaffirm the army's allegiance to the republic. Mulcahy had attempted to have first the convention and then the election of an executive averted. The events throughout the period January to March undoubtedly served to emphasise the dangers inherent in the government's relinquishing its control over the Volunteers. Mulcahy had already made it clear to the signatories that the Dáil, not he, would have to grant the necessary permission, and the Dáil, having been postponed, would not be meeting until 28 February. Mulcahy seems to have intended, at least initially, to reassure the Dáil that the proposed executive 'would harmonise the work of the Volunteers with the work of the Dáil' as had 'originally' been the case.[101] But by the 28th, though he still intended to reassure the Dáil that the proposal reverted 'control of the army back to the days before the disbandment of the Volunteer executive', he also wished to indicate that 'personally' he would 'prefer' the convention to be 'avoided'. He would not 'accept responsibility' for its being 'forced to take place'.[102] Although the matter was raised at the cabinet on the 27th, no decision was taken. It seems that Mulcahy, possibly in consultation with his colleagues, decided against bringing the 'convention' before the Dáil in order to avoid prejudicing the prospects for the

Free State bill then passing through the British parliament, but nonetheless to assume that it would proceed.[103] The position, therefore, at the beginning of March was that although it was assumed that the convention would proceed, it would do so without the blessing or encouragement of the cabinet, and without the matter being raised in the Dáil.

Limerick had, of course, changed all that. Griffith had prohibited the convention. But what is interesting is that before making the order public, Mulcahy discussed it with divisional commandants, and their reaction, if somewhat discontented, was muted. The first southern claimed that promises had been made that 'were not being kept' and insisted 'that "we can't possibly have an election"'; there was 'no increased difficulty' with the first western, while the second, third and fourth had 'nothing to say'.[104] The eastern and midland divisions were 'alright', as was 'east-Limerick', though the latter 'complained of general let down'. Of the northern divisions, the third northern, which might have given trouble, seemed to have been 'in favour of a convention' only 'as . . . increasing . . . the feeling of unity'.

If the issues involved throughout the country since January had been confused by local rivalries; by the competition to take over the barracks; by indiscipline in constituent brigades and short finances; by the confusion of insubordination with allegiance to the republic and the oath; Rory O'Connor now began to eliminate such confusions. On 23 March an interview given by him was published in the newspapers. He intended, 'notwithstanding' Griffith's announcement, to proceed with the convention, and the Volunteers, of whom he claimed to speak for 80 per cent, were not 'going into the British empire' and stood for 'Irish liberty'.[105] The Dáil had 'let down' the republic and there was no longer a government to which the Volunteers owed allegiance: 'we will set up an executive which will issue orders to the IRA' and 'in effect the holding of a convention means that we repudiate the Dáil'.[106] When asked if therefore there was to be a military dictatorship, O'Connor replied, 'You can take it that way if you like', adding that 'the army . . . is one hundred per cent republican'.[107]

The convention proceeded despite the prohibition. Those

present reaffirmed the army's allegiance to the republic and an executive was elected to supreme control of the army. Its members included O'Connor and Mellows from headquarters, and from the commands Lynch, O'Malley, Moylan and Barry.[108] The convention decided to reimpose the Belfast boycott (which had been stopped after the treaty) and there were rumours that they intended to declare the forthcoming general election 'abortive' or 'prevent' it 'being held', that they would seize government funds, and that they intended to see that the new civic guard was treated 'similarly' to 'the old RIC'.[109] The statement issued by the executive afterwards claimed that 220 delegates attended, representing forty-nine brigades, while four members of GHQ, and officers from eight of the divisional staffs and three of the independent brigades were present.[110] The government did nothing and decided, for the moment, to allow the situation to 'develop'.[111]

While Rory O'Connor had been challenging the authority of the Dáil – on the basis of its having betrayed the republic – the government was preoccupied with preparations for the establishment of the new Free State, for the new constitution and the elections, as it also was with conditions in and policy towards the north.

Relations between the twenty-six and the six counties had been eased at an 'official' level by the agreement reached between Craig and Collins in London on 21 January. In general the agreement meant that the boycott of Belfast goods and traders imposed formerly by the Dáil would now be lifted in return for the removal, by the northern authorities and employers, of 'religious and political tests'.[112] This did not mean that the government had changed its policy which, Griffith maintained in the Dáil, was aimed at 'a unified Ireland'. That policy had existed before the agreement, and the removal of the boycott was part of it.[113]

However, at an unofficial level, relations between north and south had become increasingly strained on account of the incidents on or near the border involving nationalists and loyalists and on account of the suspicion on both sides that the

respective governments condoned these activities, if they did
not actively support them. On the night of 7 February for
example, various 'Ulster loyalists' were kidnapped from their
homes in Ulster by armed forces, and subsequently detained
in the south.[114] At the same time a group of Monaghan men
on their way to the final of the Ulster gaelic football
championship, had been detained in the north, on the suspicion that they were planning a raid on Derry jail; they were
carrying guns and illegal documents.[115] On 12 February,
four Ulster 'special' constables were killed when shooting
broke out at Clones station between the constables, who
were changing trains, and Irish officials. Other 'specials'
were captured and detained.[116]

What should be noted about these incidents directed against
loyalists is that the northerners implied that the provisional
government was in sympathy, if not active collusion, with the
perpetrators. In the case of the first kidnappings, certain
reports suggested that the victims were, in fact, detained by
the provisional government; in that of the Clones specials,
the killings and detentions were unprovoked.[117] The implication in both cases was that the Irish government was in a
position to secure release and should do so.[118]

Although neither Collins nor Griffith accepted responsibility publicly, they suggested with regard to the first group
that they were 'taking steps' to find the men who, they were
'confident', would not be harmed.[119] Following a series of
interventions by Churchill, releases gradually took place on
both sides, and it emerged that if Collins were 'privately'
assured that the Monaghan footballers would be released,
then he could 'induce' the Monaghan IRA to release their
prisoners from the north.[120]

Whatever the attitude publicly maintained of judicious
impartiality between north and south, the claim was made
that the British government tended to side with the north.
Cope, still in Dublin assisting in the transfer of administration, had already suggested that the suspension of the
evacuation of British troops could be thus interpreted. Jones,
in London, was not 'happy about the action of the treasury
in allotting over a million pounds to the 'B' specials in
Ulster'[121] He feared that 'if we travel much further along

this road we shall be in trouble' and he reminded Lloyd George on 17 March that 'the essence of the bargain ... made with the south' was that the north would remain 'an integral part of the UK ... but with powers no greater and no less than under the 1920 Act'.[122] In a joint memorandum with Curtis he referred to the 3,000 RIC men in the north due for disbandment, which Craig wanted to keep, backed by over 4,000 'A' specials, 20,000 'B' specials (of whom 15,000 had been armed since the raid into Northern Ireland) and behind whom there were 'C' specials.[123] All the specials were Protestants (if only because of Catholic aversion to the oath) and they were paid by the British government under special arrangements by which the exchequer would meet the costs until 30 September 1922.[124] The British government had therefore, in Jones's view, paid and armed a force of at least 20,000, over and above the RIC, but did 'not control' it; and it seemed to him and Curtis that the northern government had assumed 'the military functions specially reserved to the British ... by simply calling the forces "police"'.[125] Moreover, the ex-chief of the imperial staff, Henry Wilson, having lost favour with the government, had been offered the seat for North Down, which he had taken. He subsequently became implicated in the various schemes for the 'defence' of Ulster and the reorganisation of the special constabulary.[126]

It was against the background of the Craig-Collins agreement on the one hand, and the border incidents on the other that the developing attitude of the provisional government must be examined, an attitude which was exacerbated by the increased numbers and organisation of the special constabulary in the north.

What seems to have been the case in January and February was, that although neither Collins nor Mulcahy was in collusion with the kidnappers, they were in a position to secure the loyalists' release. They certainly sympathised with the plight of the northern Catholics, particularly in Belfast, whose conditions had not been notably alleviated by the first agreement with Craig. Not 'one single expelled nationalist or Catholic worker' had, according to Collins, 'been reinstated in his employment'. Nor had Craig taken 'any action whatever or even publicly expressed a wish that his part of the agreement should be honoured', and there remained '9,000 unfortunate workers, all citizens of Belfast . . . driven out of their employment solely because . . . [of] different political and religious views'.[127] The Dáil ministry had, by mid March, begun to consider the reimposition of the Belfast boycott and by the 24th its members were not only dissatisfied with events in the north, but also with the way in which the British government had become implicated on account of its support for the specials.[128] Mulcahy particularly objected to the increased number of British troops who supported Craig's government 'at its order and in its spirit'.[129] But pending the passage of the Irish Free State bill through the British houses of parliament, and a visit by the Irish ministers to London at Churchill's instigation to discuss the north, no action was taken.[130] From that visit emerged the second Craig-Collins pact, that of 30 March.

But in addition to the pacts and the recriminations, the interventions of Churchill and the discussions in London, it seems that there was also an 'unofficial' policy of the headquarters staff, about which the government had some knowledge. This involved a measure of support for the northern units of the IRA in their efforts, if not to overthrow the northern government, to rouse Catholic morale and offer some defence against sectarian discrimination. This 'unofficial' policy developed particularly from March, and it coincided with the failure of the second pact with Craig — which Collins described shortly afterwards as having become a 'dead letter' — and with the split in the army when one section of it proceeded with the convention, setting up its own executive.[131]

The way in which the development of the 'unofficial' northern policy affected the government's attitude to the executive forces will be discussed later. Suffice it to say here that the problems for the provisional government of preparing for the new state — drafting the constitution, calling the elections, 'taking over' from the British — had been complicated by the divisions and dissensions in the army, by the repudiation of GHQ by some of that army, and by the unsatisfactory position of the northern Catholics (of which, indeed, much was made by de Valera's party in the Dáil). In addition to all this there were the increasing number of incidents in the country – raids on post offices, seizure of property – for which responsibility tended to be placed on the body of republican opposition.[132] Moreover, from London came demands that the Irish put their house in order, and that the elections be held. In general the confused situation in the country was mistakenly taken to be simply about the demand for a republic, by republicans, against whom it also seemed Collins was reluctant to strike the first blow.

By 5 April Churchill anticipated 'the not inconceivable contingency' of the 'proclamation of an Irish republic' during the coming weeks.[133] 'One of the main difficulties' appeared to be that Griffith and Collins considered it 'vital and indispensable to the success of . . . the treaty' to avoid 'striking the first blow against republicans' or taking 'provocative' steps.[134] The weakness of the provisional government seemed the consequence of its insisting on the withdrawal of British forces, which it then 'failed to replace' by forces on which it could 'rely'.[135] At that stage plans were discussed to deal with the possible proclamation of a republic in Dublin. These plans involved martial law and the use of two destroyers; it was also decided that the Irish government should be sent the arms it required, together with a serious note from Churchill demanding that Collins deal with the situation.[136] Churchill accordingly warned Collins that under 'no circumstances' would the cabinet 'recognise' or 'negotiate' with a republic, should it be set up, but rather, would 'stand by the treaty as representing the full and final offer'.[137] Privately he felt that the ten-day period from 10 April would be 'most critical' and 'before a month had passed' they would know whether the Free State would 'fight or endure insults'. He also felt that the provisional government, though reliable, appeared 'incapable of withstanding the extremists'.[138] On the 12th he again warned Collins that 'in the long run' the Irish government 'must assert itself or perish', and that Mr de Valera might 'gradually come to personify not a cause, but a catastrophe'. He urged that the elections should take place without further delay,

for 'we have a . . . right to ask that the uncertainty as to
whether our offer is accepted or rejected should not be
indefinitely prolonged'.[139]

By then the Irish ministers had, in any case, begun to
discuss the possibility of giving the army officers search
and raid powers. They had also decided that the election
could not be delayed beyond an agreed time and that it must
take place in June, upon the existing register.[140] The same
day the government adjourned for ten days for the Easter
period; two days later, on 14 April, the executive forces
under Rory O'Connor occupied the Four Courts.

Between January and June 1922 there was (and has been
since) a mistaken tendency to assume that de Valera's
political opposition and the dissident (later executive) IRA
men were one group. Theoretically the connection between
the politicians and the Volunteers existed, in that both
groups protested their allegiance to the republic. The politicians continued to imply that the republic was being subverted
by the provisional government and for many of the volunteers
this had become part of the rhetoric which concealed the
confusion of motives for the incidents from early January.
Despite the convention's resolution of allegiance to the
republic and O'Connor's proclamations as to the 'republican'
character of the majority of the army, the executive forces
and de Valera's party remained separate. In March
O'Connor displayed a measure of contempt for de Valera
and his document number two, which he 'had not read', and
he declined suggestions both then and later that the army
might obey de Valera, for it did not 'belong to any political
party', nor had de Valera anything 'to do with' it.[141]
Throughout April and May other army leaders confirmed the
position. While the theoretical connection of de Valera's
party with allegiance to the republic was reiterated, so too
were the demands which exemplified the incidents of the
previous three months.

Mellows, the new secretary of the Four Courts army
council, submitted his proposals for army unity to the
secretary of the Dáil.[142] He suggested not only that the

'existing republic' be maintained but that the army should be independently controlled, that the civic guard be disbanded, that 'all financial liabilities' of the army be discharged and that 'future requirements' be met by the Dáil.[143] Moreover, while 'the threat of war by England' existed, there were to be no elections on 'the issue [the treaty] at present before the country'.[144] Moylan too was concerned with the election, as were five southern army officers whose position was ostensibly 'anti-treaty'. Moylan proposed on 21 April that if held it should be 'on a nominated basis' and not 'on treaty versus republic'.[145] The anti-treaty officers – Breen, Hales, Murphy, O'Hegarty, and O'Donoghue – issued a statement on 1 May jointly with five pro-treaty officers proposing the unification of all forces and an agreed election on the basis that 'the majority of the people of Ireland are willing to accept the treaty'.[146] On the 3rd they put their statement before the Dáil, which prompted it to set up its own 'peace committee'; simultaneously the IRA leaders, both at GHQ and at the Four Courts, arranged that a 'truce' would begin on 4 May to last for four days; this was subsequently prolonged indefinitely.[147]

The attempts to arrange a peace proceeded throughout April and May and involved a multitude of groups – the Four Courts executive, de Valera and Brugha, Collins and Griffith, Mulcahy, army officers, divisional commandants, Corkmen, republicans, 'treaty' men – whose schemes were as multitudinous as their proposers. For the provisional government the problem of reaching a settlement became more urgent on account of the election being fixed for June. Without some kind of agreement, which most of the 'anti-treaty' IRA men in any case wanted, it might be impossible to hold one on account of the increasing disorder in the country, from which de Valera did not dissociate himself. In view of this urgency the government proceeded with its attempts to reach a settlement on the basis that the identity and demands of de Valera coincided with those of the Volunteers.

De Valera deliberately fostered the idea that he both influenced the Volunteers and sympathised with their demands. In the Dáil in early March he had told Hogan that

except for the fact that the Dáil was a 'sovereign assembly[,]
I would be the very first to ask the army to sweep you and
the like of you out'.[148] During the Limerick 'crisis' he had
written to Mulcahy. He reminded him of his promise to
maintain the army as the army of the republic; he referred
to the 'natural discontent' of men who 'took up arms for
the republic' at seeing the government disestablish 'that
republic'; and he warned that unless settled 'it may well be
the beginning of a civil war'.[149] De Valera's reference to the
prospect of civil war as early as 6 March may or may not
have been a calculated attempt to suggest that only he could
prevent one; and whatever the public denials of Rory
O'Connor that de Valera had any role in the affairs of the
army, by April the government had come to accept that he
had. It may have done so because it had little choice but
to do so or because by doing so de Valera's lack of responsibility for the activities of his followers could be castigated.
In any case, by 12 April it had been decided by the ministers
that de Valera and Brugha must be asked to 'disavow the acts
of aggression' committed 'by their supporters' and to promise
as part of any negotiations that there would be no interference with the elections.[150] None the less de Valera and his
colleagues seemed increasingly to associate themselves with
the 'unconstitutional and unscrupulous opposition' to the
government. They neither blamed nor castigated those
responsible for the incidents nor dissociated themselves
from them. They tended instead to accuse the government
of 'flouting' the 'authority' of the Dáil and for being therefore responsible for 'the seduction of the army of the Irish
republic'.[151]

After the Dáil peace committee failed to reach agreement,
which it did partly because the republicans felt it useless to
continue and considered their opponents were 'more concerned with committing us to ... the treaty than with working
out a detailed scheme of settlement', negotiations with
de Valera none the less proceeded.[152] On 15 May the
ministers privately considered the possible terms of an
agreement.[153] The proposals involved an agreed election in
the proportion of five to three, after which a coalition would
be formed.[154] That coalition would consist of the president

and ten ministers, with six nominations from the present
government and four from the opposition.[155] On the 18th
Collins met de Valera. At first he did not think 'much' would
'come out of it' (a meeting had been arranged with de Valera
as early as 11 April).[156] But on the 19th they met again
and by the 20th an agreement had been reached, the terms
of which were announced that day in the Dáil.[157] A 'pact' or
agreed election would take place; a national coalition panel,
representing both parties in the Dáil and the Sinn Féin
organisation would be sent forward; the number for each
party would be as 'their present strength in the Dáil'; candidates would be nominated through existing party executives;
and the government formed after the election would consist
of the president (elected as formerly), the minister of defence
(representing the army, and nine other ministers – five from
the majority party and four from the minority.[158] Each party
would choose its own nominees, but the allocation of
portfolios would be in the hands of the president.[159]

The 'manifesto' recommending the 'panel' referred to 'the
coalition of forces represented in the Sinn Féin organisation'
which had been 'Ireland's strength' during the previous five
or six years. Sinn Féin would continue 'to stand not for
party, but for nation' and the coalition government would be
formed from 'the men and women' who had been 'tested
through the time of trial' and would 'best be able to meet
the immediate national need'.[160]

But the pact, if it seemed to resolve the difficulties of
holding an election, given the apparent nature of relations
between de Valera's party and the dissident Volunteers, not
only exacerbated relations between the provisional government and Churchill but, beyond the provision for an agreed
election, did nothing to satisfy the demands of the Volunteers.

Regarding the effect of the peace talks on Churchill, even
before the pact Mulcahy had indicated that a 'strong
coalition' would not help 'our relations with England'.[161]
This was an understatement. The talks and conferences
between the government, de Valera's party and the army
executive; the toleration by Collins of the Four Courts
seizure; the continued incidents and raids throughout the
country: all had provided reason for dismay in London, if

not for mistrust of the new leaders. Even before it was ready, the new constitution had been described by Collins as 'd–d democratic' and its terms, in Jones's view, would make it necessary for Lloyd George to be 'within hail' on delivery, to prevent his colleagues turning down the document 'at first glance in their fear of diehards'.[162] The rumours about the character of the constitution coincided with the negotiations between the government on the one hand and de Valera, the various 'anti-treaty', southern, or Four Courts officers, or the Dáil peace committee, on the other. They had repercussions on the reaction of those responsible in London to the Irish requests for arms and munitions, and to the continued evacuation of British troops. Before acceding to the requests for munitions, the British 'must have proof' that the provisional government meant to 'assert its authority against insurgents'. Such proof should be given by serious measures to re-establish its authority in the capital.[163] For this purpose trench mortars would be advanced.[164] At the same time, while Cork, Ballincollig and Youghal would be evacuated on 17 May and the troops transferred to Northern Ireland by sea, no further troops were to be evacuated from Dublin.[165]

By 16 May, that is just four days before the pact, Churchill had reached the conclusion that the Irish government had shown 'no capacity' to deal firmly with the situation.[166] Not only had de Valera succeeded in having the election postponed because it would have 'gone against him', but there were now discussions about an agreed election 'between the two factions' in which 'so many seats' would be assigned to de Valera 'and so many to the Free State'. 'The Irish leaders move in a narrow world'; they had been 'men of violence and conspiracy and had hardly emerged from that atmosphere' and it seemed to Churchill that those British troops now in Dublin should remain there, for if removed 'a republic would very likely . . . be proclaimed'.[167] If Ireland fell into a 'state of anarchy, we should have to re-establish a pale again around Dublin'.[168] When, therefore, the pact was announced on 20 May, Churchill's fears about Collins and the provisional government seemed to have been confirmed. At the colonial office, Curtis believed Collins to have 'clearly capitulated to the republican party' – though not necessarily Griffith, who might not follow him.[169] By the 23rd the position was more serious. Churchill told his colleagues that although he did not envisage a 'sudden breakdown' on a 'clear' issue, he none the less feared the Free State would 'slide into an accomodation with the republicans'.[170] He explained that Collins's attitude was unsatisfactory; he had made no attempt to prevent 'all this' and resorted to defending himself on the grounds that he did not wish to make 'martyrs' of the de Valeraites.[171] Churchill now wanted it to be made clear to the Irish that if a republic were proclaimed 'before or after' the election, then 'that is war'.[172] 'We' would not 'allow ourselves to slide along into a republic' and at a certain stage 'we shall lose confidence in the provisional government'.[173]

Lloyd George was more restrained. He agreed that the position was 'grave'. They were 'drifting' to the position of having either 'to abandon or reconquer'; he would not abandon, and 'we might have to reconquer'. But it would first be necessary to make clear to the 'civilised world' that the present position was not 'our fault'.[174] He referred to the period before the treaty, when nobody liked 'what we were doing in Ireland'.[175] But an offer had been made, every chance given, and 'they' had broken faith.[176] Yet it was not clear to the 'outside world' *whose* fault it was and it was essential that Britain must not appear to take advantage of the inexperienced, for if they did then the world would say that it had never 'really meant' to grant self-government.[177] 'We may have to take stern action', but the prime minister was 'against using menace unless we mean to carry it out'.[178] Instead, 'let us tell them our views' and 'give them a chance'; and if there was to be a break ultimately, it must be on issues 'so obvious that it cannot be argued about'.[179]

Four days later, on 28 May, the Irish were in London with their constitution. Lloyd George saw Griffiths and Collins but his fears were not allayed. 'We are back where we were on the first day' he told his colleagues.[180] The constitution was 'a complete evasion of the treaty' which involved the 'setting up of a republic with a thin veneer' with, in Churchill's words, 'the king as a lackey'.[181] Lloyd George thought that if they signed the document they would be 'traitors to the king'.[182] It was a 'very serious challenge'.[183] Were the Irish prepared to accept the 'constitutional position of the other dominions' or not? That was 'the issue'.[184]

The discussion turned on the prospect of a break. Churchill alluded to Collins having said that in that event, the Irish troops 'would probably be in uniform' and able 'to conform to the laws of war'.[185] He himself thought the provisional government might resign, and doubted that Griffith would 'split' with Collins. He mentioned Cosgrave's reference to the '341 polling stations in Kerry alone' and the difficulty of protecting them from 'all' the elements — IRA 'irregulars, hooligans, bolsheviks'.[186] If there was no agreement, Collins might 'reunite himself' with de Valera, but that left Lloyd George in no doubt as to what action 'he would take then'.[187]

The British, therefore, privately anticipated and prepared for the worst — although Churchill more so than Lloyd George, who wanted to make it appear that the Irish had been given every chance. Griffith none the less stressed to the British ministers that the constitution was not intended 'to conflict with the treaty' and that if it were shown to do so, then it would be 'revised'.[188] When Churchill suggested that the election should be postponed, Griffith countered that it would be 'inconvenient' and the people would suspect a division.[189] He indicated that those 'republican' members to be brought into the government by the pact would be 'outside' ministers, and that in any case, the provisional government would be there.[190] If it could be shown that they were not complying with the treaty by having these men, then they would 'take steps to comply with it'.[191]

If the pact had exacerbated relations between the provisional government and Churchill, there was little reason for such exacerbation. The electoral arrangement aside, the government had made few concessions of substance either to the demands for a republic from de Valera's party, or those of the Volunteers. What had been done was that in order to ensure that the election could proceed without interference from either de Valera's political supporters or those Volunteers who might be said to be supporters, an arrangement was made. But the arrangement rested on the assumption that Mr de Valera could control his 'wilder' followers, that is the mutinous republican executive, or simply dissident IRA men. O'Connor had denied the existence of relations between the IRA men and de Valera but the latter had refused to do so and throughout the spring had by his public statements — or their absence — continued to suggest that he was in sympathy with the Volunteers, if not in a position of influence. Whether or not the government really considered de Valera could stop the incidents perpetrated by the dissident or republican Volunteers is doubtful, but Collins must have hoped that by including de Valera and his republican party in the proposed coalition and by agreeing to the demands made by IRA men for an agreed election, he would appear to be making provision for the republic in the new state, and in some measure, therefore, for the maintenance of the IRA as the army of the Irish republic.

The pact might mollify many to the extent of making the elections possible, but as far as the members of the Four Courts executive were concerned, it had not resolved enough. Even before the pact one officer referred to the peace moves which distorted the simple but crucial army demand, 'to revert to the old control' of the executive, rather than that of the Dáil.[192] The army, he maintained, had 'never really' been the 'army of the government'.[193] In the past its executive had acted independently, planning the war, for example, and executing those plans 'whether the cabinet was willing or not'.[194] In fact, the cabinet and the Dáil had been 'often most unwilling'.[195] Lynch too had criticised the various proposals as had Mellows on the grounds that they failed to concede the republic. Mellows, both a member of the Four Courts executive and a parliamentary representative in the Dáil, had denounced the proposals of the officers in May as clearly a 'political dodge' which ignored 'the cause of disunity' — the treaty.[196] Lynch's continued communications to Mulcahy were designed to make his position clear, if not to eliminate differences. They reiterated in the main that the IRA must be kept as the army of the Irish republic, and rejected Mulcahy's counter-suggestions, dealing with its administration, because they ignored 'the cause of the split in the army' which for him, as for Mellows, was the treaty.[197] But the most forceful antagonist of the government, headquarters, the treaty and the Collins-de Valera pact was Rory O'Connor of the executive forces. On 29 May O'Connor rejected the pact in an interview published in the *Cork Examiner*.[198] He declared that the truce of July 1921 had only been 'an interlude before the final coup for the republic'; that he would attack 'the north-east counties as soon as he was ready'; and that he regarded the agreement 'by the republicans with the Free State imperial party' as unlikely to last 'after the June elections'.[199] He would 'act independently' of de Valera who, he claimed, had 'nothing to do with the army'; he indicated that he controlled 'three-fourths' of the republican army and insisted, with some accuracy, that the seizure of the Four Courts had 'forced Collins and de Valera to make peace'.[200] But the 'expression of the popular will' would not be 'through parliamentary channels'.[201]

O'Connor, therefore, dissociated himself from de Valera and it seemed that as far as he was concerned, the pact meant nothing. This was a serious position in view of his allegation that he controlled 'three-fourths' of the republican army. Moreover, the army truce which had begun on 4 May had not, despite its 'indefinite' prolongation on the 8th, proved successful. O'Duffy and Mulcahy subsequently alleged that the anti-treaty group had continued to recruit and that 'within a week alone' of the signing, many breaches had been reported. These ranged from attacks on Protestant homes, or kidnapping, to raiding banks and post offices.[202] Though 'never formally broken', the army truce had been, according to the statement later prepared for the government, 'never kept for one day by the anti-treaty side or the section of the army which seceded to the irregulars'.[203]

These allegations are important, not because they attribute blame — even if that was important as far as the provisional government was later concerned — but because they bore out to some degree the claims of Rory O'Connor. Whatever the size of the republican army, or whatever the proportion he spoke for, there were many Volunteers who, even if they had little to do with O'Connor, had not been affected either by the army truce or the Collins-de Valera electoral pact. It seemed that if they were indifferent to the former, then they were contemptuous of the latter. For the moment the breaches were overlooked by headquarters, by Collins and Mulcahy during the protracted negotiations to reconcile the army with civil control; and if it became increasingly evident that the pact with de Valera had not reassured the dissident Volunteers, it also became increasingly the case that the Volunteers would not, or could not, be reassured.

The discussions in London at which the British had rejected the Irish draft constitution because it set up a republic 'with a thin veneer' coincided with two things. First, the culmination of what seemed to the British to be the unsatisfactory attitude of the provisional government to their republican opponents, civil and military; secondly, the final manifestation of the unofficial policy pursued by the provisional government towards the north, which arose from frustration with its failure to improve the conditions of the northern Catholics by other methods, and a sense of resentment towards the British government's attitude.

Since the agreement of 30 March, the peace which had been declared had not materialised. The border incidents had continued unhindered by the commission set up to police it in March. [204] It remained unclear to the Ulstermen and to Churchill whether the provisional government was simply unable to control the more extreme Irishmen on the border, whether it was unwilling to do so, whether it was in sympathy with those who intervened (particularly in Belfast city) or whether it was in collusion. Hints had been continually made that some of the arms sent by the British to the provisional government found their way to the north to be employed against the specials or the Ulstermen.[205] From the Ulster side, the 'peace' of 30 March had lost its character under the schemes of Henry Wilson, who had become MP for North Down after retiring as CIGS in February. At a political level he and Craig had laid plans for the north's defence, and refused to take part in the boundary commission, as agreed in the treaty.[206] At a practical level his plans for the 'defence' of Ulster included schemes for the reorganisation and increase of the special constabulary, and the appointment of Solly Flood to its command.[207] Throughout the latter part of April he had given a series of rousing public speeches, finishing up at Donaghadee on the 21st, with a warning that it was 'for Ulster men and women to prepare themselves for what may be coming and . . . to put themselves in a position to stand on their own feet'.[208]

The issue became all the more urgent during May. By 20 April Collins was complaining that his agreement with Craig had become a 'dead letter'.[209] Craig complained of the southern government's lack of co-operation, its abandonment of a railway enquiry, its failure to suppress raids into the six counties – as well as the continued activity of the IRA in Ulster – and its failure to nominate representatives to a 'police committee'.[210] On the one hand Churchill was pressing Collins to restore the joint commission, originally proposed as an 'alternative to drastic steps to secure Northern Ireland from further violation', and to make good 'any damage inflicted on loyalists'. On the other, he indicated to his British colleagues that Craig's demands for the constabulary should be met;[211] against the 'considerable objections' of his colleagues in London, Churchill urged that the demands of the Ulster government to raise their police force to 48,000 should be met, in view of the 'present weakness' of the British army.[212] On 30 May he explained that Craig's attitude had been brought about by the failure of Collins to keep order in the south and by his joining the 'avowed republicans': it was 'little wonder' that the north had gone back to its extreme and violent position and 'we have to give them assurances of help'.[213]

Collins and Griffith were in London at the time. During an interview with the British Collins had appeared truculent and distraught. On the one hand he displayed 'concern' with the north, with British payment of the special constabulary, and had brought with him 'a dossier of outrages' against the Catholics.[214] On the other he seemed disenchanted with affairs in Ireland and indicated that he was willing to give the country 'back . . . as a present'.[215] Lloyd George wondered whether he was 'manoeuvering us into a position where our case was weak', that is into a break on Ulster where 'we should get the same atmosphere of doubtful responsibility as in the case of reprisals', rather than a position which was strong, such as on the issue of republic versus monarch, where 'there would be support'.[216]

By the end of May the Ulster question had therefore become inflamed by the activities of nationalists and loyalists within the six counties; by incidents and outrages in the city of Belfast and on the border; by the failure, unwillingness or collusion of the south in the activities of their extremists; by the failure of the pact between Collins and Craig; and by the financing of the specials by Britain (which it did to preserve Ulster from the implications of disorder in the south). Lloyd George recognised the tactical weakness of breaking on Ulster, as he had always done. He would not accept Collins's offer of Ireland 'as a present': Craig would be summoned to London, for Lloyd George would not break on 'Ulster'.

But nor would Collins, by early June, break on Ulster. His unofficial northern policy had serious implications not only for the constitutional settlement of the south, but for the practical course of tolerating the Four Courts executive.

It is difficult to estimate the extent to which other members of the government were involved in that policy, though it seems clear that there was some knowledge of what was going on and that O'Duffy, in any case, was involved.

After the treaty, and particularly from April 1922, GHQ not only knew of, but sanctioned operations in the northern area against enemy forces, for which the 'stuff' was to be transported from GHQ.[217] The initiative for one such operation in April had come from the third northern division; but on account of a series of delays, the opening date for the 'move' was settled for 17 May.[218] Due to further delays and the failure of other units to come out in support of those in the third northern, the operation was dropped.[219]

However, no attempt had been made by either Mulcahy or the provisional government to demobilise the IRA units within the six-county area after the treaty, though in general they did suffer badly from financial distress and demoralisation.[220] Moreover, once the initiative had been taken by the third northern, not only did the chief-of-staff and headquarters in Dublin promise to transport material northwards, but they also undertook responsibility for conveying the instructions to other northern units and for settling a date for operations.[221] The materials, munitions and indeed men were despatched, by all available accounts, through the Four Courts.[222] The conclusion which suggests itself is that those responsible in GHQ, like O'Duffy or O'Sullivan, or in the government, like Collins, both tolerated and exploited the Four Courts executive for a number of reasons: they wished to reassure the executive forces that they agreed with their views on the north-east; that whatever their public pronouncements, they were privately willing to support active operations in the north. They hoped to afford practical defence to the Catholic population against the loyalists and the specials. On the other hand they hoped to gain the trust of the executive by this course, while simultaneously diverting its more active supporters to the north-east and away from the twenty-six counties.

It is against such a background that the final incident occurred, the Pettigo-Beleek affair. It got its name from the triangle which joined the border villages, Pettigo and Beleek. It involved clashes between British and Irish troops in late May and early June 1922. It also involved 'irregular' or 'northern bound' troops, who may have been on the border in connection with the abortive operations planned for the north from 17 May.

The accounts on both sides differed. Craig maintained that the Pettigo-Beleek triangle had been invaded by forces 'operating from Southern Ireland'.[223] He had been advised by Solly Flood that to deal with the situation, it would be necessary 'to occupy Ballyshannon on the Free State side of the border'.[224] The nature of these 'forces' which Craig claimed were operating from Southern Ireland remained unclear. At the outset there were reports that Pettigo had fallen into the hands of republicans, and that though Beleek was held by neither side, there were 'republicans' in the old fort in Free State territory commanding the village.[225]

There had been fighting between republican IRA and specials on the frontier; both villages lay partly in Ulster territory and seemed by 31 May to be in the hands of republicans, as was the area 'between the two villages'.[226] By that date permission had been given to the Irish commander-in-chief, by the war office, to 'pursue' any forces that occupied Ulster territory or attacked either Ulster or British forces 'across the border'.[227] On 3 June two companies of British troops crossed from Lough Erne to the point where southern territory almost touched the lough, and then advanced twelve miles into Irish territory.[228] They cut off Pettigo from the west while other troops closed in from the east.[229] During the ensuing operations seven of Pettigo's defenders were killed, sixteen prisoners taken, and half a dozen high explosive shells fired — to dislodge the snipers in the hills.[230] From Dublin the official army report denied that British troops were first fired on.[231] Collins demanded a joint enquiry and protested against the 'unwarrantable interference with our forces in our territory': an extension of the trouble would be 'disastrous' and would 'imperil the whole situation'.[232] The barracks at Pettigo had been in the hands of Free State troops, and seven of those killed were Free Staters; these troops had not fired on the British and 'any firing from the South ... must have been the work of irregulars'.[233] In Cope's view, the British troops 'hit the wrong people'.[234]

The provisional government in Dublin maintained an attitude of having been wronged.[235] They explained that an officer had been sent from Dublin to withdraw troops from the Pettigo border.[236] No sniping by Free State troops had occurred and a medical officer, sent by their side to explain the position of the British, had been arrested.[237] They demanded an impartial inquiry into the 'whole business'.[238]

Privately, Mulcahy's assessment had been that though the barracks was 'held by us' in Donegal, the border 'war' had been started by the irregulars. After this the British had come, occupied the village, shelled the barracks, killed seven and taken ten prisoners.[239]

In any case by that stage — 5 June — the impact of British

dissatisfaction with the failure of the Irish government to govern, its toleration of the executive troops, its pact with de Valera, its constitution which set up 'a republic with a thin veneer' had had a cumulative effect on Collins and his colleagues. So too had the failure of the pacts and negotiations to resolve the situation, and the threat implicit in the British guns in Beleek. On 2 June the Irish ministers met in Dublin. The confidence which had previously existed in their complicated scheme of arrangements to get through with the treaty, and to deal with the army and de Valera, had been undermined. Both the patience and time of the government were running out. The feeling existed that the constitution had been 'definitely rejected' in London; and there was a 'good deal of talk about war'. The 'present position in Ireland was responsible for [the] hard British attitude' and the situation was the 'same as July last', for which the shooting of British officers had been 'largely responsible'.[240] The English were now 'more hostile' and they would 'give us belligerent rights in case of war'.[241] The time had come when no further concessions should be made and although the pact would not be denounced, Collins would 'not go on any joint platform'.[242] Any breach of the treaty 'arising out of [the] pact' would be put to a vote of the house; this may have been in the interests of 'straight dealing', for after the election there would be 'no more duality'.[243] The next day, 3 June, Collins had indicated that he would not sign the draft of an appeal submitted by Boland for joint signature: while 'not refusing bluntly' he would 'get out of it gracefully until [the] election was over', with an 'appeal to uphold the pact in spirit'.[244]

But the decision to face the 'differences' and end the 'duality' was more ominous for the opposition, in view of the simultaneous resolution to abandon 'unofficial' northern policy, and to recognise the northern government.[245] At the meeting of the Irish ministers on the 3rd, the feeling seems to have predominated that the 'withdrawal of irregulars' must be secured. Cosgrave's proposal urging 'peace' and recognition of the northern parliament 'without prejudice' – the position to be 'what it was last September' – was supported by Griffith, O'Higgins and McGrath.[246] Although Collins seemed reluctant to 'force recognition' before the northern parliament 'recognises us' (by which he presumably meant the northern Catholics), it seems none the less that the 'duality' towards the north was to stop.[247] 'No troops of any kind' were 'to be sent into [the] N[orth] E[ast]'.[248] The policy of 'peaceful obstruction' should be adopted towards the Belfast government and 'no troops from the twenty-six county area, either those under official control or attached to the executive, should be permitted to invade the six-county area'.[249] At the same time any extension of powers on the part of that government should be 'strongly opposed' and care taken to prevent any powers 'other than those conferred by the 1920 act'.[250]

In a sense, therefore, it could be argued that the 'outbreak of civil war' — that is the subsequent decision on 27 June to turn the guns on the Four Courts — was inherent in the conclusions reached by the government more than three weeks previously. The government's tolerant attitude towards the Volunteer split and the dissident IRA men had been made possible only on account of its ambiguous attitude to the north of Ireland: while public pacts might be made with Craig and promises given to the British, private acquiescence and possibly encouragement might be offered to those IRA men who intervened in the north on behalf of the 'persecuted minority'. Neither the pacts nor the agreements had eliminated the persecutions.

The north, and the double policy of the government to the north, made it possible to tolerate the dissident Volunteers and the separate executive. It made it possible to anticipate that their allegiance to headquarters and the government could be secured, if not on 'the republic' then on a 'national' policy to the north. Thus while Mulcahy continued his talks with Cork IRA men and members of the Four Courts executive in order to reconcile the army to civil control, and while O'Connor publicly reiterated his army's allegiance to the republic for which the fight would yet be resumed, there had been in the background an additional policy which made other developments appear superficial by contrast. As long as the Volunteers were encouraged to intervene in the north, it was unlikely that any *impasse* with the 'irregulars' would be irreversible. As far as O'Connor was concerned, indeed, it may not have been unlikely that the fight against the British would be resumed, with the private if not the public support of the government. For while he might publicly denounce the 'Free State "imperial party"', he might privately hope for its support in his 'attack' on the 'north-east counties as soon as he was ready'.

The decision of the government on 2 and 3 June meant that there was now no more room for proposals to 'attack' the 'North East', and that therefore, there was no more room for O'Connor.

The implications of the decision to withdraw all troops from the northern area, whether official or irregular, subsequently became more pronounced. The government decided, for example, to end negotiations with the Four Courts executive once the latter insisted on having the nomination of the chief-of-staff in a proposed council of eight, which would have four representatives from each side.[251] Despite a final attempt, by either Lynch or O'Hegarty, to resolve matters to the extent that Lynch, if made chief-of-staff, would solemnly undertake not to 'overthrow the administration' formed after the elections, there was to be no arrangement.[252] Griffith objected to the 'majority' for the 'other side' involved in the proposals for an army council, as he continued to oppose the 'people being sacrificed on [the] altar of false unity'.[253] Mulcahy, who as late as 5 June felt 'we are approaching' unity, having 'scored all along... with the policy of generosity', believed by the 12th that the government had gone 'beyond what I personally consider we were entitled to go'.[254] On 12 June it was decided that there would be no further negotiations pending the formation of the new coalition.[255]

What should be noted about the decision to terminate negotiations with the executive is not so much that it was taken, but that it was taken during a period when Collins, in particular, was anxious about the escalation of outrage against Catholics in Belfast. On 6 June, for example, he had complained that Craig continued to break the bargain: three members of the police committee had been arrested and lodged in Crumlin Road jail, while the Mater hospital in Belfast had been attacked with machine-gun fire.[256] Despite Craig's rejoinder that the arrests were warranted, and accounts of the shooting exaggerated, Collins insisted that he wanted investigations made into the hospital incident, and the nature of the charges against the three imprisoned men revealed.[257] On the 8th he claimed that Craig made no 'real effort to stop outrages', forty-six Catholics having been murdered or died of wounds and 100 wounded during May (as against corresponding Protestant figures of twenty-nine and sixty-three).[258] Moreover, 108 attempted murders had occurred; and 404 Catholic families had been evacuated from their homes.[259]

Yet at the same time Collins reiterated to his colleagues, as he did on 9 June, that the 'border business' should be given up; and though it might be emphasised publicly that the border question was artificial, engineered from Belfast to distract attention, he was resolved that 'duality' should be terminated after the election. With his colleagues, he determined to stop further negotiations with the Four Courts, pending the formation of the new coalition.[260] The executive was accordingly informed that there would be no further negotiations until after the election.[261] The final discussions on the constitution took place prior to the publication of that document on the day of the election, the 16th, and on a pre-election visit to his constituents in Cork, Collins abandoned the pact, urging 'the citizens of Cork to vote for the candidate you think best of . . . whom [*sic*] . . . will carry on best in the future' the work that they want carried on'.[262]

The Irish people went to the polls on 16 June. The morning newspapers had contained drafts of the constitution and its oath. But the votes would not be counted before a week had passed. In the meantime a split had occurred in the Four Courts, when Barry proposed a resolution that an ultimatum be given to the British to withdraw their troops within seventy-two hours.[263] Mellows and O'Connor supported him, possibly because they hoped to unite the country on the pro-

posal against the British before the votes were counted.[264] But
Lynch opposed the proposal, as did two other Cork officers,
Moylan and Deasy, and withdrew from the Four Courts.[265]

In any case when the votes were counted it became clear
that despite the constitution and the oath, the Irish people
had voted for the treaty. Fifty-eight pro-treaty candidates
had been elected, and, despite the pact, only thirty-five
anti-treaty ones. There were thirty-five others, farmers,
independents and the like, most of whom supported the
treaty. But the election had solved nothing, beyond possibly
confirming the government's determination that there would
be no more 'duality'. With the news of the results came that
of the shooting dead, by two Irishmen, of Sir Henry Wilson
in London on 22 June, and the demand by Lloyd George
to the provisional government that it take action to expel
O'Connor and his followers from the Four Courts, where
they were in 'rebellion' in the 'heart of Dublin city'.[266]

In London the first of a series of emergency cabinet and
ministerial meetings occurred. Although there was no 'proof'
that 'any connection between the IRA, at any rate between
the Four Courts and the murder' existed, documents had
been found on those responsible which included a 'printed
scheme of organisation of the IRA' with reference to the
need for organisation in London.[267] These were sufficient
to form the basis of the warning to the Irish leaders. They
would be told that 'information' existed connecting the
assassins with the IRA; that preparations were being made
'among irregular IRA' to attack lives and property of British
subjects in Ulster and in England; that the ambiguous
position of the IRA could no longer be ignored; that 'it was
intolerable that Mr Rory O'Connor be permitted to remain in
open rebellion' and that the Irish government must bring
this state of affairs to an end.[268] The letter was therefore
sent to the Irish.[269] On the 23rd Macready was in London
when he discussed with the ministers the possibility of a
'*coup de main* by the imperial forces' against the republican
headquarters at the Four Courts.[270] A plan involving a
summons to surrender to the garrison had been worked out,
designed to surprise and for which everything was ready.[271]
Although some civilians would be 'killed or wounded' —

which Lloyd George did not want — Macready had enough troops 'to carry out the operation and to hold his own in Dublin in the event of 'consequential trouble'.[272] Pending a reply to the formal request to Collins to expel the garrison, Macready was to return to Dublin to make 'all arrangements for the operation.'[273]

Collins had been absent when Lloyd George's letter arrived on the 23rd and Griffith had simply despatched an 'interim reply'.[274] When it did arrive, Collins's reply was not entirely satisfactory. His letter, discussed by the ministers on the 24th, intimated that his government had the matter 'in hand', that he would give it his 'personal attention', but there was no promise that the 'immediate action demanded by the prime minister would be taken'.[275] Further preparations to take the Four Courts were made. Churchill was to draft a proclamation to be issued after the attack, and the admiralty was to order sufficient ships to Dublin to accomodate 400 prisoners.[276]

The proclamation was prepared, to be issued by Macready to the 'citizens of Dublin',[277] and when the ministers assembled later in the day they heard that the ships would reach Dublin next morning (Sunday) at 9 a.m.[278] The decision was then reached that the plan 'for surrounding the Four Courts and for securing the surrender by the present occupants' should start next day, Sunday 25 June.[279]

As it happened, Macready took it upon himself to disobey the instructions. He did so on the grounds that, because the republicans 'went away for the weekend' and because the leaders did not even sleep there, few would be captured. Moreover, seventy-two hours notice of truce termination should be given, and more seriously, the operation would endanger the troops, not at the time, but afterwards.[280] The general staff agreed with Macready; the operation 'must' in their opinion 'be of the most extreme political importance' to 'justify the risk of loss of life and . . . the unfortunate effect on our troops', while the danger existed of its bringing 'the two wings' of the IRA together.[281] Ostensibly on account of the military attitude, and of the need to provide seventy-two hours notice of the termination of the truce, the ministers dropped the plan.[282]

In Dublin chance intervened to ensure that not the British
but the Irish would storm the Four Courts. Certain republican
apologists argue that Collins acted under pressure from Britain.
No evidence exists for this; indeed the government in
London had formulated its own plan to take the Four Courts.
It may be that Collins got wind of it and determined to
forestall them but again there is no evidence that this was the
case. Ever since he had abandoned his unofficial northern
policy, the occupation of the Four Courts had been a
problem less and less likely to be resolved peacefully. The
election victory might have discouraged him from stretching
his patience; in any case it would be essential in his scheme
of ending the duality to have the garrison cleared out before
the opening of the new parliament on 1 July, for which all
preparations had been made.

As the provisional government discussed the summoning
of the new Dáil on 26 July, the assistant chief-of-staff of
the regular army, J. J. O'Connell, was arrested by 'irregular
forces' and detained in the Four Courts. He was held in
retaliation for the arrest by government troops of Leo
Henderson, a supporter of the executive who had been
involved in a raid on Ferguson's garage in Baggot Street.[283]
On 27 June the provisional government decided to 'serve
notice' on the armed men 'in illegal occupation' of the Four
Courts and Fowler Hall. They would be ordered to evacuate
the building and surrender all arms and property; if they
refused, then 'the necessary military action would be taken
at once'.[284] On the same day the government discussed the
new parliament, with regard to the appointment of the
clerk of the house, the speaker and deputy speaker.[285]

The Four Courts were surrounded, the ultimatum deliver-
ed, and ignored. The garrison may not have thought the
government in earnest, feeling that the demand had been
made to mollify the British but that it was not to be taken
seriously.[286] The government was, of course, serious and
hoped to complete the 'job' in three to four hours. Two
British eighteen-pounder guns had been lent to 'open the
attack' and it was intended to lend two more 'to hasten
the end'; but there was a shortage of shells, and despite
urgent representation by Cope to Churchill, delays occurred

before they arrived.[287] Worried lest the vital supplies would
not reach Dublin in time and thus reduce the prospect of
success, Collins wired Churchill that it was 'imperative that
our further requirements should be met tonight without
fail'.[288] Churchill's reaction was immediate; he would supply
anything, including soldiers, and orders had been sent to
Macready 'that all assistance is to be given'.[289] Even a 'broad
hint' would be sufficient.[290] But the Irish resisted the soldiers,
for as Cope explained, it would be 'fatal' to supply
troops to shoot down Irishmen.[291] While Churchill alluded
to the Irish wisdom in refusing military assistance, he
privately wondered whether Macready would 'complete the
operation if the Free State break off and when'.[292] If the
'worst' came to the 'worst' it would be 'quite impossible to
let matters stop unfinished'.[293] He promised Collins that
Macready would help in any way 'if you feel you can carry
it no further'.[294]

In any case the munitions, if not the men, were supplied.
On 29 June the war office authorised Macready to issue
arms and munitions to the provisional government, up to
10,000 rifles at his discretion, together with four eighteen
pounders and two sixty pounders.[295]

The same day de Valera, still outside the government
despite the pact, described the Four Courts men as 'the best
and bravest of our nation': 'In Rory O'Connor and his
comrades lives the unbought indomitable soul of Ireland.'
He appealed to 'Irish citizens' to 'give them support' and
'Irish soldiers' to bring them aid.[296] De Valera then, in the
words of his biographers, decided that 'for himself . . . there
was nothing left but to join up again' and he re-enlisted as a
private in his old volunteer battalion.[297]

On 30 June the Four Courts fell. Churchill wrote to
Collins that the situation had been revolutionised and he
added that, even if the archives were scattered, the 'title
deeds of Ireland' were safe.[298] The metaphor was scarcely
appropriate and definitely premature. Even if the garrison
had been routed, republicans throughout the city had begun
to seize other buildings.[299] For de Valera had announced
that 'the republic' was fighting for its life.[300]

7
Epilogue: July 1922 — May 1923

The decision to attack the Four Courts had been implicit in
that of 3 June to stop the 'border' business. But it was also
a reaction to the consistent provocation of the dissident
groups in the country, rather than a contrived and deliberate
military plan to eliminate the irregulars. The chance element
of the affair was reflected in the government's not having
the necessary equipment for the attack and their asking for
the loan of two eighteen pounders beforehand — the much
celebrated 'British guns' of the republican accounts.[1] But
the spontaneity of the attack was quickly lost as a 'wave of
sympathy' for O'Connor was reported on the 29th to be
'rapidly increasing', which, it was feared, might 'spread to
the country'.[2] While Macready in Dublin seemed slow to
produce the supplies urgently required by Collins, the
garrison held out and chance turned to design.[3] The holding
out of the garrison, combined with the shortage of shells,
the insurrection in Dublin, the collecting of republican and
Four Courts supporters throughout the country, prompted
the government to turn itself over to dealing more thoroughly
with what had become a military problem. The need to
defeat the garrison militarily — itself the culmination of the
reversals in attitude since early June — predominated, and
British demands, republican taunts, and the 'historic unity'
of the 'movement' faded from importance. Having determined to take the Four Courts as the first practical measure
in its new policy, the government had altered, if somewhat
simplified, the nature of the problem. This was partly due
to de Valera's bringing in his republican opposition.

By joining the fight de Valera assisted its prolongation.
Whereas previously many of the units of dissident IRA men

had local rather than national sympathy, implicated in incidents rather than details, de Valera brought to the fight a certain morality synonymous with his former position as 'president of the republic', as well as his allegiance to that republic and a body of republican TDs. By bringing in the political opposition de Valera helped to make the Civil War seem to be just that: a 'war' between two, rather than many, opposing groups, on the issue of the republic. The Volunteers throughout the country who had opposed the government, or headquarters, or the civic guards, or rival Volunteers, now seemed to be bound with the party into an ideological opposition, challenging more completely than hitherto the authority of the government. This in fact was not the case and it quickly became clear that de Valera and the 'politicians' continued to be regarded as a liability by the 'fighting men' (see below, p.205).

In any case the government had now to contend with what seemed to be a united republican and Volunteer opposition 'increasing in numbers and activity', spreading from Dublin to Cork, Louth and the west.[4] In Dublin de Valera and Brugha were reported to be leading the rebellion in Sackville Street, as if re-enacting 1916, and by 1 July the irregulars (as they increasingly became known) had occupied thirty-six buildings in the city, the 'main spring of the rising';[5] in Brittas, Co. Wicklow, Childers was collecting forces. On 4 July the British government authorised aeroplanes for Ireland.[6]

By 5 July the provisional government had almost recovered Dublin. Brugha was captured — and died — while heroically standing up to the guns, prompting Collins's observation that he was both a 'fanatic' as well as one who had given his 'all' for Ireland's 'freedom', and 'because of his sincerity I would forgive him everything'.[7] De Valera left Dublin and headed south, first for Co. Tipperary and then Cork, where Liam Lynch — now IRA chief-of-staff — had set up headquarters, having left the Four Courts after his split with O'Connor on 18 June.[8] The government then decided to turn its attention from Dublin to the south of Ireland.[9]

By 5 July the 'chance' nature of the decision to storm the Four Courts had been replaced by a more resolute military policy. On 1 July the peace proposals of the Labour party had been rejected by the provisional government and the decision taken that military action against the irregulars should continue.[10] Ministers also left the ministry to take up command in the field with the government's troops, which were now becoming known as the 'national forces'. Mulcahy left, as did McGrath. Collins, for the moment, would act as minister for defence.[11] On 2 July O'Hegarty left to take up duty as the governor of Mountjoy jail, now to be used exclusively for military captives.[12] On 3 July it was decided to increase the strength of the army and to enlist up to 20,000 volunteers at a cost of £3 million.[13] Simultaneously, plans were made to commandeer officially petrol supplies around Dublin, and to establish Kilmainham as a military prison.[14] The government now considered the legal and financial implications of a 'state of war' — particularly in regard to indemnity for taking over buildings, and for compensation.[15] On 12 July a war council — with Collins, Mulcahy and O'Duffy — was set up and the country was divided into five commands: the western command under MacEoin; the south-western under O'Duffy; the eastern under Emmet Dalton; the south-eastern under J. T. Prout; and the Curragh under J.J. O'Connell.[16] O'Higgins became assistant adjutant-general.[17] On the 13th a proclamation proroguing parliament was drafted and by the 17th the transformation from civil to military was almost complete: O'Higgins, McGrath and Fionan Lynch had given up their 'civil' positions; so had Collins, who told his colleagues that he wished to take up military duties as commander-in-chief and would not, therefore, act in a ministerial capacity until further notice.[18] Government became the preserve of the administrators rather than the politicians. Cosgrave succeeded Collins as acting minister for finance and chairman of the provisional government on 12 July; Hogan and Walsh remained with him; and Blythe, Fitzgerald, Gavan Duffy, Hayes, Griffith and O'Sheil attended meetings though they did not belong to the provisional government.[19]

On 8 July the government forces occupied Enniscorthy and Wexford, routing the irregulars led by O'Malley. Two days later the republicans at Blessington were dispersed, with a hundred or so captured. In Limerick Commandant

MacManus put an end to the 'truce' negotiated between
the opposing sections of the army under Lynch and Hannigan
on the basis that each side would retain present positions:
MacManus arrived from Dublin with 'definite instructions'
for 'military operations' in the area and no such agreement
could be 'admitted by GHQ'.[20] Prout took Carrick-on-Suir
on 3 August and was, according to his own account 'cheered'
as he entered — the locals having been terrorised since the
elections for having failed to vote for Breen and Robinson.[21]
O'Duffy was in Limerick where he issued a proclamation on
the 4th indicating that he would deal sternly with the
opposition: his troops had been ordered to fire on any person
discovered destroying bridges or railways, obstructing roads
or looting, and to arrest those known to aid and abet 'such
wanton destruction'.[22] By 12 August Dalton was in Cork
planning the 're-conquest' of the rest of the county and
assuring Collins that the irregulars were 'absolutely finished
in the south'.[23] Two shiploads of reinforcements had been
landed in Cork on the 11th, 200 recruits from the 'Legion
of ex-Servicemen' had been temporarily accepted, and he
planned to take Midleton on the 13th, Fermoy on the 14th
and Cobh that night.[24]

Griffith died on 12 August and Collins was killed in an
ambush ten days later in Co. Cork. Speculation continues as
to who was responsible for Collins's death: the accused range
from the British to the republicans. However, at the time
republican IRA men claimed responsibility for the ambush
and shooting, and were, in turn, praised by Lynch. The
incident was reported to Lynch on 24 August by the
commander of the first southern division, who indicated that
there were only nine republicans present during the
operation: the main party had left because the convoy was
not expected. In Lynch's view, the attack was a 'splendid
achievement' as 'these nine men with rifles were opposed by
machine-gun and greater numbers'. His only regret was that
his men had had no mines. He was satisfied that Collins's
death would badly affect the Free State who could not 'fill'
his loss. He drew the lesson that it had become necessary 'to
shoot such men as . . . Collins' whose former services to the
republic had been splendid', hoping, at the same time, that

the enemy would realise 'the folly of trying to crush the republic before it is too late'.[25]

Since 22 August 1922, the ambush and death of Michael Collins has been seen as another of the tragedies in the tragedy of Irish history, whose Euripidean proportions have been extended in retrospect. If the Free State exploited the killing of Collins to undermine the apparent patriotism of the republicans as well as their popularity, many of the republicans quickly left Lynch's view behind. Indeed, his attitude was resented, even by some of his own supporters: from Cork city came reports of one IRA officer who was 'very bitter in his conversation more particularly against Liam Lynch' on account of Collins's death.[26] Instead of accepting the killing as a 'splendid achievement' by their own men, republicans began to attribute blame for masterminding the operation to the British.

The attribution of blame to the British reflects something of the way in which the complexity of events has become tempered by those assumptions — made by all sides — which have become part of an historic memory. The suggestion that the British killed Collins rests on the view that he was going to make peace, or unite with the republicans and abandon the treaty, the Free State, and the provisional government.

It is clear that in the spring and early summer of 1922, Churchill did entertain fears on this count. He had not been reassured by the postponement of the election, followed by the pact with the republicans, by the toleration of the Four Courts executive 'in open rebellion' in the 'heart of Dublin city', by the apparent involvement or sympathy by the government with the activities of the IRA in the north, by the original draft of the constitution 'setting up the republic with a thin veneer', and by the failure to do as bid and storm the garrison after the shooting of Henry Wilson. But he had not known that just after the Pettigo-Beleek affair, which seemed to strengthen his doubts and suspicions about the Irish leaders, Collins and his colleagues had resolved to stop all involvement in the north. On the one hand they would now concentrate simply on publicising the position of Belfast city and on the other, they would extend recognition to the northern government.

Nor had Churchill known of the decision, even before the
election, to stop the 'duality'; nor had he been completely
reassured by the attack on the Four Courts.

His initial reaction of elation had given way to anxiety
which he had somewhat communicated to his colleagues. He
remained anxious to prevent any compromise between the
Irish groups. He opposed, for example, the Irish Labour
party's plan to call a meeting of TDs to discuss the position
of the country and proposals for a peace. This would 'only
encourage the rebels, prolong the fight and increase the
destruction of property' and any compromise would remove
from the provisional government the sympathy and support
they would need from his country in the coming winter.[27]
Churchill continued to be somewhat uncertain of the Irish
government's intention, or ability, to obliterate the opposition. He refused, for example, to lend Collins some southern
forts to assist in the campaign, for that would constitute a
'breach' of the treaty.[28] Nor would he make definite preparations for the evacuation of the remaining British troops
from the south. When the war office submitted their proposals for the accommodation of 900 British officers and
15,000 men in Ireland (including Ulster) over the winter,
he felt that there was 'nothing for it' but to 'wait and see'
how the situation developed; and the cabinet, on 24 July,
agreed to authorise provision for winter huttings for the
troops – 16 battalions in Northern Ireland, and six in
Dublin.[29]

But Churchill's anxieties about the country after the
outbreak of civil war, and his doubts about Collins's ability
or resolution to stamp out the opposition, do not substantiate
claims of British implication in his death; for apart from
Churchill's natural tendency to overreact to events (a tendency
which Lloyd George balanced by his more conciliatory
attitude after the treaty), it is also the case that long after
Collins's death, in October 1922, Churchill was as reluctant
as he had been when Collins was alive, to remove the troops
from Dublin. He told a conference of the British general
staff on 26 September that though it would probably not
be necessary to use British troops in Ireland in support of
the provisional government, he did not want them withdrawn:

for that might give 'much encouragement to de Valera and others to redouble their efforts against' the government.[30] When the coalition fell in October, Churchill, who was replaced at the colonial office in Law's new administration by Devonshire, referred in a farewell message to the 'unceasing, tormenting struggle' which had cost Griffith and Collins their lives and concluded that in Cosgrave, O'Higgins, and Mulcahy 'we have found Irishmen whose word is their bond'.[31]

Churchill's summing up of the new men was not a reflection on Collins's having broken his 'bond', but on his not sufficiently formulating it. Too often it seemed to him that Collins had waited and waited and that even after 28 June there had been traces of waiting. Macready had remarked on the reluctance of the Free State to kill, though that was not true of their opponents; reports had been despatched of talks between the government and extremists like Breen, or to the effect that the government was making 'no real headway'.[32] Collins had been reluctant to permit 'abuse' of opponents in the newspapers, many of whom though 'misguided' were 'sincere'; he opposed the closing down of the republican party's headquarters, for that would merely serve to drive the opposition underground, and it would be 'wrong to go in for a policy of suppression'.[33] His death on 22 August marked the end of the period of waiting, which had already begun on 3 June.

Three weeks later, on 9 September, the third Dáil met. This would be the parliament to which the provisional government would be responsible, but which had been prorogued fortnightly since 28 June. All the deputies – except those belonging to Mr de Valera's party – assembled (see below, p.206). W. T. Cosgrave, proposed by Mulcahy, as the 'trusted head' of the 'national party' and a man 'of sufficient strength of character to carry forward the work . . . of securing . . . full freedom . . . under this treaty' was elected president.[34] MacNéill, who seconded the nomination, claimed there was 'no mystery' about it: for since the deaths of Griffith and Collins, the 'burden of being chairman' of the Irish government had devolved on Cosgrave.[35] Cosgrave promised that the existence of the two ministries — the Dáil and provisional governments — would be terminated; they would be 'assimilated'; he intended to enact a constitution, reassert the authority and supremacy of parliament, and support the national army — if necessary by asking parliament for the powers essential to the restoration of order.[36]

Cosgrave's declaration at the outset of the new Dáil was the first of a series of indications that he determined to reassert the supremacy of that parliament. On 12 September Mulcahy announced in the Dáil that the only possible basis for settlement would be the surrender of arms to the government of the people, which alone could control the armed forces of the state.[37] The treaty would be honoured in spirit as well as practice. O'Higgins told the Dáil on the 18th, when the constitution was being discussed, that there were 'things in this constitution which we would wish out of it', just as there were in the treaty; but as the British had never been actually driven out of the country, those 'irksome' matters existed.[38] The constitution was to be ready for submission to the British parliament for ratification before 6 December, the date upon which the powers of the provisional government expired; its ratification would automatically bring about the establishment of the Irish Free State, which, under article 17 of the treaty, must come into existence by that date.[39] Although there were fears, when Lloyd George's coalition fell in October, that the change of government might mean a delay in the British parliament's ratifying the constitution and that the twenty-six counties might therefore be left 'up in the air', both Lloyd George and Law promised that this would not happen.[40] Law supported the treaty now — whatever his former interventions — and he promised that the new parliament would meet in time to ratify the constitution. Cosgrave had told him that nothing was 'more likely' to lead to an early settlement in Ireland than a *'fait accompli'* i.e., the final ratification of the constitution and the establishment of the Free State. He had insisted that there would be no 'terms offered to the rebels' except 'the complete surrender of their arms'.[41]

Cosgrave's resolution to restore the authority of parliament,

enact the constitution and see to the establishment of the
Free State remained paramount. He knew 'his own mind',
decided 'rapidly' and avoided 'all verbiage and . . . reference
to the past'.[42] Although he opposed the abolition of pro-
portional representation within the six counties on the
grounds that it was not a 'domestic matter' for Northern
Ireland, that it 'loads the dice against the Free State before
the boundary commission and . . . prejudices the implementation of the treaty', he would not resort to 'unofficial'
procedures.[43] He endorsed as it were the policy of abandoning such procedures and guaranteed that his forces would not
cross the border either armed or in uniform. He was prepared
to make an official declaration, when the time was 'oppor-
tune', that no government of the Irish Free State would
turn its forces against the state of Northern Ireland, for he
believed the 'national army' should deal 'only with internal
troubles and defence' and should not be used as 'an army
of aggression against the north'.[44] His meeting with Law
on 24 October when he promised that there would be no
peace in the south except on 'the complete surrender of . . .
arms' and when he urged that nothing was more likely to
lead to an 'early' settlement than a *'fait accompli'* with regard
to the constitution and the establishment of the new state,
reflected the changed nature of the bonds between both
governments: concern with constitutional, administrative,
and technical issues replaced more completely than had been
the case since the treaty was signed concern with Ireland
as a political issue. Even before the fighting was terminated,
Cosgrave had ensured and reassured that the Irish question
was and would be simply an administrative one, and that
Ireland would never again impinge significantly on the
conduct of British party politics.

In Dublin Cosgrave's administration proceeded with its
attempts to restore the authority of parliament and the
rule of law to the Irish nation. Recruitment to the civic
guard was advertised in the newspapers in October, the
notice having been prepared by the new commissioner of
the force, General O'Duffy: candidates must be unmarried,
between 19 and 27 years, with a minimum height of 5'9"
and a chest measurement of 36"; they would be examined

in reading, writing, dictation, arithmetic and composition; and they must produce a testimonial of good character from a clergyman and the local divisional or brigade commandant.[45] Already 500 guards had been despatched to country areas, unarmed, as an 'experiment',[46] and although it was decided at a staff meeting that newspapers should treat the war as a secondary news item and emphasise the 'normalisation' of affairs, the rule of law had not yet triumphed.[47] On 26 September a resolution drafted partly at Mulcahy's request had been put before parliament, designed to give the army additional powers in order to restore law.[48] Two days later the resolution was carried. The army was empowered to establish military courts with full powers to inquire into charges and to inflict punishment on those found guilty of 'acts calculated to interfere with or delay the effective establishment of the authority of the government'.[49] Four days later, on 2 October, the army council laid down the regulations governing the trial of civilians by military court, from the constitution of the court to the scale of punishments: death or any lesser penalty might be inflicted.[50] The order was published in the newspapers on the 10th, and was to take effect from the 15th; an amnesty would be offered to those who surrendered their arms or ceased hostilities against the state before that date.[51]

The proclamation of 29 June and de Valera's joining the army, though it seemed to bind the republican and IRA opposition together, did not in fact do so. Until October 1922 there was no formal connection and the two — or more — groups remained distinct, as hitherto. Lynch (now IRA chief-of-staff) particularly shunned the 'politicians'.

When de Valera left Dublin in July he travelled to the south. He went first to Tipperary and stayed at IRA headquarters in Clonmel. From there he moved to Cahir; and as the Tipperary towns fell to Prout, he went to north Cork. In August he was in Fermoy, then Ballincollig and other towns held in the region by republicans. Occasionally he stayed in 'safe' houses or at IRA headquarters.[52] At that stage no formal connection existed between the republican party and the IRA beyond certain TDs holding prominent positions in the army organisation: Stack was its director of finance; and Derrig, the TD for West Mayo, was adjutant of the northern and eastern commands.[53] Moreover, Lynch continued to resist the establishment of a formal connection, and despite de Valera's attempts to arrange a meeting with the army executive, he refused to become entangled with him – or the 'politicians' though he would be 'pleased' to receive their views at any time.[54] Throughout July and August Lynch insisted that though 'the political people' might assist the IRA generally, they should neither control nor initiate policy and definitely not 'military propaganda'.[55] National and military policy were, in his view, one: 'to maintain the established republic'. The army was finished with all compromise or negotiation, unless 'based on recognition of the republic'.[56]

Lynch particularly resisted the danger, as he saw it, of the political group's setting up a government. He had 'no notion' of doing so: for 'we . . . await such time as An Dáil will carry on as the government of the republic without any fear of compromise'.[57] In the meantime 'no other government' would 'be allowed to function'.[58] Nor would the IRA have anything to do with 'the calling of the 2nd or 3rd Dáil' though if either one of them met and carried on 'as the government of the republic' then 'all would be well'.[59] He had abandoned his attempts of the previous spring to 'compromise' or make peace, which had ultimately split him from O'Connor on 18 June. Since the outbreak of war he opposed such attempts and he feared that any association with de Valera or the party might redound against the army, or that de Valera might take 'public action that would ruin us' – particularly as de Valera seemed in mid-August to regard the position as 'hopeless'.[60]

Lynch's fears must have been exacerbated by the events surrounding the official summoning of the Dáil for 9 September. In Cork, for example, when republican TDs approached Deasy (the officer commanding) regarding whether or not they should attend, Deasy's reaction was that they might: although if the question of peace arose, it should be referred back to the army executive, for just as the party was in no way responsible for the war, so too it should play no part in ending it.[61] Lynch himself wanted it impressed on de Valera before the Dáil meeting that the military position was strong, and that the army was so sure of success that 'we ask that no action be taken by him or the republican party which would weaken us and even rob us of victory'. In any case, the 'second Dáil and army executive are the only bodies to bring about peace' and 'surely the republican party are not expected to take . . . responsibility as regards the war, and I hope they realise this.'[62]

De Valera, for his part, did not attend the Dáil, having considered the question of attendance on the grounds of 'expediency' and 'principle'.[63] The assembly was not the Dáil, and the difficulties regarding the oath would arise; moreover, his party would be the 'butt of every attack' and accused constantly of obstructing the work.[64] No, the future of the party lay with abstention, not attendance, and de Valera decided neither to issue a statement nor proclaim the meeting. Proclamation could not be enforced, while a statement would limit de Valera's future course of action. Instead he would both stay away and say nothing. 'Let them keep guessing', he wrote.[65]

The meeting of the Dáil on the 9th had therefore provoked a debate amongst the party and the IRA as to whether the party should attend, and had also encouraged Lynch to reiterate that the party should have, and had, nothing to do with the war or the peace. Moreover, he maintained that in any case it was 'a waste of time to be thinking too much of policy' and 'we should strike our hardest' for that, ultimately, would make 'policy easier to settle'.[66] None the less, the army leaders were divided on 'policy' and some of them held that a government should be set up under de Valera. From prison the Four Courts leaders had made their views clear. O'Connor had warned against 'the compromising mind of the diplomat' but McKelvey and Mellows urged the formation of a republican government.[67] McKelvey felt the time had 'come' for one, particularly after Collins's death; Mellows, too, thought it 'imperative' because of the likelihood that the English would 'take a hand sooner or later' and the war would otherwise become a 'fight of individuals'. A government was essential as 'a rallying point' and 'a focus

point' for 'the movement'.[68] From elsewhere O'Malley
wanted a government to offset the 'illegality' of the provisional government. Six army leaders — Traynor, Barney
Mellows, Corbett, Pilkington, Barry and O'Donnell — called
for a meeting of the 'third Dáil', as did the republican
deputies — including Stack and Derrig — who wanted
detailed financial and other reports considered.[69] The
politicians' demands may have been designed to impress upon
Cosgrave the need to maintain the national assembly as the
Dáil — which they would attend — and not the provisional
parliament, which they would boycott. But the army leaders,
both inside and outside prison, envisaged a separate Dáil,
as distinct from that body which had disestablished the
republic, comprising only republican deputies.

De Valera, in mid September, opposed the setting up of
a republican government, for 'we no more than the others
could get from the army unconditional allegiance without
which our government would be a farce.'[70] As public
representatives, the position of his party had become
'impossible and impracticable' and he advocated that the
army executive, rather than a government, should take
control.[71] On 14 September a meeting of the republican TDs
sanctioned this course: the military should take control 'and
we co-operate'.[72]

In one sense the military did indeed take control: an
executive meeting which had been delayed until October —
and was the first since July — unanimously resolved that 'the
final decision' regarding any peace terms 'rests with the
executive'.[73] An army council was set up to carry on the
function of the executive when not in session and to
'negotiate terms of peace' such as would not 'bring this
country into the British empire'.[74] The commands were
reorganised; Lynch would move to Dublin, joining O'Malley
and Derrig; Deasy became deputy chief-of-staff, responsible
for the southern and first western divisions.[75] But what was
most remarkable, in view of the earlier manifestations by
both Lynch and de Valera against setting up a republican
government, was the call to de Valera to form a government
of the republic.[76] De Valera seems to have changed his mind
since mid-September, and seems to have taken the initiative.

But the executive formally called on the 'former president of Dáil Éireann to form a government' which would preserve 'the continuity of the republic'. It pledged 'wholehearted support' and allegiance to such a government and empowered it to 'make an arrangement' either with the provisional or British government, provided that arrangement 'does not bring the country into the British empire'.[77]

A public proclamation was prepared and issued on the 26th by the IRA. At the same time the republican deputies met together, constituted themselves 'Dáil Éireann' and appointed de Valera as 'President of the Republic' and chief executive of the state.[78]

De Valera's former inactivity disappeared with celerity. He proclaimed the provisional parliament, its members, its debts; and he rescinded the ratification of the treaty.[79] Dáil Éireann (i.e, his Dáil) was the only legitimate authority in the country and he, as president, was in supreme control; he nominated a cabinet with Stack, Ruttledge, Barton, Moylan and O'Kelly, though he submitted the nominations to the army for approval.[80] He appointed Mellows minister for defence, but because Mellows was in prison he considered the documents relating to 'defence' should bear the signature of both himself and the chief-of-staff.[81] But in effect the connection between the government and the army remained as it always had been, more formal than real; and the subsequent events which characterised the remainder of the Civil War revealed that de Valera no more controlled the IRA than he had done hitherto. For while the president proclaimed the enemy institutions, the real campaign was conducted by the units of the IRA in the south, in the west and in parts of Dublin. For the remainder of the Civil War, most of the GHQ orders did not carry de Valera's signature, though occasionally certain important documents did — like that proclaiming the 'other' Dáil on 17 November.

In one sense de Valera's collaboration with the army, combined with the effect of the stalemate of the campaign, ultimately altered the course and the conduct of the war. For despite the initial Free State victories in July and August, there had been something of a stalemate from September to November. This had been partly due to the nature of the 'war': once the towns had been taken, little could be done beyond maintaining them and simultaneously attempting to disperse the irregular groups. Moreover, transport was scarce and there seems to have been an increase in the number of republicans in the south, apparently in excess of the number present during the election. Added to these problems for the government, there existed what one report claimed to be 'the ignorant jealousy' by Corkmen of their Dublin colleagues.[82] Even the Free State officers with good reputations during the 'Tan times' failed to make any serious impression after August; it was not until December that the 'stalemate' gave way, not to a more decisive campaign, but to a more ruthless determination to exterminate the respective leaders on both sides. This development occurred partly in consequence of the new and formal association between de Valera and the IRA, in which his government proclaimed and sanctioned the executions of members of the 'provisional parliament', and in reaction to which the Free State government for its part introduced its policy of 'reprisals'.

Before then, the story, if not one of ruthlessness, was not one of distinction. Amongst the Free State generals, for example, Sean MacEoin's command in the west lacked distinction; his organisation seemed weak, he evoked little confidence, he was hampered by a delay in receiving supplies, and had no civil administration to fall back on.[83]

In the south the republicans had occupied Kenmare in Co. Kerry on 11 September, thereby endangering Cahirciveen and Waterville and the transatlantic cable. While the national troops were satisfied by mid October that Limerick was mainly a matter of 'police work', large groups of republican forces still remained in north Cork in Millstreet, Macroom and Ballyvourney, while a few hundred irregulars threatened Tralee.[84] In Tipperary there were about 200 irregulars, and in the second southern area 600. In Cork Mulcahy believed the irregulars to be disorganised and morale to be low.[85] The east of the country had fewer republican centres, the main points being Dublin city and Dundalk. In the west there were 1,000 irregulars, though in Donegal merely fifty, in bands of eight.

Although these numbers were based on reports and cannot necessarily be verified, what can be claimed is that there were groups of irregular soldiers throughout the south and west of the country from Carlow-Kilkenny, to Cork, Kerry, Limerick and Galway; and that reports from the commands did not suggest that the Free State generals were making dramatic progress. MacEoin's command in the west has already been mentioned in this respect. In the south and south-west, the rivalries between the two leading generals, O'Duffy and Dalton, had resulted in the absence of co-operation between these two bordering commands before O'Duffy left the army for the police in September; this had its effect on the campaign once the winter set in. Dalton, for example, had been reported to be attempting to 'fix' the boundaries in his command to include parts of Kerry and north Cork which O'Duffy had 'wrested from the enemy'. O'Duffy maintained that 'we engage' the irregulars 'everywhere — teach [th]em lessons', but other commands did not. He complained that Dalton, particularly, had 'more men per post than we have but . . . has not yet got down to solid steady work', while O'Duffy considered that Dalton's early success in Cork was due to his meeting no opposition, for the irregulars were being engaged elsewhere by him.[86] In any case O'Duffy was released from army duties in September to become commissioner of the police; but the rivalry had not helped either command, and apart from the earlier victories, no startling progress was recorded.[87]

But the most hopeless command seemed to be the Kilkenny-Waterford one, where the national forces were led by Prout. Despite his own account of having been cheered as he entered the towns, Prout subsequently did not seem to enjoy the confidence of either superiors or subordinates.[88] The republicans made frequent raids into his headquarters, Kilkenny, from Tipperary, occasionally in collusion with local civilians. Prout was certainly 'not too strong and decisive'; he provoked popular dissatisfaction by his connection with the proposed promotion of his friend, a captain Cunningham (an ex-British officer); his laxity of direction resulted in the making of 'truces' by individual officers with their opponents; and his command was one of 'extreme

Epilogue, July 1922 – May 1923

lassitude', demoralised not only by the peace moves and truces or by Prout's 'lying low and taking things too easy', but by the combined effect of drinking by the troops, the shortage of adequate supplies, and the continued raids by irregulars; his difficulties were exacerbated by leaking boots and inadequate clothing for his men. On 9 December the republicans overpowered the Free State garrison at Carrick-on-Suir and proceeded to seize Thomastown and Callan two days later.[89] President Cosgrave then intervened; he interviewed the TD for the region, Gorey, and wrote to Mulcahy in January that the officers in the area should be removed.[90]

The problems for the Free State were, then, numerous and diverse: not only could the stalemate be ascribed to the character of the campaign and the winter weather, but it also could be to the rivalries between the leaders; the inefficiencies of certain commanding officers; the absence of civilian support; the scarcity of supplies, from transport to waterproof clothing; the outbreaks of influenza; the problem which Brugha had already tried to eradicate during the truce, drink; and a new one, 'immorality'. Mulcahy received reports that his officers were drinking in the Theatre Royal in Dublin; O'Duffy had had accounts of excesses in Limerick; while from Cork came accusations that the Free State soldiers were 'loose', that there was 'immorality' in the 'open street', that 'acts of immorality' were being 'photographed by the irregulars for propaganda purposes', and that even a 'Free State' priest had complained that whereas the irregulars 'broke' the fifth and seventh commandments, the Free Staters in Cork broke the sixth.[91] In addition the weather and winter helped neither side, though they may have given the republicans a marginal advantage. Moreover, the loyalties of local populations were not to be relied on by either side; and although the republicans were obstinate, many were righteous and the setting up of the 'republican government' under de Valera in October may have helped to improve their 'moral' standing. There was also the feeling by some republicans that Cosgrave might eventually be 'scared' out: O'Connor, for example, had reminded O'Malley in September that during the black-and-tan terror, Cosgrave had run away to Manchester to a priest, telling O'Higgins to close down his department.[92]

But Cosgrave would not be 'scared out'. It became increasingly apparent that the government had enough determination to make up for the deficiencies of its troops. Preparations were being made to provide barrack accommodation for up to 25,000 recruits by 1 February 1923, and to secure adequate accommodation for prisoners and internees, at home and abroad. Negotiations with the British government took place between September and November to secure the island of Saint Helena to intern irregulars, and at home by December, camps were established or approved at Newbridge, Gormanstown, Templemore, Portlaoise and the Curragh.[93] By December, the formal procedure for military arrests had been established and the government therefore had all preparations made for trial by military court with the power of inflicting the death sentence, and for arrest and detention of opponents.[94] Moreover, irregular funds lodged in banks were to be seized and recruiting for the civic guard proceeded, despite all attempts by the opposition to have it stopped.[95] To emphasise, as it were, the new course, an army council was set up, replacing the war council of July, its formal approval by Cosgrave having coincided with the passing of the emergency power resolution in the Dáil.[96] Mulcahy, McMahon, O'Sullivan, O'Hegarty, and McGrath would now replace what had been Collins's war council of three.[97]

What is more, the emergency powers were to be used. On 17 November, four men, who had been 'tried by military courts for having revolvers in their possession', found 'guilty and sentenced to death', were executed — the 'unknown dupes', as the government would have it, of de Valera — Fisher, Cassidy, Tuohy and Gaffney.[98] The same day a well-known leader, arrested on the 10th, was tried for possession of a revolver: Erskine Childers was found guilty, sentenced to death and executed, although beforehand Cosgrave had seemed 'undecided as to which was the right course to pursue'.[99] The executions were said to have had a 'salutary effect' and they led to a new phase of the war, one which had been encouraged by the new relationship between the IRA and de Valera's government of the republic, the war of reprisals.

De Valera and Ruttledge, as president and minister for

home affairs respectively in the government of the republic, issued a proclamation rescinding the Dáil's approval of the treaty. They declared that those who called themselves the provisional government or their adherents belonged to an illegal body, and were guilty of rebellion against the republic.[100] On the 18th the IRA suppressed the 'enemy' courts, and on the 22nd, it proclaimed the civic guard.[101] But despite the proclamation, it seems that de Valera was in ignorance of its implications, as far as the IRA was concerned, and was not consulted when Lynch resolved on a policy of reprisals.[102] On 28 November Lynch wrote to the speaker of the 'provisional parliament' referring to the guilt of both the provisional government and the members of its parliament who had voted for the emergency powers resolution 'by which you pretend to make legal the murder of soldiers'.[103] He warned that unless 'your army recognises the rules of warfare . . . we shall adopt very drastic measures to protect our forces'.[104] On the 30th, Lynch circulated to his divisions a list of those to be shot on sight: members of the provisional parliament who had voted for the 'murder bill'; Free State army officers who approved it or behaved 'aggressive[ly]' against IRA forces; and ex-British army officers who had joined the Free State army since December 1921.[105]

On 7 December the first casualty of the IRA order occurred: deputy Sean Hales was shot dead in Dublin, while his comrade, Padraig Ó Máille was wounded. 'As a reprisal' for this shooting and as 'a serious warning to those involved' four more prisoners were executed the next day. This time they were well known: Rory O'Connor, Liam Mellows, Joseph McKelvey — all taken from the Four Courts — and a Munster man, Dick Barrett: one for each province.

The reprisals continued. Lynch ordered that hostages should be taken to be held against the safety of prisoners and shot in retaliation for any executions.[106] At the same time the 'national' commands were reorganised and plans laid to bring in fresh drafts. The south-west, or at least Kerry, could shortly be marked off 'as finished', while MacEoin had reports that 'another month' would 'finish the west'.[107]

By the end of December it seemed that success would be won by the side which held out longest. It also seemed that the Free State had the edge over its opponents on account of its access to British as well as national resources, its ability to recruit troops and provide them with uniforms and victuals, not to mention wages and separation allowances. Although parallels with the 'Tan period' between the position of the British and provisional governments are neither appropriate nor part of a historical exercise, one related point should be made: the new Irish leaders were in a position to deal with the 'rebels' in a way that the British government before them could not and would not have done. The new men had neither to consider the survival of a coalition, nor the matter of 'public opinion'. Party alignments were irrelevant to them. They would use terror to stamp out terror, and would continue to do so, whatever the cost. The determination of W.T. Cosgrave ultimately rendered the Civil War finite and ensured that it would not continue even in small measure. His government turned down peace proposals before Christmas for it was 'hardening in its determination' to use 'every . . . means for the speedy and complete suppression of crime and disorder'.[108] J. J. Walsh, his postmaster-general, wanted 'fascisti' set up, but Kevin O'Higgins did not.[109] Like Cosgrave, O'Higgins believed in 'democracy' and Cosgrave intended that 'the rule of democracy' would be maintained 'no matter what the cost'.[110]

On 6 December 1922 the formal establishment of the Irish Free State occurred, one year after the signing of the treaty. The 'provisional' nature of the parliament elected in the main to enact the new constitution was now terminated.[111] In London preparations had been made to withdraw the remaining British forces from Ireland after that date.[112] Even the garrison at Pettigo was to be withdrawn, despite the petition the previous September against such a course by its inhabitants; Beleek, too, was to be left to the Irish, although that decision was not taken until almost a year later.[113] In any case the final evacuation of British troops from Ireland strengthened the case made by the Irish ministers that the treaty did give real independence and sovereignty to Ireland.

Moreover, the formal end to British military involvement in Ireland was marked by formal arrangements, on both sides, to avoid the long-term legal implications of that involvement: Cosgrave introduced an 'amnesty' or 'indemnity' bill into the Dáil on 20 December. The amnesty was to extend to 'all members of the naval, military, police or civil services of the British government . . . by whom acts of hostility against the Irish people were committed, aided or abetted . . . during the past six years'.[114] The amnesty or indemnity was, however, to be conditional upon the release by the British government of the Connaught Rangers (who had mutinied in India in 1920) and certain other prisoners detained by the British government; and although the British were prepared to release the Rangers, they would not release one prisoner, Dowling, arrested in connection with the German plot of 1918.[115] Although the Irish senate at first refused to pass the bill until all the prisoners were released, Cosgrave advised that this object could be best achieved by passing the bill and thus the Indemnity Act became law on 10 February 1923.[116] The release of the Connaught Rangers and the eventual promise, made by Devonshire in July 1923 to release Dowling, as a 'mark of recognition' for the manner in which the Indemnity Bill had been passed, combined with that act, marked the formal and legal end of British military involvement in Saorstát Éireann.[117]

The establishment of the Free State seemed to coincide with, and promote, the determination of Cosgrave's government 'to restore order no matter what the cost'. The commands were reorganised to take effect from 24 January; the eastern command now became the 'Dublin' command, the western the 'Athlone'; the battalions would be reorganised too, with an average strength of 500 and a new number-name.[118] Headquarters sent investigators to examine the particular circumstances of the Cork and Waterford commands and steps were taken to pay off the controversial Skibbereen army accounts, where allegations had been made that local troops dishonoured their debts.[119] In Dublin plans were laid for joint meetings between the cabinet and army council to discuss 'the most effective way 'of dealing with 'the lawlessness prevailing throughout the country' with a view 'to bringing it to a speedy end'.[120] The ministers were united that there must be unmitigated resolution to defeat the armed opposition and the country must be left in no doubt that the government intended to do so. O'Higgins, who claimed that the opposition was due only in a small degree to the treaty, that there were groups with a 'vested interest' in disorder and debt, that as the first sign of a 'crumbling civilisation . . . the bailiff . . . has failed', recommended full military protection in the enforcement of decrees and stern treatment of lawlessness and illegal possession of land.[121] 'We are not engaged in a war,' he maintained, but 'rather organised sabotage'.[122] Hogan, the minister for agriculture, insisted that all peace talks, compromise and negotiations must be put to an end. 'We are engaged in a war . . . with . . . no alternative but to win'; and it must be made clear to the public that the government meant business.[123]

On 8 January a new army council order was made known to the Dáil, which showed that the government 'meant business'. It specified a list of offences, from possession of a document or Free State uniform unlawfully, to revealing a tendency to conspire against the safety of the state, for which persons so charged could be tried by military court and sentenced to death (or a lesser penalty); and it was made in pursuance of the powers given by the Dáil to the army the previous September.[124] Cosgrave told the Dáil that the government could not 'economise on the death penalty'; both in public and private he insisted that the executions would continue.[125] On 1 January he wrote to a Kilkenny clergyman who had previously worked for Cosgrave in his constituency, but whose admiration for him had dwindled with the executions. Cosgrave 'regretted' them as much as anybody else but there would be more if what was called, in his opinion libellously, 'civil war' did not cease.[126] Cosgrave meant it. During the month of January, thirty-four executions occurred throughout the country.

In the Dáil Hogan spoke up for policy of the government. On 17 January, when advocating the new army order, he declared that the government was doing what every government under similar circumstances did, in giving itself 'untrammelled powers' to deal with the situation. With regard to martial law, the position, he maintained, was not complicated: where armed rebellion existed, so too did martial law; declarations or proclamations were quite unnecessary, for the one demanded the other.[127] The members of the cabinet all agreed that there was 'armed rebellion'. O'Higgins described it as anarchy 'let loose', for which the only solution was force. On 23 January he told the Dáil that there were no real 'laws of war'; that these were, if anything, more honoured in the breach than in practice; that it was ridiculous to suggest that 'force settles nothing' for 'we have no talisman except force' and 'we are not able to devise any other weapon to meet the situation that exists here, except force'.[128] Blythe too refused to consider that the position could be dealt with in any but a military fashion, and said that the military courts were not intended to be a judicial process engaged on judicial work; they were engaged simply in military work.[129] O'Higgins, when he introduced on 19 January the Enforcement of Law Bill to deal with the breakdown and 'partial paralysis of the executive machinery of the courts', referred to the resolution to combat this 'anarchy', this 'greed'; and the commandeering of land or property throughout the country would cease, with the assistance of the army.[130]

The government therefore suggested publicly that the war was not in fact war, but 'armed rebellion', 'anarchy', 'lawlessness' and 'greed'; that the situation demanded force; that force would be used. Cosgrave, who heard reports that the irregulars admitted to being 'beaten' by late January but intended to 'do much damage before it is over', urged that the damage be made 'as expensive as possible' for them and reiterated that there would be no peace talks, no negotiations, no clemency.[131] Simultaneously his government played on the anonymity of the irregular leaders and denigrated the opposition as the forces of 'disorder' who exploited as 'pawns' the youths of the country. In the Dáil Cosgrave read letters from those mothers whose sons were sacrificed at the behest of such leaders. Yet one leader was known, de Valera, and O'Higgins described the young men as the 'dupes' of his 'vanity'.[132] He also alluded to the 'irony' of de Valera's calling them out 'in the name of the republic', for de Valera had 'taught us the necessity of compromise, and . . . the immorality . . . of persisting when there was no hope of success, and of keeping the country under the harrow of British oppression simply for a formula'.[133] Mulcahy implied that de Valera was neither truthful nor responsible; that he had, the previous September, disclaimed responsibility for what was being done; but that the orders for destruction and assassination had since then been issued under his name.[134] Although the government overestimated, as it had done since the treaty was signed, the degree of collaboration or unity between de Valera and the IRA, it none the less continued to do so to undermine the 'moral' position of the republicans: their idealism and constancy to the cause were castigated, as were their leaders for the manipulation of the young for purposes of personal 'vanity' and 'political nonsense'.

While the Free State government undermined the ideological and moral position of the republican forces, while it strengthened its powers for arresting the 'disorder' resulting from the war, whether kidnapping (which would result in the execution of the prisoners[135]) or illegal occupation of land or property, its campaign in the country had persisted. It is difficult to estimate the degree of truth in stories which Cosgrave had heard in which the 'irregulars' admitted to 'being beaten and badly beaten'.[136] But it seems clear that the capture, imprisonment, execution or death of the republican leaders had some effect on the morale of certain members of the IRA. This was evident from the manifestations of discontent against de Valera or the republican 'politicians'.

From the west, for example, the followers of the IRA commanders Maguire and Kilroy, who had been captured in the autumn, displayed more solicitude for the safety of their leaders, than for the cause for which they fought.[137] John O'Dowd, a Volunteer from Louisburgh, had 'no use' for the republican politicians Derrig and Ruttledge 'up there in Dublin, using the fighting men as pawns'; and he lamented that 'de Valera and the wild women are hopeless'.[138] He wanted Kilroy's life spared, and peace; and he wanted the so-called neutral IRA men (the group of former IRA members who had taken no part in the Civil War) to do something.[139] Although O'Dowd was reprimanded by his commanding officer, his was not an isolated case.[140] There were rumours that the men from the west were 'out against Derrig'; that they would 'plug de Valera'; and that their present attitude derived as much from having accumulated debts and fearing to return home to unemployment, as a rejection of the government; they would accept the Free State for practical purposes, as the 'only authoritative executive in the country'; and although they would 'hate' to give up their arms, they could be got round to doing this'.[141]

But more divisive for the movement nationally was the capture and sentence to death of Liam Deasy, deputy chief-of-staff of the IRA and responsible for the southern command. Deasy was captured near Cahir in Co. Tipperary on 18 January. Although he had in the past incurred Lynch's displeasure for his dubious attitude towards peace or settlement, it was none the less reported that whereas Lynch carried 'no weight with the Cork irregulars', Deasy was 'the only leader of any use'.[142] In any case Deasy was removed to Clonmel barracks under Prout's supervision. He was charged with illegal possession of a parabellum revolver and twenty-one rounds of ammunition, tried by court martial on 25 January, and sentenced to death by firing squad on the 27th. Even before his trial Deasy had submitted proposals for ending the conflict and had requested facilities for getting in touch with IRA leaders. But Mulcahy, despite receiving the proposals on the evening of the 25th, none the less confirmed the sentence on the 26th, and instructed Prout to make arrangements to have the execution carried out on the morning of the 27th.[143] Deasy requested a stay of the sentence in the cause of peace and reconciliation and 'for the future of Ireland'.[144] But Mulcahy would not grant a stay unless Deasy guaranteed in writing the immediate and unconditional surrender of 'all arms and men' and 'issues orders accordingly'. Although Deasy claimed he had not the power to do this, he did indicate he could stop the war on terms 'agreeable to the Free State', and would sign a promise to 'accept and ... aid ... the immediate and unconditional surrender of all arms and men as required by ... Mulcahy'.[145] At 4.45 a.m. on the morning of the execution Prout wired that Deasy had signed.[146] Deasy was then removed to Dublin and on 29 and 30 January in the company of certain Free State officers, he prepared a demand, to be sent to those involved, requesting the immediate and unconditional surrender of the members of de Valera's cabinet and of the army executive, whom he named individually.[147]

In the country the reaction of the IRA leaders was certainly not unanimous. On 2 February Lynch denounced both the appeal and the presumption on which it was made, i.e., that the position of the IRA was weak.[148] Lynch insisted that the 'vital' moment was at hand to make the final effort.[149] Three members of the executive also rejected the appeal, Frank Barrett, Sean MacSweeney and Frank Carthy, although Barrett privately assured Deasy that he believed the latter had made a 'great sacrifice'.[150] On 5 February, Lynch, on behalf of the army command, officially rejected the appeal, declaring that the IRA would 'fight to the finish to maintain Irish independence'.[151] But there were others in the 'movement'. In Athlone a whole company, the Fahereen, surrendered with arms on the 6th; in Kerry an officer named Pierce, who led two columns, promised to do so, but needed time to contact the men.[152] In Limerick prisoners in the county jail volunteered to surrender, that is if headquarters issued the instruction, and they sought parole to arrange for peace. They believed that to continue the struggle was 'a waste of blood', that the fight had developed into 'a war of extermination', that it had gone 'far enough', and that it 'ought to stop now'.[153] In Cork arrangements were made to grant parole to some prisoners and from Tralee came the support of others for Deasy, who requested parole to discuss the matter with their leaders.[154]

On 9 February the government offered its last chance. It published the Deasy communication to the republican leaders, and simultaneously offered an amnesty to those who surrendered before 18 February.[155] After that date no further opportunity was to be given to the prisoners to sign and the army council decided on the 12th that the recent 'bad' cases were to be prepared for execution the following week.[156] On 17 February, Cosgrave's statement was published

in the newspapers: the government was 'determined to put
down this revolt against democracy, regardless of the cost';
if anyone persisted 'in this unnatural war . . . he must be
prepared to pay the price in full', for there would be 'no
going back on this'.[157] There would be no meeting for
negotiations with de Valera or Lynch 'or any of their collab-
orators in destruction'.[158]

Lynch remained obdurate. The war would proceed until
the independence of the country was recognised by its
enemies, both 'foreign and domestic' and there could be
no compromise on this 'fundamental condition'.[159] The
order, first issued the previous December, which prohibited
peace moves by any officer, was re-issued. Violation would
result in suspension from the army and court-martial on
release from prison.[160] Yet the divisions remained: on the
one hand the IRA's adjutant-general reassured Lynch that
the amnesty had been a 'complete fiasco' and all now
awaited the 'next turn of the wheel and full speed ahead';
on the other, Tom Barry, the Cork IRA officer, submitted
a personal peace offer and requested the suspension of executions, pending Mulcahy's receipt of the proposals.[161] At
the same time, surrenders were reported from Kerry,
Limerick and Newmarket.[162]

Barry had called for a meeting of the full IRA executive
and the Free State's General Reynolds reported from Cork
that the first southern division was prepared to make terms
of absolute surrender.[163] Con Moylan, another Cork IRA
man, and one who had surrendered after the Deasy appeal,
left for Dublin to meet Mulcahy and confirmed the dissip-
ated morale among the irregulars: they were 'down and out';
and when Mulcahy insisted that any agreement must involve
acceptance of the treaty position, Moylan saw no 'other way
out of it' and personally hoped it would be accepted.[164] On
26 February the first southern divisional council was held.
Lynch and Barry were reported to be 'at loggerheads':
Barry and his comrades did not feel they could hold out
much longer, for it was '800 against 80,000', and no matter
what orders were given to the prisoners in Cork jail, it was
clear that they intended to sign Deasy's document, for it
was 'preferable to being executed'.[165] They demanded a

meeting of the executive, but Lynch procrastinated. They had lost their sense of proportion, forgetting that conditions and morale in the rest of the country were good.

Although Lynch continued to hold out for the republic throughout March, he could not bring all the men in the south with him. Moreover de Valera — whose position on peace was becoming ambiguous — had brought himself forward as a spokesman. He had written to the neutral IRA group regarding their intervention; his letter had followed a statement in the newspapers on 17 February. Whereas he rejected the prospect of a truce which would not bring peace and insisted that 'their national heritage' would not be surrendered, it was none the less clear that the peace movement had a large following in Cork, where it was more thoroughly organised than elsewhere.[166] Moreover de Valera's attitude, despite the reply to the neutral IRA men's proposals on behalf of the 'government and army' of the republic, was not clear. Word went round that he would settle on document number two, and he neither affirmed nor denied the rumour, leaving it to Derrig to clarify his attitude. Derrig declared that although de Valera did not sponsor document number two, he would not oppose it. De Valera himself had indicated in a public statement on 17 February that 'our minimum will be the maximum that conditions of the moment will enable us to obtain'.[167] In any case if a truce were contemplated, it was the business of his government to establish what the position of its army was, and the government should be approached.[168]

Against de Valera's ambiguous attitude and Barry's call for peace, Lynch remained obdurate. Reports from the south indicated that Lynch would not 'budge from war policy'.[169] On 8 March his headquarters issued the order that any Volunteer who surrendered would be shot.[170] The peace moves, the form signing, the 'humbug' as Lynch called it, must stop. On the 12th he suggested that the sound, over-all national military position be put to the executive, for the southerners were unduly pessimistic about the campaign.[171] On 23 March the executive met and de Valera was admitted, with all rights, except voting, Aiken having proposed the admission and Robinson having seconded it.[172] Barry pro-

posed to the executive that further 'armed resistance' would
not help the national cause but the motion was defeated.[173]
The executive meeting was not decisive and although the
differences between Barry and Lynch which had emerged
during the southern council on 24 February were again
brought out, in general there was a reluctance to take a
decision, whether to call off the campaign, or insist on 'full
steam ahead'.[174] Instead the executive decided that it alone
was the body to negotiate a peace – or else the army council –
and a further meeting was convened for 10 April.[175]

If the executive meeting demonstrated that its members
did not unanimously consider the IRA to have been utterly
and irrevocably 'beaten', it also revealed that the leaders
were divided. They were simultaneously anxious to avoid
calling off the war (which would be tantamount to an
admission of defeat) and reluctant to lay down that it must
be proceeded with. On the one side was Lynch who upheld
the war and the reason for its continuation: the republic. He
refused to allow that the situation was hopeless, although he
did admit that it might be reconsidered in three weeks time.
On the other, Barry emerged again as the spokesman for the
pessimists of the first southern, which had initially been the
strongest and most militantly obstinate division. Former
self-confidence had turned to confessions of defeat and a
sense of having lost. This feeling had led to the interventions
of Deasy, MacSweeney, O'Hegarty, Barry and the neutral
IRA men like Florrie O'Donoghue; and although the republic
had been for them a moral issue, it had not been the only
consideration – as evidenced by their activities and interventions since the truce had been declared in July 1921.
During the truce, for example, Barry's attempts to gain
'recognition' for his status from the British had led to
Lynch's observations on his vanity. After the treaty
MacSweeney, O'Hegarty and O'Donoghue had been among
the 'anti-treaty' officers who had put their plans to the
Dáil in May for a peace on the basis that the 'majority'
accepted the treaty, but they had been denounced by Mellows
for making a proposal which would better come from the
Free State, as it was a Free State document.[176] In the Four
Courts split on 18 June, Lynch and Deasy had abandoned

O'Connor, Mellows and McKelvey on the Barry motion, although on the 28th they forgot their differences when the Four Courts were stormed. The point is, of course, that there were and had been differences, during the truce, after the treaty, and after the outbreak of the Civil War, and that views and attitudes continued to change. Lynch had become 'more extreme' since June 1922 and Barry less. If similarities existed, they were tenuous, bound up with the links between the Corkmen and the largest division as against headquarters, discipline, Dublin, the treaty — although even these were complicated by the continued connections and consultations after the treaty with Collins and the possible influence of the IRB. But there were also the other IRA men, like Aiken who was wanted by the northern and southern governments, who ran a northern IRA unit, who advocated de Valera's inclusion at the executive, but had not voted for cessation at the meeting of 23-26 March.[177] On 6 April Derrig was captured; on the 10th Lynch was killed en route for the executive meeting.[178] By 16 April seven members of de Valera's cabinet were under arrest[179] and on the 20th, when the IRA executive met, Frank Aiken succeeded Lynch as chief-of-staff, having been proposed by Barry and seconded by MacSweeney.[180] Aiken had not previously supported peace, though his proposal to include de Valera at the March meeting indicated that he may not have been averse to such a course. The executive set up a new army council, comprising Barry, Aiken and Pilkington and together with de Valera's government it was empowered to make peace with the 'Free State government' on the basis that 'the sovereignty of the Irish nation and the integrity of its territory' were 'inalienable'.[181] Although the republic was not part of the motion, it was too strong for Barry who proposed an amendment simply 'to call off all armed resistance', with no conditions.[182] But the executive was not ready for that and the formula of 'the sovereignty' of the Irish nation being the basis for peace remained, even if its rejection was not to lead to the war being carried on.[183]

A week later, on 26 April, the new army council and de Valera's cabinet resolved to issue the 'suspension of offensive' order to the army.[184] The president would issue a proclamation giving the terms upon which the republicans were prepared to negotiate, and he was also entrusted with responsibility for any possible negotiation and was to summon a joint meeting if and when necessary.[185]

Aiken, as chief-of-staff, issued the suspension order on 29 April and de Valera simultaneously announced the principles upon which his government was willing to negotiate peace.[186] No reference occurred to the surrender of arms; Aiken instructed that all units 'take adequate measures to protect themselves and their munitions'.[187] De Valera maintained that no individual could be excluded from his share in 'determining national policy' by any oath, and he indicated that the suspension order was being issued to provide 'evidence of our good will'.[188]

Cosgrave had no interest in negotiating peace. In late February he had reiterated that there would be no peace, except on the basis of surrender; that he had, at the end of June 1922, made up his mind 'definitely' that he was 'not going to make any further effort to meet the republicans'; that he would not 'hesitate if . . . we have to exterminate 10,000 republicans' for 'the 3 millions of our people is bigger than this 10,000; and that 'a bad peace in the south means absolute partition in the north for many a generation'.[189] On 27 March a war council had been set up, and three days later a council for defence had been announced.[190] The duties of the former were not clear, but those of the latter were: to inquire into the administration of any military department and to interrogate many or all the high officers.[191] Although this reflected Cosgrave's concern with the plans of certain Free State officers to reintroduce the 'old ideals' into the national army and to develop an organisation therein, it was a general reflection of his continued determination to assert the supremacy of civil control, whether over the irregulars or over his own officers.[192] By April he was resolved that there could be peace only if the irregulars surrendered their arms. He told Luzio, the papal nuncio, this on the 11th of the month, though he had difficulty in convincing Luzio that the government was not unreasonable in refusing to offer terms to its opponents; and the cabinet decided that a letter to the pope should be drafted and that the minister for external affairs should go to Rome, to put the 'true facts' before the pontiff.[193] On 17 April – just ten days before the Aiken-de Valera declarations ordering the suspension of the offensive and laying down the points upon which peace could be made – Cosgrave reiterated that he would not discuss terms with de Valera.[194]

Cosgrave, O'Higgins, Mulcahy and Hogan had been fighting since September for the supremacy of parliamentary authority, for the right of the people to choose their government, as they had done in the June election. At the first session of the Dáil elected in June 1922, Mulcahy had insisted that 'the sword be not thrown into the situation' and since then Cosgrave remained adamant that the possibility of resorting to the 'sword' be removed by its surrender to the government. If the principle was acknowledged, the government would facilitate its practice. Cosgrave, for example, was reported to be willing to accept certain proposals 'if [the] arms were given to priests'.[195] Therefore, reaction to the Aiken-de Valera declarations was unanimous. Kennedy described the de Valera statement as verbose, 'with empty pretensions labelled as principles', and urged his colleagues to have 'no futile nonsense on this matter'.[196] O'Higgins was emphatic that the arms must be surrendered and maintained that the national army was not the army of a party, but the army of the people; the government had no intention of tampering with the oath, and besides there were two parties to the treaty.[197] Cosgrave would not see de Valera, although he authorised the businessmen Douglas and Jameson, now senators, to do so. He insisted that military action would cease by his government only when arms had been surrendered and prisoners released on the same condition.[198] De Valera's meetings with the senators took place between 1 and 8 May. Cosgrave's written conditions were put to him, but he submitted counter-proposals and attempted to secure the abolition of the oath.[199]

Cosgrave rejected the de Valera counter-proposals as a 'long and wordy document inviting debate, where none is possible'.[200] The government would not depart from its specified conditions and there could be no further communication with de Valera, save one 'indicating his definite

acceptance . . . in writing'.[201] De Valera would not or could
not agree and Cosgrave had no intention of granting him a
'lease of political life' by removing the oath.[202] De Valera
had nothing to offer but seemed 'so anxious' to get out of
his present predicament that he would 'bring all his party'
to meet the government, and would agree to 'anything'
which would 'save his face'. His bearing seemed to them to
be that 'of a defeated man', and his attitude 'the reverse of
that . . . in the old days when he was president'; he was
beaten and 'he knew it.'[203]

There was, therefore, to be no agreement. Cosgrave would
not concede on the oath, or anything else. But the IRA
executive had made provision for such a development, to the
extent that the war need not necessarily be carried on.[204] On
24 May the IRA formally abandoned its war for the republic.
Aiken issued the order to 'ceasefire' and 'dump arms', though
these were not to be surrendered. De Valera provided a
message to the 'Soldiers of the Republic', the 'Legion of the
Rearguard': the republic could no longer be successfully
defended by arms; but the efforts and sacrifices of the
soldiers and their dead comrades had 'saved the nation's
honour', preserved its 'sacred . . . tradition' and 'kept open
the road of independence'.[205] The time had come to seek
other means 'to safeguard the nation's right'; de Valera now
abandoned war in favour of the 'constitutional' means of
settling his differences.

Abbreviations

Certain abbreviations are referred to specifically in the course of the references. In addition the following are used generally:

I. To designate collections*

BL	Bonar Law Papers
CAB	Cabinet Office
CO	Colonial Office
DE	Dáil Éireann files
DER	Derby Papers
LG	Lloyd George Papers
Montagu (AS- . . .)	Montagu Papers
MP	Mulcahy Papers
MS Asquith	Asquith Papers
EOM	O'Malley Papers
'R'	Rialtas Sealadach files
'S'	Provisional Government and first Executive Council of the Irish Free State files
LWE	Worthington-Evans Papers

*(For the details of those and other collections, see Bibliography Sections A I and II)

II. To designate Irish personnel

A/G	Adjutant General
(A/A/G)	Assistant Adjutant General
C in C	Commander in Chief
C/S	Chief of Staff
(A/C/S)	Assistant Chief of Staff
(D/C/S)	Deputy Chief of Staff
D/I	Director of Intelligence
D/O	Director of Organisation
GHQ	General Headquarters
M/D	Minister for Defence
O/C	Commanding Officer

O/C 1SD 2SD 3SD	Commanding Officer first, (second, third,) Southern Division.
O/C 1WD 2 WD 3WD	Commanding Officer first, (second, third,) Western Division.
O/C 1ND 2ND 3ND 4ND	Commanding Officer first, (second, third, fourth,) Northern Division.
O/C 1ED	Commanding Officer, first Eastern Division
QMG	Quartermaster-General

References

Chapter 1
INTRODUCTORY, 1914-18
(pp. 1—27)
1. Asquith to the King, 23 Jan. 1914, MS Asquith 7.
2. Asquith to the King, 4 Mar. 1914, MS Asquith 7.
3. Asquith to the King, 11 Mar. 1914, MS Asquith 7.
4. Asquith to the King, 5 May 1914, MS Asquith 7.
5. Asquith to the King, 5 May 1914, MS Asquith 7.
6. ibid.
7. Asquith to the King, 'Memorandum on the Irish Situation, 17 July, 1914, MS Asquith 7.
8. ibid.
9. ibid.
10. Rothermere to Montagu, undated, but c. July 1914, Montagu papers AS—1—8.
11. Asquith to the King, 17, 24 July 1914, MS Asquith 7.
12. Suspensory Act 1914, in Worthington Evans papers, C. 903.3.
13. Asquith to the King, 10/11 Aug. 1914, MS Asquith 7.
14. Asquith to the King, 12 Oct. 1915, MS Asquith 8.
15. ibid.
16. ibid.
17. ibid.
18. Asquith to the King, 29 Apr. 1916, MS Asquith 8.
19. Gavan Duffy to Fitzgerald, 10 May 1916, NLI MS 5581.
20. ibid.
21. ibid.
22. Asquith to the King, 27 Apr. and 6 May 1916, MS Asquith 8.
23. Asquith to the King, 6 May 1916, MS Asquith 8.
24. Maxwell to Asquith, 5 June 1916, MS Asquith 37, and Maxwell to Asquith, 9 June 1916, MS Asquith 37.
25. Maxwell to Asquith, 5 June 1916, Maxwell to Bonham Carter, 7 June 1916, Maxwell to Asquith, 17 June 1916, all in MS Asquith 37.
26. Asquith to the King, 18 Oct. and 2 Nov. 1916, MS Asquith 8.
27. Gavan Duffy to Fitzgerald, 10 May 1916, NLI MS 5581.
28. ibid.

29. Gavan Duffy to O'Connor, 9 Mar. 1917, NLI MS 5581.
30. For the debate about amalgamation or dissolution, see NLI MS 5581.
31. Acting Honorary Secretary, Irish Nation League, to Plunkett, 24 Mar. 1917, NLI MS 5581.
32. Gavan Duffy to Dixon, 9 Feb. 1917, NLI MS 5581.
33. Acting Secretary, Irish Nation League to Plunkett, 24 Mar. 1917, NLI MS 5581.
34. McCartan to Gavan Duffy, 25 Mar. 1917, and 'Sean T.' to Gavan Duffy, 27 Mar. 1917, NLI MS 5581.
35. McCartan to Gavan Duffy, 30 Mar. 1917, NLI MS 5581.
36. Gavan Duffy to McCartan, 29 Mar. 1917, Gavan Duffy to O'Connor, 10 Apr. 1917, Nicholls to Gavan Duffy, 4 Apr. 1917, NLI MS 5581.
37. O'Connor to Gavan Duffy, 15 Apr. 1917, and Gavan Duffy to O'Hegarty, 29 May 1917, NLI MS 5581.
38. Gavan Duffy to PSO'H, 29 May 1917, NLI MS 5581.
39. ibid. Dillon, Hon. Sec. Mansion House Committee, to the Supreme Council, Irish National League, 10 June 1917, NLI MS 5581.
40. ibid. For the amalgamation/dissolution discussion, see NLI MS 5581.
41. Sinn Féin scheme of rules, 25 Oct. 1917, NLI P 3269.
42. Sinn Féin, tenth convention, 25 Oct. 1917, NLI P 3269.
43. ibid.
44. ibid.
45. ibid.
46. ibid.
47. ibid.
48. ibid.
49. Asquith to the King, 10 May 1916, MS Asquith 8.
50. Asquith to the King, 27 June, 5 July, 19 July 1916, all in MS Asquith 8.
51. Asquith to the King, 27 June 1916, MS Asquith 8.
52. For Lloyd George's description of himself as a 'Gladstonian Home Ruler', see cabinet, 13 Oct. 1920, CAB 23/23.
53. Derby to Lloyd George, 25 Jan. 1917 in Lloyd George papers (hereafter abbreviated as LG) F/14/4/18.
54. Midleton memo, 23 Jan 1917, LG F/14/4/18.
55. Lloyd George to Duke 26 Jan. 1917, LG F/37/4/8.
56. ibid.
57. Duke memorandum, 30 Jan. 1917, LG F/37/4/10.
58. ibid.
59. Montagu account, 17 May 1917, Montagu papers AS—1—8 and Lloyd George to Midleton, 13 June 1917, LG F/38/1/1; Law to Lloyd George to Midleton, 13 June 1917, LG F/38/1/1.
60. Law to Campbell, 2 Apr. 1918, BL 84/6/70. Dunraven to prime minister, 31 May 1917, LG F/15/6/2.
61. ibid. and Derby to prime minister, 26 May 1917, LG F/14/4/46.

62. Midleton to Milner, 2 June 1917, LG F/38/2/9, Addison to prime minister, 6 June 1917, LG F/1/3/22 and Midleton to prime minister, 21 June 1917, LG F/38/1/2.
63. Midleton to prime minister 21 June and 12 July 1917, LG F/38/1/2 and LG F/38/1/6; Midleton to Law, 19 June 1917, BL 82/1/17.
64. Mond to prime minister, 22 June 1917, LG F/36/6/19.
65. Lloyd George to Healy, 20 July 1917, LG F/27/2/2.
66. Draft minute, 6 June 1917, in NLI MS 5581.
67. Gavan Duffy to PSO'H, 29 May 1917, NLI MS 5581. Extract from the *Irishman*, 12 June 1917, BL 85/B/10.
68. Duke to prime minister, 6 Oct. 1917, LG F/37/4/38.
69. Midleton to prime minister, 22 Feb. 1918, LG F/38/1/10.
70. ibid.
71. ibid.
72. Dunraven to prime minister, 23 Feb. 1918, LG F/15/6/3.
73. Lloyd George to Plunkett, 25 Feb. 1918, BL 85/B/11.
74. Lloyd George to Law, 10 Apr. 1918, LG F/30/2/31.
75. ibid.
76. Stamfordham to prime minister, 25 Apr. 1918, LG F/29/2/33.
77. Duke to prime minister, 22 Mar. 1918, LG F/37/4/47.
78. Midleton to prime minister, 30 Apr. 1918, LG/F/38/1/12.
79. Lloyd George to Chamberlain, 4 May 1918, LG F/7/2/12.
80. Fisher to Lloyd George, 27 Apr. 1918, LG F/16/7/24.
81. Hankey to Jones, 20 Apr. 1918; Long to Law, 4 Apr. 1918, BL 83/2/2; Londonderry to Derby, 7 May 1918, Derby papers, DER(17)28; Carson to Law, 8 Apr. 1918, BL 83/2/9.
82. Sinn Féin Standing Committee (hereafter SF Standing C/tee) 10 Apr. 1918, NLI P 3269.
83. O'Neill to O'Brien, 10 Apr. 1918, NLI MS 7998.
84. ibid.
85. SF Standing C/tee, 6 May 1918, resolution passed in order to be inserted in the minutes of SF Standing C/tee, 4 Apr. 1918, NLI P 3269.
86. Duke memorandum, 'Developments in Ireland', 16 Apr. 1918, LG F/37/4/51.
87. ibid.
88. Midleton memorandum, 30 Apr. 1918, LG F/38/1/12.
89. ibid.
90. ibid.
91. ibid.
92. Law to Campbell, 15 Apr. 1918, BL 84/7/20.
93. SF Standing C/tee, 17 May 1918, NLI P 3269.
94. ibid.
95. Carson to Law, 27 Apr. 1918, BL 83/2/33.
96. Chamberlain to prime minister, 10 Apr. and 3 May 1918, LG F/7/2/8 and F/7/2/11.
97. Chamberlain to prime minister, 3 May 1918, LG F/7/2/11.
98. ibid.

99. Long to prime minister, 7 May 1918, BL 83/3/17.
100. Londonderry to Derby, 7 May 1918, 920 DER(17)28 and Cecil to Law, 8 May 1918, BL e3/3/21.
101. Salisbury to Law, 15 May 1918, BL 83/3/29.
102. Law to Carson, 28 Apr. and Law to Cecil, 10 May, BL 84/7/25, 84/7/30.
103. Thomas Jones, *Whitehall Diary*, 3 vols., London 1971, ed. K Middlemas, vol. III entry for 9 May 1918.
104. Cabinet, 16 May 1918, CAB 23/17.
105. For the list of those arrested see SF Standing C/tee, 21 May 1918, NLI P 3269.
106. Leaflet issued by SF Standing C/tee, c. 20 May 1918, NLI P 3269.
107. ibid.
108. ibid.
109. ibid.
110. SF Standing C/tee, letter to the editors of Dublin newspapers, 20 May 1918, NLI P 3269.
111. Extract from draft minutes of meeting of the war cabinet, 9 July 1918 with additional documents in LG F/23/3/8.
112. Jones *diary*, 4 June 1918.
113. ibid. Also Mond to prime minister, 5 June 1918, LG F/36/6/26; Law to Shortt, 16 Aug. 1918, BL 84/7/61; Law to Midleton, 27 Sept. 1918, BL 84/7/91.
114. See SF Standing C/tee, 27 May and 21 June 1918, NLI P 3269.
115. SF Standing C/tee, 27 June 1918, NLI P 3269.

Chapter 2
NOVEMBER 1918 – OCTOBER 1920
(pp. 28–68)
1. For the King's reservations see Stamfordham to prime minister, 14 Dec. 1916, LG F/29/1/2; Stamfordham to prime minister, 9 Jan. 1919, LG F/29/3/1; Stamfordham to Law, 17 Apr. 1919, BL 97/2/11.
2. Londonderry to Derby, 12 May 1918, Derby MS 920 DER(17)28.
3. Long to Law, 17 July 1918, BL 83/5/17.
4. See above chapter 1; also Law to Middleton, 27 Sept. 1918, BL 84/7/91.
5. See Mond to prime minister, 5 June 1918, LG F/36/6/26; Law to Shortt, 16 Aug. 1918, BL 84/7/61; Montagu notes, 6 and 7 Nov. 1918, Montagu AS–1–12.
6. *Dáil Éireann. Minutes of Proceedings of the First Parliament of the Republic of Ireland, 1919-21.* Official Record (Dublin), 21 Jan. 1919 (hereafter Dáil Éireann, *Record*).
7. ibid.
8. ibid.
9. ibid.
10. ibid.
11. ibid.

12. ibid.
13. Dáil Éireann, *Record*, 22 Jan. 1919.
14. Dáil Éireann, *Record*, 1 and 2 Apr. 1919.
15. Dáil Éireann, *Record*, 10 Apr. 1919.
16. ibid.
17. ibid.
18. ibid.
19. ibid.
20. ibid.
21. SF Standing C/tee, 13 June and 18 July 1918, NLI P 3261.
22. Collins to Stack, 19 Aug. 1918, NLI MS 5848.
23. ibid.
24. Collins to Stack, 22 Aug. 1918, NLI MS 5848.
25. See Collins to Stack, 11 May 1919, NLI MS 5848; for lists of membership see SF Standing C/tee, 8 Apr. 1919 and 6 May 1919, P3269.
26. Collins to Stack, 17 May 1919, NLI MS 5848.
27. ibid.
28. ibid.
29. Collins to Stack, 18 May 1919, NLI MS 5848.
30. There is, of course, little or no surviving contemporary documentation for the raids and attacks; for subsequent accounts see Robert Kee, *The Green Flag*, London 1972; F. O'Donoghue, *No Other Law*, Dublin 1954. See also the *Fighting Story* series, *Told by the Men who Made it*, booklets published in the 1940s by *The Kerryman*.
31. P. Beaslai, *Michael Collins and the Making of a New Ireland*, 2 vols., London 1926, vol. 1, pp.269-70.
32. Collins to Stack, 17 May 1919, NLI MS 5848; Rex Taylor, *Michael Collins*, Four Square ed., 1961, p.105.
33. Dáil ministry, 15 Aug. 1919, DE 1/1. Dáil Éireann, *Record*, 20 Aug. 1919.
34. Long to Law, 21 Feb. 1919 enclosing Ross to Long, BL 96/10/8.
35. Cabinet, 14 May 1919, CAB 23/15.
36. ibid.
37. ibid.
38. French to Law, 19 May 1919, BL 97/3/28.
39. Cabinet, 14 May 1919, CAB 23/15; MacPherson to Law, 16 May 1919, BL 97/3/24, and 21 May 1919, BL 97/3/29.
40. Macpherson to Law, 21 May 1919, BL 97/3/29.
41. Jones to Davies, 23 May 1919, LG F/23/4/69.
42. Cabinet, 14 May 1919, CAB 23/15.
43. ibid.
44. Long to Law, 21 May 1919, BL 97/3/30.
45. Law to Macpherson, 15 May 1919, BL 101/3/69.
46. Law to Macpherson, 15 and 16 May 1919, BL 101/3/69 and 71; Law to prime minister, 18 May 1919, LG F/30/3/63; cabinet, 14 May 1919, CAB 23/15.

47. French message, 24 June 1919, LG F/23/4/81 (attached to Jones to Davies).
48. Jones to Davies, 25 June 1919, LG F/23/4/81.
49. Cabinet, 26 June 1919, CAB 23/15.
50. ibid.
51. ibid.
52. ibid.
53. Note of telephone message from Paris for Jones, 26 June 1919, LG F/23/4/82.
54. Law to Stamfordham, 14 and 17 Sept. 1919, BL 101/3/146 and /148.
55. *The Political Diaries of C.P. Scott, 1911-1928*, (London, 1970), ed. T. Wilson, (hereafter Scott, *diary*) Spender to Scott, 23 Aug. 1919, p.377.
56. Cabinet, 5 Aug. 1919, CAB 23/15.
57. ibid.
58. ibid.
59. Grey memo, 5 Aug. 1919, LG F/12/1/35; Lloyd George to Grey, 7 Aug. 1919, LG F/12/1/35.
60. Cabinet, 5 Aug. 1919, CAB 23/15.
61. ibid.
62. Cabinet, 15 Aug. 1919, CAB 23/15.
63. Cabinet, 5 Aug. 1919, CAB 23/15.
64. ibid.
65. ibid.
66. ibid.
67. Spender to Scott, 23 Aug. 1919, in Scott, *diary*, p.377.
68. Macpherson to Law, 13 Sept. 1919, BL 98/2/12.
69. ibid.
70. ibid.
71. Law to Stamfordham, 17 Sept. 1919, BL 101/3/148.
72. French to Law, 13 Sept. 1919, BL 98/2/11.
73. Law to Stamfordham, 17 Sept. 1919, BL 101/3/148.
74. The committee was to be chaired by Long and was appointed to 'examine the situation in Ireland'. Committee on Ireland, c. 8 Oct. 1919, LWE Ms. Eng. Hist. C.903.
75. Law to Balfour, 9 Oct. 1919, BL 101/3/159.
76. Cabinet, committee on Ireland, c. 8 Oct. 1919, LWE Ms. Eng. Hist. C.903.
77. Committee on Ireland, C.1, 14 Oct. 1919, LWE Ms. Eng. Hist. C:905.
78. ibid.
79. Law to Balfour, 8 Oct. 1918, BL 101/3/159.
80. ibid.
81. ibid.
82. Hankey note to prime minister, 23 Oct. 1919, with 'summary of position' LG F/24/1/19.
83. Fisher diary, 15 and 20 Oct. 1920.

84. Committee on Ireland, 4 Nov. 1919, LWE Ms. Eng. Hist. C.905.
85. Irish committee: joint note by Worthington-Evans and Birkenhead, 11 Nov. 1919, LWE Ms. Eng. Hist. C.905.
86. ibid. also additional note by Birkenhead, attached.
87. Fisher diary, 3 and 11 Nov. 1919.
88. Cabinet, 11 Nov. 1919, CAB 23/18.
89. ibid. See also committee on Ireland, 4 Nov. 1919, LWE Ms. Eng. Hist. C.905.
90. Cabinet, 3 Dec. 1919, CAB 23/18.
91. ibid.
92. Cabinet, 3 Dec. 1919, CAB 23/18.
93. ibid.
94. ibid.
95. ibid.
96. ibid.
97. Cabinet, 10 Dec. 1919, CAB 23/18.
98. ibid.
99. Cabinet, 19 Dec. 1919, CAB 23/18.
100. ibid.
101. Cabinet, 3 Dec. 1919, CAB 23/18.
102. Cabinet, 3 Dec. 1919, CAB 23/18.
103. ibid.
104. Cabinet, 10 Dec. 1919, CAB 23/18.
105. Fisher diary, 6 Nov. 1919.
106. Cabinet, 15 Dec. 1919, CAB 23/18.
107. ibid.
108. ibid.
109. Balfour to prime minister, 10 Feb. 1920, LG F/3/5/2.
110. Fisher diary, 2 Dec. 1919.
111. Fisher diary, 9 Dec. 1919.
112. Cabinet, 10 Dec. 1919, CAB 23/18; Balfour to prime minister, 10 Feb. 1920, LG F/3/5/2.
113. Cabinet, 19 Dec. 1919, CAB 23/18.
114. ibid.
115. ibid.
116. The decision had been taken despite the recommendation of Long's committee that the whole of the province of Ulster should be the unit. See committee on Ireland, report, 17 Feb. 1920, (CP 664), LWE Ms. Eng. Hist. C.907; also Fisher diary, 24 Feb. 1920; also Cabinet 24 Feb. 1920, CAB 23/20.
117. Cabinet, 4 Feb. 1920, CAB 23/20.
118. *Field Marshal Sir Henry Wilson. His Life and Diaries*, 2 vols., London 1927, ed. C.E. Calwell (hereafter Wilson, *diary*) 22 and 31 Dec. 1919.
119. French to prime minister, 29 Dec. 1919, LG F/31/1/17(a).
120. Lloyd George to Law, 30 Dec. 1919, BL 98/5/23.
121. Wilson, *diary*, 13-14 Feb. 1920; Law to Campbell, 24 Mar. 1920, BL 100/4/20.

122. Scott, *diary*, 16-17 Mar. 1920.
123. ibid.
124. Law to Lloyd George, 23 Apr. 1920, LG F/31/1/25.
125. Note of conversation, 30 Apr. 1920, CAB 23/21, (i.e. between ministers and Irish officials).
126. ibid.
127. ibid.
128. ibid.
129. ibid.
130. ibid.
131. ibid.
132. ibid.
133. Macready to prime minister, 1 May 1920, LG F/36/2/13.
134. ibid.
135. ibid.
136. ibid. also Macready memo, 24 May 1920, LG F/36/2/14.
137. ibid.
138. ibid.
139. ibid.
140. Fisher memo, 15 May 1920, LG F/31/1/33.
141. Fisher memos, 12 and 15 May 1920, LG F/31/1/32 and /33.
142. ibid.
143. ibid.
144. ibid.
145. ibid.
146. ibid.
147. Fisher memo, 15 May 1920, LG F/31/1/33.
148. Note of conversation (i.e. between ministers and Irish officials) 30 Apr. 1920, CAB 23/21.
149. ibid.
150. ibid.
151. ibid.
152. ibid.
153. ibid.
154. Law to Storey, 6 Apr. 1920, BL 101/4/25. Law to Lloyd George, 7 May 1920, LG F/31/1/29.
155. Law to Lloyd George, 7 May 1920, LG F/31/1/29; Law to French, 31 Dec. 1919, BL 101/3/180.
156. Law to Lloyd George, 11 May 1920, LG F/31/1/30; conference of ministers, 11 May 1920, appended to cabinet, 19 May 1920, CAB 23/21.
157. Wilson, *diary*, 11 May 1920.
158. Conference of ministers, 11 May 1920, appended to cabinet, 19 May 1920, CAB 23/21.
159. ibid.
160. ibid.
161. Law to Lloyd George, 11 May 1920, LG F/31/1/30.
162. ibid. Cabinet, 21 May 1920, CAB 23/21.

163. ibid.
164. Macready memo, 24 May 1920, LG F/36/2/14. Conference of ministers, 31 May 1920, appended to cabinet, 7 June 1920, CAB 23/21.
165. Jones, *diary*, 31 May 1920.
166. ibid.
167. ibid.
168. Conference of ministers, 31 May 1920, CAB 23/21.
169. Fisher diary, 14 and 24 Feb. and 2 and 12 Mar. 1920.
170. See Montagu note of conversation with prime minister in November 1918, 6 and 7 Nov. 1918, Montagu AS—1—12; Wilson, *diary*, 22 Dec. 1919; for his refusal of the Irish 'job' in 1916, see Montagu to prime minister, 2 May 1916, Montagu AS—1—12.
171. Macready, *Annals of an Active Life*, London 1924, vol. 2, p.459.
172. Lord Riddell, *Intimate Diary of the Peace Conference and After, 1919-23*, London 1933 (hereafter Riddell, *diary*), 6 and 11 June 1920.
173. Riddell, *diary*, 6 June 1920.
174. Cope to Fisher, extract from Fisher to prime minister, 17 June 1920, LG F/17/1/2.
175. Anderson to chief secretary, 20 July 1920, LG F/19/2/14.
176. ibid.
177. Anderson to chief secretary, 20 July 1920, LG F/19/2/14.
178. ibid.
179. Jones, *diary*, 23 July 1920.
180. ibid. also Macready to Greenwood, 17 July 1920, LG F/19/2/12.
181. ibid.
182. ibid.
183. Jones, *diary*, 23 July 1920.
184. ibid.
185. ibid.
186. ibid.
187. ibid.
188. ibid.
189. ibid.
190. ibid.
191. ibid.
192. ibid.
193. ibid.
194. ibid.
195. ibid.
196. Riddell, *diary*, 11 and 13 June 1920; Scott, *diary*, 4 June 1920.
197. Scott, *diary*, 4 June 1920; Riddell, *diary*, 13 June 1920; Jones, *diary*, 26 July 1921; Cabinet, 2 June 1920, CAB 23/21; and 2 Aug. 1920, CAB 23/22.
198. Cabinet, 7 June 1920, CAB 23/21; Riddell, *diary*, 6 June 1920.
199. Cabinet, 2 June 1920, CAB 23/21; Jones, *diary*, 4 Aug. 1920;

Wylie to Anderson enclosed to Miss Stevenson, 4 Aug. 1920, LG F/19/2/18; Stamfordham to prime minister, 12 Aug. 1920, with Shaftesbury to Stamfordham, 12 Aug. 1920, LG F/29/4/23.
200. Jones, *diary*, 4 Aug. 1920.
201. ibid.
202. ibid.
203. ibid.
204. ibid.
205. Jones, *diary*, 4 Aug. 1920.
206. ibid.
207. Cabinet, 13 Aug. 1920, CAB 23/22.
208. ibid.
209. ibid. also appended draft of prime minister's statement.
210. ibid.
211. Fisher to Lloyd George, 11 Sept. 1920, LG F/16/7/59. Montagu to Fisher, 25 Nov. 1920, Fisher papers, box 8.
212. Conference of ministers, 13 Oct. 1920, CAB 23/23.
213. ibid.
214. ibid.
215. ibid.
216. ibid.
217. ibid.
218. ibid.
219. Montagu to Fisher, 25 Nov. 1919, Fisher papers, box 8.
220. Long memo, committee on Ireland, 29 Sept. 1920, LWE Ms Eng. Hist. C, 907.
221. Law to Ashley, 30 July 1920, BL 101/4/72; Jones, *diary*, 23 July 1920.
222. Dáil Éireann, *Record*, 29 June 1920.
223. ibid.
224. ibid.
225. ibid; also Dáil Éireann, *Record*, 20 Aug. 1919, 29 June 1920.
226. Dáil Éireann, *Record*, 29 June 1920.
227. Memo on proposal to collect income tax, unsigned but title in Collins's hand, 28 June 1920, MP P7A/1/12. The proposal had been raised already, by, amongst others MacSwiney; See MacSwiney to Collins, 16 June 1920, MP P7A/12.
228. Jones, *diary*, 4 Aug. 1920.

Chapter 3
OCTOBER 1920 – JULY 1921
(pp.68–98)

1. Draft account of meeting, 25 Aug. 1920, LG F/31/1/40; conference of ministers, 2 Sept. 1920, CAB 23/22; Harmsworth to prime minister, 6 Sept. 1920, LG F/13/1/17.
2. Conference of ministers, 25 Aug. 1920, LG F/31/1/40; Lloyd George to Law, 4 Sept. 1920, LG F/31/1/44; also Davies to Stamfordham, 17 Sept. 1920, LG F/29/4/28.
3. Lloyd George to Law, 4 Sept. 1920, LG F/31/1/44.

4. Conference of ministers, 1 Oct. 1920, CAB 23/22.
5. ibid.
6. ibid. Also conference of ministers 17 and 18 Oct., CAB 23/23.
7. Conference of ministers, 18 Oct. 1920, CAB 23/23.
8. Conference of ministers, 1 Oct. 1920, CAB 23/22.
9. ibid.
10. Memo by secretary of state for war, 'The Irish situation', 3 Nov. 1920, appended to conference of ministers, 10 Nov. 1920, CAB 23/23.
11. ibid.
12. Scott to Hobhouse, c. 4 Nov. 1920, in Scott, *diary*, p.389.
13. Bishop of Ardagh to Devlin in Devlin to prime minister, 8 Nov. 1920, LG F/15/1/2.
14. Fisher to prime minister, 16 Nov. 1920, LG F/16/7/61.
15. ibid.
16. ibid.
17. Montagu to Fisher, 25 Nov. 1920, Fisher papers, box 8.
18. Smuts to prime minister, 27 Sept. 1920, LG F/39/2/20.
19. Law to Lloyd George, 7 Oct. 1920, LG F/31/1/47.
20. Midleton to Derby, 20 Sept. 1920, Derby 920 DER(17)28.
21. Conference of ministers, 1 Oct. 1920, CAB 23/22.
22. Memo by secretary of state for war, 'The Irish situation', 3 Nov. 1920, appended to conference of ministers, 10 Nov. 1920, CAB 23/23.
23. ibid.
24. Conference of ministers, 10 Nov. 1920, CAB 23/23.
25. Cabinet, 1 Dec. 1920, CAB 23/23; Jones, *diary*, 1 Dec. 1920.
26. ibid.
27. ibid.
28. ibid. See also Hankey draft of Lloyd George to Greenwood, 1 Dec. 1920, LG F/19/2/22.
29. Jones, *diary*, 1 Dec. 1920.
30. Greenwood to prime minister, 5 Dec. 1920, LG F/19/2/28.
31. Cabinet, 1 Dec. 1920, CAB 23/23. ibid. Jones, *diary*, 1 Dec. 1920.
32. Greenwood to prime minister, 5 Dec. 1920, LG F/19/2/28.
33. ibid.
34. ibid.
35. Lloyd George to Greenwood, 2 Dec. 1920, LG F/19/2/26.
36. ibid.
37. Cabinet, 8 Dec. 1920, CAB 23/23.
38. ibid.
39. Lloyd George to Greenwood, 2 Dec. 1920, LG F/19/2/26.
40. ibid.
41. ibid.
42. ibid.
43. ibid.
44. Cabinet, 9 Dec. 1920, CAB 23/23; telegram to O'Flanagan appended.

45. ibid.
46. ibid.
47. Jones, *diary*, 20 Dec. 1920.
48. ibid.
49. *Aide Memoire*, prime minister's verbal remarks, cabinet, 13 Dec. 1920, CAB 23/23.
50. ibid.
51. Cabinet, 24 Dec. 1920, CAB 23/23.
52. ibid.
53. Cabinet, 29 Dec. 1920, CAB 23/23.
54. Cabinet, 24 Dec. 1920, CAB 23/23.
55. Cabinet, 29 Dec. 1920, CAB 23/23.
56. ibid.
57. ibid.
58. ibid.
59. ibid.
60. ibid.
61. ibid.
62. ibid.
63. ibid.
64. ibid. Jones *diary*, 20 Dec. 1920.
65. Cabinet, 29 Dec. 1920, CAB 23/23.
66. Cabinet, 30 Dec. 1920, CAB 23/23.
67. Macready to Derby, 31 Dec. 1920, Derby, 920 DER(17) 33.
68. Greenwood memo on Clune, December 1920, LG F/19/2/31.
69. Greenwood to prime minister, 3 Dec. 1920, LG F/19/2/27 and ibid. (i.e. memo).
70. Greenwood to prime minister, 26 Jan. 1921, LG F/19/3/2.
71. ibid.
72. ibid.
73. Irish Office report, weekly survey (hereafter survey) week ending (hereafter WE) 7 Feb. 1921, CAB 24/119.
74. Survey, WE 14 Feb. 1921, CAB 24/120.
75. Greenwood memo, 27 Feb. 1921, CAB 24/120.
76. ibid.
77. Law to Campbell, 11 Jan. 1921, BL 101/5/7.
78. ibid.
79. ibid.
80. Jones, *diary*, 30 Jan. 1921.
81. ibid.
82. ibid.
83. ibid.
84. ibid. also Jones, *diary*, 27 Apr. 1921 and 12 May 1921.
85. Jones, *diary*, 27 Apr. and 12 May 1921.
86. Jones, *diary*, 15 Feb. 1921; Greenwood to Lloyd George, 26 Jan. 1921, LG F/19/3/12.
87. Cabinet, 14 Jan. and 14 Feb. 1921. CAB 23/24.
88. Note of conference at 10 Downing Street, 15 Feb. 1921, CAB 23/24.

89. Lloyd George to Greenwood, 25 Feb. 1921, LG F/19/3/4.
90. Jones, *diary*, 15 Feb. 1921.
91. ibid.
92. Derby to Macready, 2 Jan. 1921, Derby 920 DER(17)33.
93. Derby to Macready, 6 Jan. 1921, Derby 920 DER(17)33.
94. Fisher to Miss Stevenson for prime minister, 11 Feb. 1921, LG F/17/1/9.
95. ibid.
96. Macready report, WE 29 Jan., also WE 5 Feb. 1921, CAB 24/119.
97. Macready report, WE 19 Feb. 1921, CAB 24/120.
98. Macready to Miss Stevenson, 11 Feb. 1921, LG F/36/2/16.
99. ibid.
100. Macready to Miss Stevenson, 21 Mar. 1921 enclosing Macready to chief secretary, 19 Mar. 1921, LG F/36/2/18.
101. ibid.
102. Fisher memo 'The position in Ireland', 1 Mar. 1921, CAB 24/120.
103. ibid.
104. ibid.
105. Montagu to prime minister, 4 Apr. 1921, LG F/41/1/11.
106. Addison memo, 'The Irish elections and an offer of Truce', 13 Apr. 1921, CAB 24/122.
107. Midleton to prime minister, 7 Mar. 1921, LG F/38/1/13.
108. Greenwood to prime minister, 8 Apr. 1921, LG F/19/3/10; also Lloyd George to Lord Bishop of Chelmsford and others, 19 Apr. 1921, LG F/19/3/12.
109. Cabinet, 8 Mar. 1921, CAB 23/24.
110. ibid.
111. Cabinet, 22 Mar. 1921, CAB 23/24.
112. Cabinet, 24 Mar. 1921, CAB 23/24.
113. ibid. Midleton to prime minister, 26 Apr. 1921, LG F/38/1/14.
114. Jones, *diary*, 27 Apr. 1921.
115. ibid.
116. ibid.
117. ibid.
118. ibid.
119. ibid.
120. Jones, *diary*, 12 May 1921; Cabinet, 12 May 1921, CAB 23/25; Winter to chief secretary, 11 May 1921, LG F/19/4/10; Greenwood to prime minister, 11 May 1921, LG F/19/4/10 and enclosed, i.e. Macready to chief secretary.
121. Cabinet, 12 May 1921, CAB 23/25; Jones, *diary*, 12 May 1920.
122. Macready report, WE 17 May 1921, CAB 24/123.
123. Survey, WE 16 May 1921, CAB 24/123.
124. Macready report, WE 17 May 1921, CAB 24/123.
125. Cabinet, 24 May 1921, CAB 23/25; Macready's two memoranda 'A' and 'B', 23 May 1921 and Wilson memorandum, 24 May 1921, in CAB 24/123.
126. ibid.

127. ibid.
128. Cabinet, 24 May 1921, CAB 23/25.
129. ibid.
130. Report by chairman of the 'Irish Situation Committee' (hereafter ISC) 27 May 1921, CAB 24/123; Cabinet, 2 June 1921, CAB 23/26.
131. Worthington-Evans to prime minister, 10 June 1921, LG F/16/3/26.
132. Secretary's record of meeting, ISC, 15 June 1921, CAB 27/107 and appended draft proclamation.
133. ibid.
134. ibid.; also Jones to Lloyd George, 15 June 1921, LG F/25/1/42.
135. Secretary's record of ISC, 15 June 1921, CAB 27/107, and note.
136. ibid. also Jones to Lloyd George, 15 June 1921, LG F/25/1/42.
137. ibid.
138. Jones, *diary*, 12 May 1921; Lloyd George to Bishop of Chelmsford and others, 19 Apr. 1921, LG F/19/3/12.
139. Smuts to prime minister, 14 June, in Jones, *diary*, pp.74-5; 'GHS' note to prime minister, c. 15 June 1921, LG F/29/4/48.
140. Conference of ministers, 17 June 1921, LG F/181/2/2; Lloyd George to Stamfordham, 18 June 1921, LG F/29/4/41; message from Stamfordham in Miss Stevenson's hand, received afternoon 24 June 1921, LG F/29/4/55; Cabinet, 24 June 1921, CAB 23/26.
141. Collins to O'Hegarty, 7 Dec. 1920, DE 2/234A; Fitzgerald to O'Hegarty, 6 Dec. 1920, DE 2/234A.
142. O'Brien to Collins, 25 Nov. 1920, DE 2/251; Collins to O'Brien, 2 Dec. 1920, DE 2/251; Fitzgerald to O'Hegarty, 29 Nov. 1921, DE 2/234A.
143. See for example cabinet, 29 Dec. 1920, CAB 23/23.
144. Griffith to secretary, ministry, 3 Dec. 1920, DE 2/234A; Griffith to Collins, 10 Dec. 1920, DE 2/251.
145. Griffith memo on Clune visit, 13 Dec. 1920, DE 2/
146. Griffith to O'Hegarty, undated, DE 2/234A (c. December 1-6).
147. Collins to O'Brien, 6 Dec. 1920, DE 2/234A.
148. Collins to MacDonagh, 12 Dec. 1920, DE 2/234A.
149. Collins to Editor, *Irish Independent*, 7 Dec. 1920, DE 2/234A.
150. Collins to O'Brien, 10 Dec. 1920, DE 2/234A.
151. Dáil ministry, 30 Nov. 1920, DE 1/3; O'Hegarty to Fitzgerald, 1 Dec. 1920, DE 2/234A.
152. Collins to O'Brien, 6 Dec. 1920, DE 2/234A.
153. Secretary of ministry to director propaganda, 6 Jan. 1921, DE 2/3.
154. Secretary to O'Flanagan, 17 Feb. 1921, DE 2/3; also 'P' (i.e. president) to O'Hegarty, 19 Feb. 1921, DE 2/3; also de Valera to O'Hegarty, 13 Mar. 1921, DE 2/14.
155. De Valera to Collins, 18 Mar. 1921, DE 2/244.
156. List of decisions made at Dáil meeting, 11 Mar. 1921, DE 2/14; secretary of ministry to president, 15 Mar. 1921, DE 2/14.
157. O'Hegarty to O'Brien, 23 Mar. 1921, NLI MS 8428.
158. Secretary to Irish businessmen, 6 Apr. 1921, DE 2/132.

159. ibid. See also the protracted correspondence for the month of April in DE/2/132; also de Valera to secretary of the ministry, 22 Apr. 1921, DE 2/1.
160. De Valera to secretary of ministry, 22 Apr. 1921, DE 2/1; de Valera to O'Brien, 24 Apr. 1921, NLI MS 8429.
161. Hughes to de Valera 26 Apr. 1921 and de Valera to Hughes, 27 Apr. 1921, both in Derby 920 DER(17)34.
162. De Valera to O'Hegarty, 10 Feb. 1921, DE 2/3.
163. 'AL' to O'Hegarty, 12 Jan. 1921, DE 2/3.
164. Hughes to Miss Archer (telegram) and unsigned note, 26 Apr. 1921, DE 2/258; also de Valera to Derby, 26 Apr. 1921, DE 2/258.
165. De Valera to D/Publicity, 24 Apr. 1921, NLI MS 8429; see also secretary to Jameson, 2 May 1921, DE 2/132.
166. President to O'Brien, 4 May 1921, NLI MS 8429.
167. ibid.
168. Secretary of the ministry to president, 19 May 1921, DE 2/1; de Valera to secretary of ministry, 23 and 29 May, DE 2/262; de Valera to Collins, 14 June 1921, DE 2/244. ibid.
169. De Valera to O'Brien, 14 June 1921, NLI MS 8429.
170. ibid.
171. ibid.
172. The phrase to 'control the murder gang' was Greenwood's; for Lloyd George to de Valera, 24 June 1921, see below.
173. O'Hegarty to C/S, 10 Mar. 1921, MP P7A/17.
174. The Earl of Longford and T. P. O' Neill, *Eamon de Valera*, London 1970, see parts I and II, i.e. up to chapter 15.
175. PGOD to Collins 14 and 27 Apr. 1921, MP P7A/5.
176. Collins to PGOD 1 July 1921, MP P7A/6; PGOD to Collins, 27 Apr. 1921, MP P7A/5.
177. 3 page memo on divisional area, c. Mar./Apr. 1921, MP P7A/17.
178. De Valera to O'Brien, 24 Apr. 1921, NLI MS 8429.
179. O/C Belfast Bde, report, 15 May 1921, MP P7A/18; Dublin brigade, diary of operations, May 1921, MP P7A/21.
180. Collins to Griffith, 26 Jan. 1921, DE 2/242.
181. Dáil ministry, 8 Mar. 1921, DE 1/3; Collins to D/Propaganda, 29 Mar. 1921 (correspondence re de Valera), NLI MS 22,769.
182. O'Hegarty to president, 9 Mar. 1921, DE 2/14.
183. O/C mid-Clare to C/S, 11 Apr. 1921, MP P7A/17; O/C 2ND to D/Org., 28 Apr. 1921, MP P7A/21. (See also D/Org to O/C 2ND, 20 Apr. MP P7A/17).
184. A/G to Carney, 14 May 1921, MP P7A/18; D/Org. to O/C 2ND, MP P7A/18.
185. Dublin brigade, diary of operations, May 1921, MP P7A/21.
186. Collins to O'Brien, 4 May 1921, NLI MS 8430; Collins to president, 16 June 1921, DE 2/244.
187. Collins to president, 16 June 1921, DE 2/244.
188. De Valera to Lloyd George, 28 June 1921, LG F/14/6/4.

189. Midleton to prime minister, 4 and 7 July 1921, LG F/38/1/18, /19. undated, unsigned memo in Midleton's hand, July 1921, LG F/181/2/3.
190. Dáil ministry, 1 July 1921, DE 1/3.
191. Midleton to prime minister, 4 and 7 July 1921, LG F/38/1/18, /19; also Midleton memo, July 1921, LG F/181/2/3.
192. Lloyd George to Midleton, 7 July 1921, LG F/38/1/20; de Valera to Lloyd George, 8 July 1921, LG F/14/6/5.
193. Macready to Midleton, 8 July 1921, DE 2/247, with Collins's MS notes in margin; also Collins memo, 9 July 1921, DE 2/247.
194. ibid.
195. HQ cypher, c. 10 July, DE 2/247.
196. C/S to officers commanding all units, 9 July 1921, MP P7A/21.
197. *Irish Bulletin*, special issue, 9 July 1921, MP P7A/21.

Chapter 4
JULY — OCTOBER 1921
(pp.99—112)

1. De Valera to Lloyd George, 28 June 1921, LG F/14/6/4; Jones, *diary*, 6 July 1921.
2. Jones, *diary*, 6 July 1921; Collins to O'Brien, 6 July 1921, DE 2/2.
3. Collins to de Valera, 27 June 1921, DE 2/296; Stack to Collins, 4 July 1921, DE 2/296; De Valera to Lloyd George, 13 July 1921, LG F/14/6/9; Lloyd George to de Valera, 13 July 1921, LG F/14/6/10; Collins to president, 11 July 1921, DE 2/244.
4. De Valera to Collins, 15 July 1921, DE 2/244; Collins to president, 11 July 1921, DE 2/244.
5. Collins to de Valera, 16 July 1921, DE 2/244.
6. Lloyd George to the King, 14 July 1921, LG F/29/4/57; Cabinet, 20 July 1921, CAB 23/26.
7. Cabinet, 20 July 1921, CAB 23/26.
8. ibid.
9. ibid.
10. ibid.
11. ibid.
12. ibid.
13. ibid.
14. See cabinet, 20 July 1921, CAB 23/26. Also Lloyd George to the King, 21 July 1921, LG F/29/4/60.
15. Lloyd George to the King, 21 July 1921, LG F/29/4/60.
16. Cabinet, 20 July 1921, CAB 23/26.
17. ibid. Lloyd George to the King, 21 July 1921, LG F/29/4/60.
18. ibid.
19. ibid.
20. See Macready report, 26 July 1921, CAB 25/126.

21. Lord privy seal to prime minister, 9 Aug. 1921, LG F/17/4/19; prime minister to lord privy seal, 8 Aug. 1921, LG F/7/4/18.
22. Montagu to prime minister, 30 June 1921, LG F/41/1/18.
23. Chamberlain to Lloyd George, 21 July 1921, LG F/7/4/14.
24. Cabinet, 20 July and 5 Aug. 1921, CAB 23/26.
25. Lloyd George to the king, 21 July 1921, LG F/29/4/60.
26. Ibid.
27. Stamfordham to prime minister, 21 July 1921, LG F/29/4/61.
28. Jones, *diary*, 13 July 1921 and Lloyd George to the King, 15 July 1921, LG F/29/4/58.
29. Law to Jones, 30 July 1921, Jones, *diary*, pp.91-2.
30. Chamberlain to Lloyd George, 11 Aug. 1921, LG F/7/4/24.
31. Dáil ministry, 25 and 27 July and 6 Aug. 1921, DE 1/3; de Valera to Lloyd George, 10 Aug. 1921, LG F/14/6/14.
32. ibid; Chamberlain to Lloyd George, 11 Aug. 1921, LG F/7/4/24. Jones to Lloyd George, 11 Aug. 1921, in Jones, *diary*, p.95.
33. Chamberlain to Lloyd George, 11 Aug. 1921, LG F/7/4/24; Jones to Lloyd George, 11 Aug. 1921, Jones, *diary*, p.95.
34. ibid.
35. Jones to Lloyd George, 11 Aug. 1921, in Jones, *diary*, 11 Aug. 1921.
36. ibid; also Chamberlain to Lloyd George and Lloyd George to Chamberlain, both 11 Aug. 1921, in LG F/7/4/25 and /26; cabinet, 11 Aug. 1921, CAB 23/26.
37. Lloyd George to Chamberlain, 11 Aug. 1921, LG F/7/4/26; cabinet, 13 Aug. 1921, CAB 23/26; Jones, *diary*, 13 Aug. 1921; Lloyd George to the King, 13 Aug. 1921, LG F/29/4/66.
38. Cabinet, 15 Aug. 1921, CAB 23/26.
39. ibid. Cabinet, 17 Aug. 1921, CAB 23/26.
40. Cabinet, 17 Aug. 1921, CAB 23/26.
41. ibid ; and Jones, *diary*, 17 Aug. 1921.
42. ibid.
43. Cabinet committee on Ireland 17 and 18 Aug. 1921, CAB 27/130.
44. Cabinet, 18 Aug. 1921, CAB 23/26.
45. Wilson memo, 16 Aug. 1921, CAB 24/127.
46. ibid.
47. ibid.
48. Macready memo, 19 Aug. 1921, LG F/16/3/21(a); Macready to Worthington-Evans, 24 Aug. 1921, LG F/16/3/22.
49. ibid.
50. Greenwood to prime minister, 9 July 1921, LG F/19/5/13.
51. Cope to Jones, 15 Aug. 1921, Jones, *diary*, p.99.
52. Fitzalan to prime minister, 20 Aug. 1921, LG F/17/2/9.
53. Fitzalan to prime minister, 23 Aug. 1921, LG F/17/2/10.
54. Fitzalan to prime minister, 18 Aug. 1921, LG F/17/2/8.
55. Cabinet, 25 Aug. 1921, CAB 23/26; Jones, *diary*, 25 Aug. 1921.
56. Interview with Sinn Féin representatives, 26 Aug. 1921, CAB 24/127.

57. ibid.
58. Derby to prime minister, 29 Aug. 1921, Derby 920 DER(17)34.
59. Stamfordham to prime minister, 26 Aug. 1921, LG F/29/4/69.
60. Fisher to prime minister, 5 Sept. 1921, LG F/25/2/13.
61. Hewart to prime minister, 5 Sept. 1921, LG F/27/4/31. Derby to prime minister, 5 Sept. 1921, Derby 920 DER(17)34.
62. Jones, *diary*, 7 Sept. 1921.
63. ibid.
64. ibid.
65. Note by acting secretary of the cabinet, 12 Sept. 1921, CAB 24/128.
66. Jones, *diary*, 19 Sept. 1921; Fisher to prime minister, 13 Sept. 1921, LG F/16/7/71.
67. Lloyd George to Chamberlain, 21 Sept. 1921, LG F/7/4/27.
68. ibid.
69. Jones, *diary*, 21 Sept. 1921.
70. Prime minister to Chamberlain, 28 Sept. 1921, LG F/7/4/28.
71. Dáil Éireann, *Report*, 26 Aug. 1921; memorandum by law department, 5 Aug. 1922, SPO K4; De Valera to Lloyd George, 10 Aug. 1921, LG F/14/6/16.
72. Stack and Ó Caoimh to each TD, 25 Aug. 1921, MP P7A/23; Secretary to each minister, 7 Sept. 1921, DE 2/36; de Valera to secretary each cumann and comhairle 7 Sept. 1921, MP P7A/24.
73. President's itinerary, 10-13 Aug. 1921, MP P7A/23; Dáil ministry, 15 Sept. 1921, DE 1/3.
74. Collins to PGOD, 19 and 21 Sept. 1921, MP P7A/7.
75. GOS to A/G ISD, 20 Sept. 1921, EOM P17E/1.
76. *An tÓglach*, 23 Sept. 1921, MP P7A/24.
77. Memo by the law department, 22 Aug. 1922, SPO K4.
78. ibid.
79. Dáil ministry, 27 Aug. 1921, DE 1/3.
80. Dáil ministry, 9 Sept. 1921, DE 1/3.
81. De Valera to O'Brien, 31 Aug. 1921, NLI MS 8429.

Chapter 5
OCTOBER – DECEMBER 1921
(pp. 113–145)

1. Macready report, 27 Sept. 1921, CP 3357, CAB 24/129 and Worthington-Evans memo, 13 Oct. 1921, CP 3358, CAB 24/128 and Cabinet, 6 Oct. 1921, CAB 23/27.
2. Midleton to Derby, Derby papers, 920 DER(17)33.
3. Conclusions of a meeting of the British representatives to the conference with Sinn Féin (i.e. only British representatives) hereafter referred to as British reps. SFB, 10 Oct. 1921, LG F/182/2.
4. ibid.

5. Committee on the Observance of the Truce, hereafter referred to as Truce committee, 12 Oct. 1921, LG F/182/3.
6. ibid.
7. ibid.
8. British reps. SFB, 13 Oct. 1921, LG F/182/2.
9. ibid.
10. Jones, *diary*, 13 Oct. 1921 and Jones's notes on the conference on Ireland, (hereafter referred to as Jones's notes), 13 Oct. 1921, CAB 21/253.
11. Jones's notes, 13 Oct. 1921, CAB 21/253.
12. Truce committee, SFC, 13 Oct. 1921, LG F/182/3.
13. Joint meeting of British and Irish representatives to the conference on Ireland, (hereafter designated by British and Irish reps. and normally followed by letters SFC) 14 Oct. 1921, LG F/182/3; also Jones's notes, fourth session, 14 Oct. 1921, CAB 21/253.
14. Jones's notes, fifth session, 17 Oct. 1921, CAB 21/253.
15. Truce committee, 20 Oct. 1921, LG F/182/3.
16. ibid.
17. ibid.
18. British reps., 21 Oct. 1921, LG F/182/2; Jones's notes, 17 Oct. 1921, CAB 21/253
19. Duggan memo, 24 Oct. 1921, MP P7A/72 and Secretary of delegation to president, 21 Oct. 1921, DE 2/304:6.
20. M/D to C/S, 22 Oct. 1921, MP P7A/72 and C/S to O/Cs, 31 Oct. 1921, MP P7A/46.
21. HMSO CMD 1534 1921, copy in DE 2/302.
22. British reps., SFB 27 Oct. 1921, LG F/182/2.
23. Collins to A/G, 13 Oct. 1921, MP P7A/72 and Collins to de Valera, 15 Oct. 1921, DE 2/244.
24. Childers to de Valera, 13 Oct. 1921, MP P7A/72.
25. Secretary of delegation to president, 21 Oct. 1921, DE 2/304:6 and Duggan memo, 24 Oct. 1921, MP P7A/72.
26. Collins to A/G, 13 Oct. 1921, MP P7A/72.
27. Collins to A/G, 13 Oct. 1921, MP P7A/72.
28. Collins to de Valera, 15 Oct. 1921, DE 2/244.
29. Childers to de Valera, 13 Oct. 1921, MP P7A/72 and Collins to A/G, 13 Oct. 1921, MP P7A/72.
30. Collins to A/G, 13 Oct. 1921, MP P7A/72.
31. Memo from president to Griffith, 14 Oct. 1921, DE 2/304:6.
32. De Valera to Collins, 19 Oct. 1921, DE 2/244.
33. General order No. 15, December 1920, in MP P7A/45.
34. ibid.
35. C/S to O/C ISD, 8 July 1921, MP P7A/21.
36. O'Hegarty to O/C Mid Clare, 22 Sept. 1921, MP P7A/24.
37. O'Hegarty to M/D with draft reply, 20 Sept. 1921, MP P7A/26 and Brugha note at foot.
38. C/S to Acting Bde. O/C No. 2 Derry Bde., 20 Apr. 1921, MP P7A/21; M/D to C/S, 20 Oct. 1921 and C/S to M/D, 24 Oct. 1921, both in MP P7A/24.

39. C/S to M/D, 24 Oct. 1921, MP P7A/24.
40. De Valera to Collins, 19 Oct. 1921, DE 2/244.
41. SF Standing C/tee, 21 Feb. 1918, NLI P 3269.
42. Collins to president, 21 Oct. 1921, DE 2/244 and O'Hegarty to president, 28 Oct. 1921, DE 2/238.
43. Dáil ministry 4 Nov. 1921 and Dáil cabinet, 9 Nov. 1921, DE 1/3.
44. Special memo to all O/Cs on levies and collections, 25 Oct. 1921, EOM P17 E/31.
45. Dáil ministry, 15 Sept. 1921, DE 1/3.
46. ibid.
47. ibid.
48. ibid.
49. Secretary to ministry to Griffith, 22 Nov. 1921, DE 2/421.
50. Collins to C/S, 23 Nov. 1921, MP P7A/72 and Dáil cabinet, 25 Nov. 1921, DE 1/3.
51. Dáil cabinet, 25 Nov. 1921, DE 1/3.
52. ibid.
53. C/S to all divisional commanders, 30 Nov. 1921, EOM P17/E/1.
54. For details of the arrangements, see C/S to O/C 1WD, 11 Nov. 1921, MP P7A/28, C/S to O/C 2SD, 11, 17 Nov. 1921, EOM 17E/1, C/S to O/C 2SD, 21 Nov. 1921, EOM P17E/1 and C/S to O/C 1WD, MP P7A/28, C/S to Gallagher, 17 Nov. 1921, MP P7'A/28.
55. ibid.
56. C/S to O/C 1WD, C/S to P. Ó Caoimh, C/S to Gallagher, each on 17 Nov. 1921 and in MP P7A/28.
57. Chief of police to C/S, 12 Nov. 1921, MP P7A/28.
58. O/S 1SD to C/S, 4 Oct. 1921, MP P7A/26.
59. C/S to O/C 1SD, 7 Oct. 1921, MP P7A/21; See also S. Lawlor 'Ireland from truce to treaty', *Irish Historical Studies*, XXII/85, pp.49-64.
60. Barry to C/S 19 Oct. 1921 and C/S to O/C 1SD, 27 Oct. 1921 in MP P7A/26, and C/S to Collins, 21 Oct. 1921, MP P7A/72.
61. M/D to C/S, 24 Oct. 1921, MP P7A/30. Draft general order c. 24 Oct. 1921, MP P7A/30.
62. O/C 2SD to C/S, 3 Nov. 1921 and Report on Mid-Limerick Brigade by D/C/S, Nov. 1921, in MP P7A/28.
63. C/S to O/C mid-Clare, 12 Sept. 1921, MP P7A/26 and O/C mid-Clare to C/S, 27 Oct. 1921, MP P7A/26; C/S to O/C mid-Clare, 21 Sept. 1921, O/C mid-Limerick to C/S, c. 4 Oct. 1921, C/S to O/C mid-Limerick, 18 Oct. 1921, in MP P7A/27.
64. A/G to O/Cs, 20 Sept. 1921, MP P7A/24 and O'Hegarty to each department, 24 Nov. 1921, MP P7A/28.
65. Fitzalan to Lloyd George, 20 Aug. 1921, LG F/17/2/9.
66. QMG to M/D, 19 Dec. 1921, EOM P17E/31.
67. Table of numbers IRA c. Oct. 1921, MP P7A/27, ditto c. Dec. 1921, MP P7A/32. The tables bear a pencilled date.
68. Chief of police to C/S 25 Aug. 1921, MP P7A/23 and draft general order, c. 24 Oct. 1921, MP P7A/30.

69. Derby to Lloyd George, 18 Nov. 1921, LG F/14/5/33.
70. Jones, *diary*, 11 Oct. 1921.
71. Jones, *diary*, 14 Oct. 1921.
72. ibid.
73. ibid.
74. ibid.
75. ibid. Lloyd George to Jones, 17 Oct. 1921, printed in Jones, *diary*, p.137.
76. Jones's notes, 17 Oct. 1921, CAB 21/253 and Jones, *diary*, 17 Oct. 1921.
77. Jones, *diary*, 17 Oct. 1921.
78. Jones's notes, 21 Oct. 1921, CAB 21/253, also Jones, *diary*, 21 Oct. 1921.
79. Jones, *diary*, 24 Oct. 1921.
80. ibid.
81. ibid.
82. ibid. and British reps., SFB 24 Oct. 1921, CAB 43/1.
83. Jones, *diary*, 25 Oct. 1921.
84. ibid.
85. Jones, *diary*, 7 Sept. 1921.
86. Jones, *diary*, 25 Oct. 1921.
87. ibid.
88. ibid.
89. ibid.
90. Jones, *diary*, 27 Oct. 1921.
91. Griffith to president, 24 Oct. 1921, MP P7A/72.
92. Jones, *diary*, 24 Oct. 1921.
93. ibid.
94. Collins to A/G, 24 Oct. 1921, MP P7A/72.
95. ibid.
96. ibid.
97. Jones, *diary*, 25 Oct. 1921.
98. Jones to Childers, 29 Oct. 1921, LG F/25/2/38 with appended note of telephone messages and agreements, also Jones, *diary*, 28 Oct. 1921.
99. Jones to Childers, 29 Oct. 1921, LG F/25/2/38 with appended messages and notes, also Jones, *diary*, 29 Oct. 1921.
100. Greenwood to Lloyd George, 29 Oct. 1921, LG F/19/5/36.
101. Jones, *diary*, 29 Oct. 1921.
102. ibid.
103. ibid.
104. Jones, *diary*, 30 Oct. 1921.
105. ibid.
106. ibid.
107. Griffith to president, 31 Oct. 1921, MP P7A/72.
108. ibid.
109. ibid.
110. ibid.

111. Collins to A/G, 31 Oct. 1921, MP P7A/72.
112. Jones, *diary*, 31 Oct., 1 Nov., 1921.
113. Riddell, *diary*, 30 Oct. 1921.
114. ibid.
115. ibid., 31 Oct. 1921.
116. ibid.
117. Scott, *diary*, 28-29 Oct. 1921.
118. ibid.
119. ibid.
120. ibid.
121. ibid.
122. ibid.
123. Riddell, *diary*, 30 Oct. 1921.
124. ibid.
125. Jones, *diary*, 1 Nov. 1921.
126. Griffith to Lloyd George, 2 Nov. 1921, LG F/183/1.
127. ibid. The words in brackets were not in the first letter, but were added in a subsequent draft.
128. Griffith to president, 3 Nov. 1921, MP P7A/72.
129. Jones, *diary*, 7 Nov. 1921.
130. ibid.
131. ibid.
132. ibid.
133. ibid.
134. Jones, *diary*, 8 Nov. 1921.
135. ibid.
136. ibid.
137. ibid.
138. Jones, *diary*, 9 Nov. 1921.
139. ibid.
140. ibid.
141. Churchill to Lloyd George, 9 Nov. 1921, LG F/10/1/40.
142. ibid.
143. Griffith to president, 9 Nov. 1921, MP P7A/72.
144. Cabinet, 10 Nov. 1921, CAB 23/27.
145. ibid, and Jones, *diary*, 10 Nov. 1921. See also draft memo to government of Northern Ireland, 10 Nov. 1921 (SFB 21 and 22A), CAB 43/2.
146. Cabinet, 10 Nov. 1921, CAB 23/27 and Jones, *diary*, 10 Nov. 1921.
147. ibid.
148. Lloyd George to Craig, 10 Nov. 1921, LG F/11/3/19.
149. ibid.
150. Craig to prime minister, 11 Nov. 1921, LG F/11/3/20.
151. ibid.
152. ibid.
153. Chamberlain to prime minister, 11 Nov. 1921, LG F/7/4/31.

154. ibid.
155. ibid.
156. ibid.
157. ibid.
158. Jones,*diary*, 12 Nov. 1921.
159. ibid.
160. Chamberlain to prime minister, 11 Nov. 1921, LG F/7/4/31.
161. ibid.
162. ibid.
163. ibid.
164. British reps., SFB, 12 Nov. 1921, CAB 43/1 and Jones, *diary*, 12 and 14 Nov. 1921.
165. Lloyd George to Craig, 14 Nov. 1921, LG F/11/3/19.
166. Jones, *diary*, 16 Nov. 1921.
167. Jones, *diary*, 17 Nov. 1921 and Birkenhead to Salvidge, 11 Nov. 1921, LG F/4/7/33.
168. Derby to prime minister, 18 Nov. 1921, LG F/14/5/33.
169. Craig to prime minister, 17 Nov. 1921, LG F/11/3/22.
170. Jones, *diary*, 17 Nov. 1921.
171. Derby to prime minister, 18 Nov. 1921, LG F/14/5/33.
172. Lloyd George to Craig, 18 Nov. 1921, LG F/11/3/23.
173. Craig to prime minister, 11 Nov. 1921, LG F/7/4/31.
174. Chamberlain to prime minister, 11 Nov. 1921, LG F/7/4/31.
175. Secretary of delegation to secretary of ministry, 11 Nov. 1921, DE 2/238.
176. Dáil cabinet, 13 Nov. 1921, handwritten account in DE 2/238.
177. Griffith to president, 3 Nov. 1921, MP P7A/72.
178. Dáil cabinet, 13 Nov. 1921, handwritten account, DE 2/238.
179. ibid, also Griffith to president, 3 Nov. 1921, MP P7A/72.
180. Jones, *diary*, 16 Nov. 1921.
181. ibid.
182. Dáil cabinet, 20 Nov. 1921, DE 1/3 and Jones, *diary*, 22 Nov. 1921.
183. Jones, *diary*, 22 Nov. 1921.
184. ibid.
185. ibid.
186. Chamberlain to prime minister, c. 23 Nov. 1921, LG F/7/4/34.
187. ibid.
188. Jones, *diary*, 23 Nov. 1921.
189. Jones, *diary*, 23 and 24 Nov. 1921.
190. Collins to A/G, 23 Nov. 1921, MP P7A/72.
191. Dáil cabinet, 25 Nov. 1921, DE 1/3.
192. Jones, *diary*, 28, 29, 30 Nov. 1921.
193. Jones, *diary*, 1 Dec. 1921; British reps., SFB, 1 Dec. 1921, LG F/182/2.
194. Jones, *diary*, 2 Dec. 1921; Secretaries' note, proposed articles of agreement, SFC, 2 Dec. 1921, F/182/3.
195. Dáil cabinet, 3 Dec. 1921, DE 1/3 and Dáil cabinet and deleg-

ation, 3 Dec. 1921, DE 1/3. The views and statements made at each of the meetings have been taken together, in order to clarify here what were at the time, overlapping and somewhat inconclusive meetings.
196. ibid.
197. ibid.
198. ibid.
199. ibid.
200. ibid.
201. ibid.
202. ibid.
203. ibid.
204. ibid.
205. ibid.
206. ibid.
207. ibid.
208. ibid.
209. ibid.
210. ibid.
211. Secretary to Markham, 28 Nov. 1921, NLI AOB MS 8428.
212. Jones to prime minister, 4 Dec. 1921, LG F/25/2/51.
213. ibid.
214. ibid.
215. For details of the revision, the discussions during the 5th, the chronology of the day see Jones, *diary*, 5 Dec. 1921, Birkenhead, F.E., *Earl of Birkenhead* (London 1935) 11, p.161, Taylor, R., *Michael Collins*, (London 1961) p.148, Cabinet, 5 Dec. 1921, CAB 23/27.
216. For the letter to Craig advising that the articles of agreement had been signed – no copy of the 'other' one has yet been discovered by the author – see Lloyd George to Craig, 5 Dec. 1921, LG F/11/3/24.
217. In the letter to Craig he did warn that if the government of Northern Ireland did not enter the Irish Free State, 'we should be unable to defend existing boundary which must be subject to revision on one side and another by a boundary commission'. Lloyd George to Craig, 5 Dec. 1921, LG F/11/3/24.
218. As Jones had put it, Jones to prime minister, 4 Dec. 1921, LG F/25/2/51.

Chapter 6
DECEMBER 1921 – JUNE 1922
(pp.146–194)

1. When the arrangements for the visit were being made in November, de Valera intended to be away from Dublin at least until Tuesday 6 December. See Secretary to Markam, 28 Nov. 1921, NLI MS 8428.

2. See for example Longford and O'Neill, *De Valera*: the chapters entitled 'The Thumbscrew', 'Peace v. Principle', and 'The Drift to Disaster'.
3. Dáil cabinet, 7 Dec. 1921, DE 1/3.
4. ibid.
5. Dáil cabinet, 8 Dec. 1921, DE 1/3.
6. ibid.
7. ibid.
8. *Dáil Éireann. Official Report. Debate on the Treaty between Great Britain and Ireland signed in London on 6 December 1921*, Dublin 1922 (hereafter *Treaty Debates*), 14 Dec. 1921.
9. ibid. 14 and 15 Dec. 1921.
10. ibid.
11. Officers 1SD, communication, c. 12-16 Dec. 1921, MP P7A/32.
12. ibid.
13. O/C Cork No. 1 to all TDs, 12 Dec. 1921, MP P7A/33.
14. C/S to O/C 1SD, 17 Dec. 1921, MP P7A/33; also O/C Cork No. 1 to Div./Adj. 1SD, c. 20 Dec. 1921, MP P7A/33.
15. See de Valera statement issued 9 Dec. 1921, also see M/D to C/S, 29 Dec. 1921, MP P7A/33.
16. O'Keefe to de Valera, 22 Dec. 1921, MP P7A/32.
17. ibid.
18. See Brugha note written as M/D to C/S on 2 Jan. 1922 at foot of O'Keefe to de Valera, 22 Dec. 1922, MP P7A/32.
19. Resolution by farmers and labourers, west Limerick, 26 Dec. 1921, MP P7A/26.
20. ibid.
21. O/C 1SD to C/S, 4 Jan. 1922, MP P7A/32.
22. O/C 1SD to C/S, 6 Jan. 1922, MP P7A/32.
23. Clarke to Street, 16 Dec. 1921, LG F/20/1/10, for the description of the country.
24. *Treaty Debates*, 7 Jan. 1922.
25. For the cabinet's initial reaction, Cabinet, 6 Dec. 1922, CAB 23/27.
26. ibid.
27. Clarke to Street, 16 Dec. 1921, LG F/20/1/10.
28. Chamberlain to prime minister and lord chancellor, 11 Dec. 1921, LG F/7/6/35 and Craig to prime minister, 14 Dec. 1921, LG F/11/3/28.
29. ibid. The 'automatic' provision meant that unless Ulster voted herself out (which she would undoubtedly do) she would be included in the new state. See Jones to Hankey, 13 Dec. 1921 and Jones, *diary*, 14 Dec. 1921. Jones, *diary*, III, pp.187-8; also Craig to Chamberlain, 15 Dec. 1921, ibid., p.190.
30. Jones, *diary*, 14 Dec. 1921; Grigg to Hemming enclosing Lloyd George to Griffith, 2 Dec. 1921, LG F/20/1/7.
31. ibid. Grigg to Hemming.

32. Conclusions of the cabinet committee on Irish affairs, hereafter referred to as Cabinet committee, 21 Dec. 1921, CAB 21/246.
33. Macready to Derby, 21 Dec. 1921, Derby MS 920 DER(17)33; Greenwood to prime minister, 29 Dec. 1921, LG F/20/1/13, also Wilson, *diary*, 9 and 11 Jan. 1922.
34. Greenwood to prime minister, 29 Dec. 1921, LG F/20/1/13.
35. For views as to the coalition in late December, and the effect which the Irish settlement might have on its reputation, see Derby to Davis enclosing letter to prime minister, 22 Dec. 1921, LG F/14/5/35, Derby to prime minister enclosing letter from Woodhouse, 23 Dec. 1921, LG F/14/5/36, and from Stockton, LG F/14/5/37; see also Jones to Hankey, 30 Dec. 1921, in Jones, *diary*.
36. DCM 11 Jan. 1922, DE 1/4.
37. DCM 13 Jan. 1922, DE 1/4.
38. See below p.155.
39. Notes taken by the secretary to the Dáil cabinet, 'COM' (Ó Murachadh) of what seem to have been meetings of that cabinet reveal that the agenda and discussions coincided almost exactly with the accounts taken of meetings of the provisional government, on the same day. See for example the notes in the State Paper Office, Dublin, under the file number 'M2' for June 1922 (hereafter referred to as SPO M2) and the minutes of the provisional government for the same month in MP P7B/24. Note also that the first 'official' meeting of the provisional government, or that recorded as the first, did not take place until 22 March; and that presumably before then, the Dáil cabinet 'doubled' as the provisional government. See MP P7B/242.
40. W.T. Cosgrave (1880-1965), elected as MP in 1917, by-election (see p.13), Minister for Local Government in the Dáil government and member of the provisional government.
41. E.J. Duggan, a solicitor, had become involved with IRA intelligence, before the truce; had been chief liaison officer after the truce and a member of the delegation to London. He was Minister for Home Affairs in the Dáil as well as a member of the provisional government from 10 and 13 January respectively.
42. Patrick Hogan was Minister for Agriculture and Fisheries from 10 January and a member of the provisional government from the 13th.
43. Joseph McGrath was Minister for Labour in the Dáil and a member of the provisional government from 10 and 13 January respectively.
44. Kevin O'Higgins, assistant Minister for Local Government before 9 January 1922 and Minister for Economic Affairs afterwards in the Dáil government was also a member of the provisional government.
45. Mulcahy replaced Brugha as Minister for Defence in the Dáil; he seems to have remained as chief-of-staff until later in January

1922 when O'Duffy was appointed. Gavan Duffy had become Dáil Minister for Foreign Affairs in January 1922. Neither belonged to the provisional government, though practically, the distinction was irrelevant as they attended its meetings.

46. *Dáil Éireann, Official Report for the periods 16-26 August 1921, and 28 February — 8 June 1922*, Dublin 1922 (hereafter Dáil Éireann, *Report*), 28 Feb., 1 and 2 Mar. 1922.
47. ibid. For Griffith's rejection of the opposition questions as 'propaganda', ibid., 1 Mar. 1922, p.132.
48. ibid., 28 Feb. 1922.
49. Tadh Saor to Collins, 17 Jan. 1922, DE 2/486.
50. Crowley to Collins, 27 Jan. 1922, DE 2/486.
51. Collins to Crowley, 31 Jan. 1922, DE 2/486.
52. SF Standing C/tee, 23 and 31 Jan. 1922, NLI P 3269
53. ibid.
54. Ó Tuathail to Miss Barton, 2 letters 24 Jan. 1922, NLI 8786 (2).
55. Dunne to Miss Barton, 29 Jan. 1922 and Ó Cuilean to Miss Barton, 18 Jan. 1922, NLI MS 8786 (2).
56 Cumann na mBan circular enclosed in 'L' to 'M', 1 Feb. 1922, DE 2/486.
57. Stack and Boland circular, 17 Jan. 1922, MP P7A/75; SF Standing C/tee 3 Feb. 1922, NLI P 3269; Notice issued by secretary to ministry, 6 Feb. 1922, SPO M2; SF Standing C/tee, 2 or 3 Mar. 1922, NLI P 3269.
58. Wilson, *diary*, 9, 11, 16 Jan. 1922.
59. Rory O'Connor and signatories to Mulcahy, 11 Jan. 1922, MP P7B/191.
60. ibid.
61. For a copy of the Volunteer constitution with its provisions for calling a convention, see MP P7B/193.
62. Dáil cabinet, 12 Jan. 1922 DE 1/4; M/D and C/S to individual O/Cs, 13 Jan. 1922, MP P7B/191.
63. ibid.
64. O'Connor to C/S, 18 Jan. 1922, MP P7B/191.
65. C/S to all division and brigade commandants, 21 Jan. 1922, MP P7B/191.
66. ibid.
67. ibid.
68. O/C 1SD to C/S, 13 Jan. 1922, MP P7B/191.
69. Minutes of general staff meeting, 24 Jan. 1922, MP P7A/66.
70. ibid.
71. Minutes of general staff meeting, 31 Jan. 1922, MP P7B/191; D/Org. to M/D, 9 Feb. 1922, MP P7B/191.
72. ibid.
73. D/Org. to M/D, 9 Feb. 1922, MP P7B/191.
74. ibid.
75. ibid.
76. ibid.

77. D/Org to C/S, 13 Dec. 1921, MP P7A/33.
78. ibid.
79. Dáil cabinet, 17 Feb. 1922, DE 1/4.
80. Battalion officers, 4th batt., 1st bde, 3 ND, to O/C 1 bde, 2 July 1922, MP P7A/49.
81. Dáil Éireann, Report, 28 Apr. 1922, p.340.
82. ibid.
83. ibid.
84. ibid.
85. Dáil Éireann, Report, 26 Apr. 1922, Mulcahy statement p.249 and appendix C, p.255.
86. ibid.
87. Interview between Griffith and Mayor O'Mara, 9 Mar. 1922, MP P7B/191.
88. Brennan to A/C/S, 8 Mar. 1922, and memo. NLI MS 22, 127.
89. ibid, and Brennan memo c. 8 Mar. 1922, NLI MS 22, 127.
90. Collins to M/D, 14 Mar. 1922, NP P7B/191.
91. S. MacCaoilte to Ceann Coganta an Airm, 14 Mar. 1922, NLI MS 22, 127.
92. Brennan to A/C/S, 8 Mar. 1922 and Brennan memo, c. 8 Mar. 1922, both in NLI MS 22, 127. Also Griffith O'Mara interview, 9 Mar. 1922, MP P7B/191.
93. Dáil cabinet, 15 Mar. 1922, DE 1/4.
94. ibid. Mulcahy 'notes', c. 15 Mar. 1922, MP P7B/192.
95. ibid.
96. M/D to C/S 16 Mar. 1922, MP 7B/191; see also M/D memo to A/G and officers, 24 Mar. 1922, MP P7A/49, and attached to C/S, 23 Mar. 1922.
97. Treaty debates.
98. Minute of staff meeting, 31 Jan. 1922, MP P7B/191.
99. Typed notes, RJM, 'Wed', 15 Mar. 1922, MP P7B/192.
100. ibid. Also memo on offer made by the M/D at a meeting of the first southern division, and terms submitted by the O/C and Adj. 1SD, 20-22 (Feb.?) Mar. 1922, MP P7B/191.
101. Typed memo entitled, 'Dáil', 25 Feb [sic] 1922, MP P7B/191.
102. Mulcahy's 'personal notes on Dáil meeting, 28 Feb. 1922, MP P7A/67.
103. Gavan Duffy to M/D, 24 Mar. 1922, MP P7B/191.
104. Typed notes, unsigned, but evidently Mulcahy's, on events 'Wed', 15 Mar. 1922, MP P7B/192. Basis for following sentence too.
105. Interview with O'Connor published in the newspapers, 23 Mar. 1922.
106. ibid.
107. ibid.
108. Thornton to M/D enclosing two reports on 25 and 26 Mar. MP P7B/191. Barry had been the martial law liaison officer during the truce. See above p.121.

109. Thornton to M/D, enclosing two reports on 25 and 26 Mar. MP P7B/191.
110. Official statement, released after the convention and published in the newspapers on 27 Mar. 1922.
111. Dáil cabinet, 31 Mar. 1922, DE 1/4.
112. 'Heads of Working Arrangement', 24 Jan. 1922 and appended Collins-Craig agreement of 21 Jan. 1922, MP P7A/66. DCM, 24 Jan. DE 1/4.
113. Dáil Éireann, *Report*, 1 Mar. 1922, p.133.
114. Craig to prime minister, 8 Feb. 1922, LG F/11/3/35 and Spender to Downing Street, 8 Feb. 1922, LG F/11/3/34.
115. Churchill to Craig, 11 Feb. 1922 and Collins to Churchill, 11 Feb. 1922 in CO 906/20.
116. Craig to Churchill, 12 Feb. 1922, LG F/11/3/36; Collins to Churchill, 13 Feb. 1922, CO 906/20; Cope to Anderson, 13 Feb. 1922, CO 906/20.
117. Spender to Downing Street, 8 Feb. 1922, LG F/11/3/34; Craig to Churchill, 12 Feb. 1922, LG F/11/3/36; Craig to prime minister, 8 Feb. 1922, LG F/11/3/35.
118. See memo by Chamberlain on his interview with Craig and Griffith, 10 Feb. 1922, CAB 21/250.
119. Cope to chief secretary, 9 Feb. 1922, CO 906/20.
120. Cope to Churchill, 14 Feb. 1922, Churchill to Craig, 15 Feb. 1922, Collins to Churchill, 16 Feb. 1922, CO 906/20.
121. Cope to Anderson for Churchill, 14 Feb. 1922, CO 906/20; Hankey to Lloyd George, 14 Mar. 1922, LG F/26/1/3.
122. ibid. Also Jones to prime minister, 17 Mar. 1922, LG F/26/1/17.
123. Jones Curtis memo on the imperial government and Northern Ireland, 18 Mar. 1922, CO 739/4.
124. ibid.
125. ibid.
126. See p.182. Also Wilson, *diary*, 15 and 16-18 Mar. 1922.
127. Collins statement, c. late March 1922, draft on invitation to meet Craig, NLI MS 22, 777.
128. Dáil cabinet, 15 Mar. 1922, DE 1/4.
129. Mulcahy to Griffith, 24 Mar. 1922, MP P7B/32.
130. Dáil cabinet, 24 Mar. 1922, DE 1/4. Provisional government minutes (hereafter PG minutes), 24 Mar. 1922, MP P7B/243.
131. See below p.184 for 'unofficial' policy. Collins to Churchill, 20 Apr. 1922, CO 739/5.
132. See Griffith statement, 26 Apr. 1922 referring to the 'language of menace and incitement' with its 'consequences of bloodshed and attempted bloodshed' by the 'unconstitutional and unscrupulous opposition to the Government' which had broken its agreement to act in a 'constitutional way'. Dáil Éireann, *Report*, p.235.
133. Cabinet, 5 Apr. 1922, CAB 23/30.
134. ibid.

135. ibid.
136. ibid.
137. Churchill to Collins, 6 Apr. 1922, CO 739/5.
138. Cabinet, 10 Apr. 1922, CAB 23/30. Also summary of note by Churchill appended to cabinet minutes, 11 Apr. 1922, CAB 23/30.
139. Churchill to Collins, 12 Apr. 1922, SPO S.1322.
140. PG minutes, 12 Apr. 1922, MP P7B/242.
141. Irish daily newspapers, 23 Mar. 1922 and *Cork Examiner*, 29 May 1922.
142. Mellows to secretary, Dáil Éireann, 14 Apr. 1922, SPO G4.
143. ibid.
144. ibid.
145. Moylan, suggestions, 21 Apr. 1922, MP P7B/152.
146. Mulcahy 'statement' or chronological account of events between 4 May and 28 June, MP P7B/192.
147. ibid.; also Dáil Éireann, *Report*, 3 May 1922; 'The Army Truce, how it was brought about', May 1922, MP P7B/192.
148. Dáil Éireann, *Report*, 1 Mar. 1922, pp.156 and 157.
149. De Valera to Mulcahy, 6 Mar. 1922, MP P7B/192.
150. ibid. Also Dáil cabinet, 10 and 13 Apr., DE 1/4 and PG minutes, 12 Apr. 1922, MP P7B/242.
151. Dáil Éireann, *Report*, 26 Apr. 1922, p.235; 27 Apr. 1922, p.294.
152. For the announcement of the failure made in the Dáil, see Dáil Éireann, *Report*, 10 May 1922, p.379, and the reports given, 11 May 1922, pp.401-4. See also 'Report of Republican Delegation', 11 May 1922 in MP P7B/192 and notes by COM, Dáil cabinet, 6 May 1922 in SPO M2.
153. Points or terms of agreement, appended to Dáil cabinet, COM notes, 15 May 1922, SPO M2.
154. ibid.
155. ibid.
156. Dáil cabinet, 18 May 1922, COM notes, SPO M2. For April meetings see Dáil cabinet 10 and 13 Apr. 1922, DE 1/4; PG minutes, 12 Apr. 1922, MP P7B/243; Dáil Éireann, *Report*, 26 Apr. 1922.
157. Dáil cabinet, COM notes, 18 and 19 May 1922, SPO M2; Dáil Éireann, *Report*, 20 May 1922, p.479.
158. Dáil Éireann, *Report*, 20 May 1922, p.479.
159. ibid.
160. Manifesto, 29 May 1922, MP P7B/192.
161. Dáil cabinet, COM notes, 18 May 1922, SPO M2.
162. Jones to Hankey, 5 May 1922, in Jones, *diary*, p.198.
163. Cabinet committee, 12 May 1922, CO 739/5.
164. ibid.
165. ibid.
166. Cabinet, 16 May 1922, CAB 23/30.
167. ibid. Also Jones, *diary*, 16 May 1922.

168. ibid.
169. Curtis note on Collins-de Valera pact, 21 May 1922, CO 739/4.
170. Note of meeting of British representatives, 23 May 1922, CAB 43/1.
171. ibid.
172. ibid.
173. ibid.
174. ibid.
175. ibid.
176. ibid.
177. ibid.
178. ibid.
179. ibid.
180. Conference of British ministers, 27 May 1922, CAB 43/1.
181. ibid.
182. ibid.
183. ibid.
184. ibid.
185. ibid.
186. ibid.
187. ibid.
188. Conference with Irish representatives, 27 May 1922, CAB 21/249.
189. ibid.
190. ibid.
191. ibid.
192. Document addressed to the M/D, c. 28 Apr. 1922, MP P7B/191.
193. ibid.
194. ibid.
195. ibid.
196. Dáil Éireann, *Report*, 3 May 1922, p.360.
197. Memo on proposals towards army unity, 4-8 May 1922, MP P7B/192; document headed 'Four Courts criticism', 10 May MP P7B/192; RJM diary for period 12-16 May, MP P7B/193; Lynch to O'Duffy, 12 May 1922, MP P7B/192.
198. *Cork Examiner*, 29 May 1922.
199. ibid.
200. ibid.
201. ibid.
202. RJM statement or chronological account of events 4 May-28 June, MP P7B/192.
203. ibid.
204. The commission had been proposed after the disturbances of mid February. It involved representatives from the south, the north and the British, to police the border area in cooperation. For the initial proposals see Churchill to Craig, 14 Feb. 1922, CO 906/20; Macready to CIGS, 16 Feb. 1922, CO 739/4; Macready to Collins, 17 Feb. 1922, CO 739/4.
205. Curtis correspondence, Feb.-Mar. 1922, CO 739/4.

206. Wilson, *diary*, 8 Feb. 1922.
207. ibid., 15, 16-18 Mar. 1922.
208. Callwell, *Wilson*, 11, pp.336-7.
209. Collins to Churchill, 20 Apr. 1922, CO 739/5.
210. Craig to Collins, 25 Apr. 1922, CO 739/5.
211. Churchill to Collins, 3 May 1922, CO 739/5; Curtis to Masterson-Smith, 3 May 1922, CO 739/5; meeting of British signatories, 23 May 1922, LG F/182/2.
212. Meeting of British signatories, 23 May 1922, LG F/182/2.
213. Cabinet, 30 May 1922, CAB 23/30.
214. ibid.
215. ibid.
216. ibid.
217. 'S MacC' (MacCaoilte) memo, 28 July 1922, MP P7B/77.
218. ibid.
219. ibid.
220. See p.162 above for the example of one of the battalions in the Belfast brigade area of the third northern division.
221. S. MacC memo, 28 July 1922, MP P7B/77.
222. The accounts were and have remained since mainly 'oral'; though in view of the written evidence indicating the involvement of GHQ and the government in the despatches northwards, they do have some measure of corroboration.
223. Memo by Curtis on operations for clearing Pettigo-Beleek triangle, 6 June 1922, LG F/185/14.
224. ibid.
225. Situation Report from GHQ Dublin, 31 May 1922, CO 739/11.
226. Curtis memo on British operations for clearing Pettigo-Beleek triangle, 6 June 1922, LG F/185/1/4.
227. ibid.
228. ibid.
229. ibid.
230. ibid.
231. ibid.
232. Collins to Churchill, 5 June 1922, CO 906/21.
233. Cope to Jones, 5 June 1922, CO 906/21.
234. ibid.
235. Cope to Churchill, 5 June 1922, CO 906/21.
236. ibid.
237. ibid.
238. Collins to Churchill, 5 June 1922, CO 906/21, also Dáil cabinet, COM notes, 5 June 1922, SPO M2.
239. Dáil cabinet, COM notes, 5 June 1922, SPO M2.
240. ibid., 2 June 1922.
241. ibid.
242. ibid.
243. ibid.
244. COM notes, 3 June 1922, SPO M2.

245. ibid.
246. ibid.
247. ibid.
248. ibid.
249. ibid. Also PG minutes, 3 June 1922, MP P7B/243.
250. ibid.
251. Note in Mulcahy's hand, 5 June 1922, MP P7B/243; M/D to S. O'Hegarty, 6 June 1922, MP P7B/192; COM notes, 7 June 1922, SPO M2; PG minutes, 7 June 1922, P7B/243.
252. Undertaking signed by Lynch, 8 June 1922, written up by O'Hegarty, MP P7B/192.
253. COM notes, 5 June 1922. SPO M2.
254. ibid., also M/D to Sec. Four Courts executive, 12 June 1922, MP P7B/192.
255. PG minutes, 12 June 1922, MP P7B/243; COM notes, 3 June 1922, MP P7B/243; COM notes, 3 June 1922, SPO M2.
256. Collins to Churchill, nos. 72 and 73, CO 906/21.
257. Churchill to Collins, 8 June 1922, CO 906/21; Collins to Churchill, 8 June 1922 CO 906/21.
258. Collins to Churchill, 8 June 1922, CO 906/21.
259. ibid.
260. COM notes, 9 and 12 June 1922, SPO M2; PG minutes, 9 and 12 June 1922, MP P7B/243.
261 PG minutes, 12 June 1922, MP P7B/243; COM notes, 12 June 1922, SPO M2; M/D to Sec. Four Courts, 12 June 1922, MP P7B/192.
262. COM notes 15 June 1922, SPO M2; PG minutes, 15 June 1922, MP P7B/243.
263. Account of convention, 18 June 1922, from a notebook the property of Sean MacBride, captured at Newbridge in 1923, MP P7B/90.
264. ibid.
265. ibid.
266. Lloyd George to Collins, 22 June 1922, MP P7B/244.
267. Cabinet, 22 June 1922, Cabinet 21/255; appendix to conclusions of a conference of ministers on Sat. 24 June, 11 a.m., CAB 21/255; conference of ministers, 22 June 1922, LG F/185/1/5.
268. Conference of ministers, 22 June 1922, LG F/185/1/5.
269. Above, note 266.
270. 'Most secret' supplement, in Hankey's hand and signed by Hankey, to conclusions of conference of ministers, 23 June 1922, CAB 21/255.
271. ibid.
272. ibid.
273. ibid.
274. COM notes, 23 June 1922, SPO M2 and PG minutes, 23 June 1922, MP P7B/244.
275. 'Most secret' appendix to conclusions of conference of ministers, in Hankey's hand, 24 June 1922, CAB 21/255 (11 a.m.).

276. ibid.
277. When Lloyd George's coalition fell the following October, Churchill ordered Hankey to destroy the draft proclamation. See 'most secret' appendix to conclusions of conference of ministers, in Hankey's hand, CAB 21/255 (5.30 p.m.); see also attached note by Hankey indicating that on 23 Oct. 1922 he had received orders from Churchill's private secretary to destroy draft proclamation. For a copy of the proclamation see LG F/185/1/6.
278. ibid, i.e. 'most secret' appendix by Hankey to conference of ministers, CAB 21/255 (5.30 p.m.).
279. ibid.
280. Conference of ministers, 25 June 1922, 11.30 a.m., CAB 21/255.
281. ibid.
282. ibid.
283. COM notes, 26 June 1922, SPO M2, PG minutes 26 June 1922, MP P7B/244.
284. PG minutes, 27 June 1922, P7B/244.
285. ibid.
286. For a subsequent statement by O'Connor that no demand had been made, ever, to evacuate the building, see D. Macardle, *The Irish Republic*, (4th edn. 1951) p.971.
287. Cope to Curtis, 28 June 1922, CO 906/21. For Cope's requests, CO 906/21.
288. Collins to Churchill, 28 and 29 June 1922 CO 906/21; Cope to Curtis, 28 June 1922, CO 906/21; message from the War Office, 10 p.m., CO 906/21.
289. Churchill to Cope, 28 June 1922 and Churchill to Collins, 28 June 1922, both in CO 906/21.
290. ibid.
291. Cope to Curtis, 28 June 1922, CO 906/21.
292. Churchill to Cope for Macready, 28 June 1922, CO 906/21.
293. Churchill to Cope, 28 June 1922, CO 906/21.
294. Churchill to Collins, 29 June 1922, CO 906/21.
295. Curtis to Cope, 29 June 1922, CO 906/21; Churchill to Collins, 29 June 1922, CO 906/21.
296. Poblacht na hÉireann, *War News*, 29 June 1922.
297. Longford and O'Neill, *De Valera*, p.196.
298. Churchill to Collins, 30 June 1922, CO 906/21.
299. See below p.000.
300. Above, note 296.

Chapter 7
EPILOGUE: JULY 1922 – MAY 1923
(pp.195–227)

1. See Cope to Curtis, 28 June 1922, CO 906/21.
2. Cope to Curtis, 29 June 1922, CO 906/21.
3. Cope to Curtis, 29 June 1922, CO 906/21 and Collins to Churchill, 28 June 1921, CO 906/21.

4. Cope to Sturgis, 2 July 1922, CO 906/21.
5. Cope to Sturgis, 2 July 1922, CO 906/21.
6. Curtis to Cope, 4 July 1922, CO 906/21.
7. Collins to O'Kane, 17 July 1922, in Taylor, *Michael Collins*, p.193.
8. For reference to the Four Courts split see above p.190, also 'memo of GHQ staff at the Four Courts surrender', EOM P17/B/2/4.
9. Cope to Sturgis, 1 July 1922 and Cope to Curtis 5 July 1922, CO 906/21.
10. PG minutes, 1 July 1922, MP P7B/244.
11. ibid.
12. PG minutes, 2 July 1922, MP P7B/244.
13. PG minutes, 3 and 5 July 1922, MP P7B/244.
14. PG minutes, 3, 4, 7 and 8 July 1922, MP P7B/244.
15. PG minutes, 8 July 1922, MP P7B/244.
16. Memo on meeting held on 12 July 1922, MP P7B/177. PG minutes, 12 July 1922, MP P7B/244.
17. ibid.
18. PG minutes 12 and 17 July 1922, MP P7B/244.
19. ibid.
20. Proposed terms between Hannigan and the executive forces led by Lynch in Limerick, 3 July 1922, EOM P17/E33. MacMaghunsa to Lynch, 5 July 1922, EOM P17/B/1/5.
21. Prout to GHQ, 4 Aug. 1922, MP P7B/18.
22. O'Duffy proclamation, 4 Aug. 1922, MP P7B/68.
23. Dalton to C in C, 12 Aug. 1922, MP P7B/20.
24. ibid.
25. C/S to A/C/S, 27 and 30 Aug. 1922, EOM P17/E17; and C/S to O/C 1SD, 28 Aug. 1922, MP P7B/90.
26. C/S to O/C 1SD, 28 Aug. 1922, MP P7B/90; Adj. Cork No. 1 Bde to Adj. 1SD, 30 Aug. 1922, MP P7B/90.
27. Churchill to Cope, 17 July 1922, CO 906/21.
28. W. Maxwell Scott to Macready, 1 Aug. 1922, CO 739/11.
29. Worthington-Evans to Churchill, 6 July 1922, CO 739/11; Churchill to Worthington-Evans, 7 July 1922, CO 739/11; Cabinet, 24 July 1922, CAB 23/30.
30. Cabinet, 5 Oct. 1922, CAB 23/31.
31. Churchill to Cosgrave, 25 Oct. 1922, CO 906/22.
32. Macready appreciation, 7 Sept. 1922, LG F/102/2; Curtis to Cope, 7 Sept. 1922, CO 739/6; for Breen's approach to Collins see O'Duffy to Collins, 11 Aug. 1922, MP P7B/39.
33. Collins to Cosgrave, 25 July 1922, MP P7B/29; Collins to the government, 30 July 1922, SPO S 1446.
34. *Dáil Éireann, Parliamentary Debates, Official Report*, vol. 1 (Dublin 1922), 9 Sept. 1922, cols 17-20 (hereafter Dáil Éireann, *Report*).
35. ibid.

36. ibid, 9 Sept. 1922, cols 29-30.
37. ibid, 12 Sept. 1922, cols 173-4.
38. ibid, 18 Sept. 1922, cols 358-61.
39. Article 17 of the *Articles of Agreement* . . . provided for the constitution of a provisional government to administer Southern Ireland between 6 December 1921 and the date upon which the Free State institutions were constituted, an arrangement which could not 'continue in force . . . beyond 12 months'.
40. Cope to Freeston, 15 Oct. 1922, CO 906/22 and Lloyd George to Cosgrave, 19 Oct. 1922, CO 906/22.
41. Account of a meeting between Law and Cosgrave, 24 Oct. 1922, CO 739/17.
42. Curtis to Churchill, 17 Sept. 1922, CO 906/22.
43. Cosgrave to Churchill, 8 Sept. 1922, CO 906/22.
44. Craig to Churchill, c. 14 Sept. 1922, CO 739/1; Cope to Curtis, 22 Sept. 1922, CO 739/1; Curtis to Churchill, 17 Sept. 1922, CO 906/22; and draft letter to Cosgrave, September 1922, CO 739/9.
45. O'Duffy notice for the press on recruitment for civic guard, 2 Oct. 1922, SPO S 1810.
46. Dáil Éireann, *Report*, 29 Sept. 1922, cols. 955-6.
47. Staff meeting, agenda and report, 15 Oct. 1922. MP P7B/177.
48. PG minutes 15 and 29 Sept. 1922, MP P7B/245; Dáil Éireann, *Report*, 26, 27 and 28 Sept. 1922.
49. ibid, Dáil Éireann, *Report*, 26, 27, 28 Sept. 1922.
50. ibid, General regulations, 2 Oct. 1922, SPO S 1764.
51. The amnesty notice to the newspapers was signed by L. T. MacCosgair, on behalf of the government of Saorstát Éireann; PG minutes, 3 Oct. 1922, SPO G1/3.
52. IRA General Order No. 9, 22 July 1922, made it possible to billet also in houses (often mansions) usually owned by those hostile to republicans, EOM P17/E/16.
53. Derrig was TD for West Mayo; he had been in the IRA before the truce, and became prominent as a staff officer during it. He subsequently became a member of the Four Courts executive, and his name appeared on the Lynch call to arms of 28 June; he then became adjutant of the northern and eastern command, combining the post with that of assistant adjutant general.
54. C/S to de Valera, 30 Aug. 1922, MP P7B/86.
55. C/S to A/C/S, 27 Aug. 1922, EOM P17/E17.
56. C/S to A/C/S, 25 July 1922, EOM P17/E/16.
57. ibid.
58. ibid.
59. C/S to O/C 2SD, 29 July 1922, EOM P17/E/33.
60. A/G for C/S to A/C/S, 5 Sept. 1922, EOM P17/E/18.
61. Deasy to A/C/S, 5 Sept. 1922, EOM P17/E/18; div/adj to Miss MacSweeney, 5 Sept. 1922, MP P7B/86.
62. A/G for C/S to A/C/S, 5 Sept. 1922, EOM P17/E/18; C/S to O/C 1SD, 1 and 6 Sept. 1922, in EOM P17/E/35 and SPO S 2210.

63. De Valera to 'A chara', 7 Sept. 1922, MP P7B/86.
64. ibid.
65. ibid.
66. C/S to O/C 1SD, 1 Sept. 1922, EOM P17/E/35.
67. O'Connor to O'Malley, 12 Sept. 1922, EOM P17/E/18.
68. McKelvey to O'Malley, 24 Aug. 1922, MP P7B/83; Mellows ('LOM') to O/C N and E command, 9 Aug. 1922, EOM P/17/E/17; Mellows to A/G, 11 Sept. 1922, EOM P17/E/18.
69. A/C/S to C/S, 24 Sept. 1922, EOM P17/E/13; memo to O'M, 8 Sept. 1922, MP P7B/86; signed request for convening 2nd Dáil by 8th September, MP P7B/86.
70. De Valera to COM, 13 Sept. 1922, MP P7B/86.
71. ibid.
72. Minutes of meetings of republican TDs, 14 Sept. 1922, MP P7B/86.
73. It is not clear on what date the previous meeting occurred, whether on the 15 or 21 July. See A/G to O/C 3 batt., 1D bde, 22 July 1922, EOM P17/E/33 and O'Donoghue, *No Other Law*; for the October executive see report of IRA executive, 16-17 Oct. 1922, EOM P17/E/37.
74. Report of IRA executive, 16-17 Oct. 1922, EOM P17/E/37.
75. ibid.
76. ibid.
77. ibid., second day. For de Valera's initiative, see O'Donoghue, *No Other Law*. There is no record among the available primary materials; Longford and O'Neill, *De Valera* suggest that de Valera took the initiative on the matter and submitted a memorandum to the executive; O'Donoghue, *No Other Law* quotes from this document in which de Valera set out the reasons for the establishment of a government: as a rallying point, in order to preserve the continuity of the republic and to establish a claim to the funds and other resources, of the republic. De Valera pointed out that the proper body to set up such a government would be the elected representatives of the people, but the republican party was prevented from meeting. He then interpreted the present circumstances as arising out of army action, rather than being the result of the policy of the republican party; and because there was 'no doubt' as to 'whether the army would give ... wholehearted allegiance to any other than its own executive' it was, therefore, 'obvious that the army must take the initiative in causing the government to be set up'. Longford and O'Neill, *De Valera*, p.200; O'Donoghue, *No Other Law*, pp.275-6.
78. IRA proclamation, 28 Oct. 1922, MP P7B/87; Dáil Éireann official communique (English translation), 26 Oct. 1922, MP P7B/87.
79. See proclamation in *Freeman's Journal*, 8 Nov. 1922; also de Valera-Ruttledge proclamation, 17 Nov. 1922 in *Freeman's Journal*, 21 Nov. 1922.

80. ibid. Also de Valera to each member of the army council, 13 Nov. 1922, MP P7B/87.
81. De Valera to each member of the army council, 13 Nov. 1922, MP P7B/87.
82. Report on Cork command circulated to HQ staff, 18 Nov. 1922, MP P7B/67.
83. C-in-C to MacEoin, 19 Oct. 1922, MP P7B/74; 'phone message from western command, 24 Oct. 1922, MP P7B/74.
84. Mulcahy report to cabinet, 17 Oct. 1922, MP P7B/259.
85. ibid.
86. Dalton to C/S, 2 Sept. 1922, MP P7B/71; O'Duffy to C/S, 6 Sept. 1922, MP P7B/71.
87. Dalton had served with the British army during the war, and subsequently returned to Dublin where he became associated with the headquarters group. During the truce he became chief liaison officer, and after the treaty was made responsible on the Irish side for the details connected with the British evacuation. After 28 June he was appointed to the command in Cork; and after Collins's death he considered – as apparently others did also – the possibility of his succeeding Collins as C-in-C, the prospect of which he discussed in October with Curtis. See Curtis to Masterson Smith, 19/20 Oct. 1922, CO 739/7.
88. See below, pp.210-11.
89. Wireless message from Kilkenny, interview with Phelan, 11 Dec. 1922, MP P7B/64; Kilkenny command to D/I, 17 Dec. 1922, MP P7B/64; report by Price on Kilkenny command, c. early Jan. 1923, MP P7B/64; wireless message from MacCarthy at Kilkenny, 12 Dec. 1922, MP P7B/64; Prout to Mulcahy 16 Dec. 1922, MP P7B/64; C.1/7, 15 Dec. 1922, MP P7B/245; memo of president's interview with Gorey, December 1922 and Cosgrave to Mulcahy, 15 Jan. 1923, MP P7B/64.
90. President's interview with Gorey, December 1922 and Cosgrave to Mulcahy, 15 Jan. 1923, MP P7B/64.
91. Mulcahy to A/G, 2 Sept. 1922, MP P7B/44; O'Duffy to Mulcahy, 6 Sept. 1922, MP P7B/71; Capt. Walpole to Capt. Murray, 28 Sept. 1922, MP P7B/71; intelligence report to C-in-C, Oct./Nov. 1922, SPO S 1719.
92. O'Connor to O'Malley, 12 Sept. 1922, EOM P17/E/18.
93. Note for staff, 9 Oct. 1922. MP P7B/177. For the negotiations with the British see PG minutes, 19 Sept. 1922, NP P7B/245; Churchill to governor of Seychelles and governor of St Helena, 28 Sept. 1922, CO 906/22; governor of Seychelles and governor of St Helena, respectively to Churchill, 30 Sept. 1922, CO 906/22; Curtis note, 4 Oct. 1922, CO 739/7; Masterson Smith to Devonshire, 20 Nov. 1922, CO 739/8; PG minutes 16 and 23 Nov. 1922, MP P7B/245. See also PG minutes 9 and 30 Oct. 1922, MP 07B/245; staff meeting, 15 Oct. 1922 and Mulcahy memo 19 Oct. 1922, both in MP P7B/177.

94. See above p.204. For military arrests see minutes of staff meeting, 8 Nov. 1922, MP P7B/177 and general routine order no. 6, 4 Dec. 1922, MP P7B/167.
95. Minutes of staff meeting, 14 Nov. 1922, MP P7B/177.
96. PG minutes, 28 Sept. 1922, MP P7B/245.
97. ibid.
98. Official army report issued after the four executions, 17 Nov. 1922.
99. See Loughnane to Curtis, 20 Nov. 1922, CO 739/8.
100. Proclamation signed by de Valera and Ruttledge, 17 Nov. 1922 in *Freeman's Journal* of 21 Nov. 1922; list of those affected in MP P7B/87.
101. List of those affected by proclamation of 17 Nov. 1922, MP P7B/87; also IRA proclamation 'civic guard' and C/S to all O/Cs, 22 Nov. 1922, EOM P17/E/38.
102. Longford and O'Neill, *De Valera*, p.207.
103. C/S army council to speaker, provisional parliament, 28 Nov. 1922, EOM P17/E/38.
104. ibid.
105. C/S to O/Cs all divs., 30 Nov. 1922, EOM P17/E/38.
106. Operation order no. 14, C/S to O/C third Cork brigade, 20 Nov. 1922, EOM P17/E/39.
107. Murphy to C-in-C, 7 Dec. 1922, MP P7B/72; MacEoin to C-in-C, 19 Dec. 1922, MP P7B/75; C-in-C to Murphy, 11 Dec. 1922, MP P7B/72; memo. on Cork command, 2 Dec. 1922, MP P7B/67; cmd. adj. to C/S, 22 Dec. 1922, MP P7B/67.
108. C.1/13, 20 Dec. 1922, MP P7B/245.
109. Mulcahy memo, 12 Jan. 1923, MP P7B/325.
110. Dáil Éireann, *Report*, 22 Nov. 1922, col 2283; 28 Nov. 1922, cols 2364-6.
111. For reference to the object and limitations of the third Dáil, see Dáil Éireann, *Report*, 13 Sept. 1922, cols 221-2 and 1 Nov. 1922, cols 2038-40.
112. Cabinet, 29 Nov. 1922, CAB 23/32.
113. For developments and discussions regarding the evacuation of Pettigo and Beleek see Curtis to Cope, 1 Sept. 1922 and Curtis to Masterson-Smith, 6 Nov. 1922, in CO 906/22; Loughnane to Curtis, 29 and 31 Oct 1922, CO 906/22; Masterson-Smith to Loughnane, 3 Nov. 1922, CO 906/22; Tallents' note on Pettigo for Masterson-Smith, 13 Nov. 1922, CO 739/1; Masterson-Smith to O'Higgins, 17 Nov. 1922, CO 739/1; Cabinet, 29 Nov. 1922, CAB 23/32; Sturgis to O'Higgins, 1 Dec. 1922, Tallents to Freeston, 21 Dec. 1922, Loughnane to Whiskard, 11 Jan. 1923, in CO 739/1; Tallents to Masterson-Smith, 13 Nov. 1922, CO 739/1; Anderson to Tallents, 31 Oct. 1923, CO 739/17; Tallents to Anderson 1 and 2 Nov. 1923, CO 739/21.
114. Dáil Éireann, *Report*, 20 Dec. 1922, cols 407-8.

115. Curtis memo, 9 Nov. 1922, CO 739/8; Cosgrave to prime minister, 16 Dec. 1922 in Cabinet, 19 Dec. 1922, CAB 23/32; Cabinet, 29 Dec. 1922, CAB 23/32; Loughnane to Masterson-Smith, 3 Jan. 1923 and Devonshire to Healy, 3 Jan 1923, both in CO 739/17.
116. Dáil Éireann, *Report*, 30 Jan. 1923, col 1090. See *The Public General Acts* passed by the Oireachtas of Saorstát Éireann during the year 1923 (Stationery Office, 1925), no. 2, pp.9-11.
117. For developments before Dowling's release see: Loughnane to Masterson-Smith, 5 Jan. 1923, CO 739/17; Loughnane to Curtis, 17 Mar. 1923 and to Sturgis, 5 June 1923, both in CO 739/18; Sturgis to Anderson, 6 June 1923, Masterson-Smith to Devonshire, 9 June 1923, and to S o S for War, 3 July 1923, in CO 739/18; Hill-Dillon to Sturgis, 18 June 1923, CO 739/18.
118. General routine order no. 16, 24 Jan. 1923, MP P7B/168.
119. Price preliminary report, c. early Jan. 1923, MP P7B/64; correspondence regarding Skibereen army accounts, Jan. 1923, SPO S 1944; Ó Muirthile report on Cork command, 23 Jan. 1923, MP P7B/67.
120. C.1/27, 10 Jan. 1923, MP P7B/245.
121. O'Higgins memo, Jan. 1923, MP P7B/321.
122. ibid.
123. Hogan memo to president, 11 Jan. 1923, MP P7B/321.
124. General order of the army council, 8 Jan. 1923, MP P7B/318; Dáil Éireann, *Report*, 17 Jan. 1923, cols 876-9.
125. Dáil Éireann, *Report*, 17 Jan. 1923, col 930.
126. Ayres to Cosgrave, 12 Dec. 1922 and draft reply (though not clear whether sent) of 1 Jan. 1923, SPO S1369/13.
127. Dáil Éireann, *Report*, 17 Jan. 1923, cols 897-9.
128. ibid, 8 Dec. 1922, cols 67-71.
129. ibid, 17 Jan. 1923, col 919.
130. ibid, 19 Jan. 1923, cols 966-73.
131. Cosgrave to Mulcahy, 25 Jan. 1923, MP P7B/101.
132. Dáil Éireann, *Report*, 7 Feb. 1923, col 1359.
133. ibid.
134. ibid, 31 Jan. 1923, cols 1213-4.
135. For the preparations to deal with kidnapping, GOC-in-C to each GOC, 23 Jan. 1923 and note on 'kidnapping by irregulars', 22 Jan. 1923, MP P7B/177; Hogan warning, published in the newspapers, 31 Jan. 1923.
136. Cosgrave to Mulcahy, c. 25 Jan. 1923, MP P7B/101.
137. Thomas Maguire, O/C 2WD, had been captured on 24 Oct. 1922; Michael Kilroy, O/C 4WD had been captured on 24 Nov. 1922.
138. Letter signed J.F. O'Dowd, 4 Jan. 1923 (found on the occasion of the arrest of P.J. McDonnell of the 4WD), MP P7B/90.
139. ibid.
140. O/C 4WD to J.F. O'Dowd, 17 Jan. 1923, EOM P7B/1/6.
141. Notes of conversation with 'O'M', 23 Feb. 1923, MP P7B/178.

142. For Deasy's attitude and Lynch's reaction, see for example, Lynch to Deasy, 6 Sept. 1922, SPO S 2210; Deasy statement, 8 Feb. 1923, MP P7B/284; for this account of the relative popularity of Lynch and Deasy, see Mulcahy report to cabinet, 16 Oct. 1922, MP P7B/259.
143. Prout to Mulcahy, 25 Jan. 1923 enclosing proposals; Deasy statement, 8 Feb. 1923; Mulcahy memo, 9 Feb. 1923; Mulcahy to Prout, 26 Jan. 1923, r. 11.45 a.m.; Prout to Mulcahy, 26 Jan. 1923, s. 2.55 p.m.; all in MP P7B/284.
144. Prout to Mulcahy, 26 Jan 1923, s. 6.47 p.m., MP P7B/284.
145. Mulcahy to Prout, 26 Jan. 1923, r. 11.15 p.m.; Prout to Mulcahy, 27 Jan. 1923, s. 12.38 a.m.; D/I for Mulcahy to Prout, 27 Jan. 1923, s. 2.55 a.m.; all in MP P7B/284.
146. Prout to Mulcahy, 27 Jan. 1923, s. 4.45 a.m.; and Mulcahy to Prout, 27 Jan. 1923; both in MP P7B/284.
147. Prout to Mulcahy, 27 Jan. 1923; statement by Deasy, 29 Jan. 1923; Deasy statement of events since 18 Jan., 8 Feb. 1923, Mulcahy memo, 9 Feb. 1923, all in MP P7B/284.
148. C/S to O/Cs 2 Feb. 1923, EOM P17/E/45; C/S to O/C Britain, Feb. 1923, MP P7B/89.
149. ibid.
150. F. Barrett to Deasy, 5 Feb. 1923 (private and official); S. MacSweeney to Deasy, 5 Feb. 1923; Carty to Deasy, 6 Feb. 1923; all in MP P7B/284.
151. C/S to Deasy, 5 Feb. 1923 and with enclosures, c. 5 Feb. 1923, MP P7B/284.
152. First battalion surrender, 6 Feb. 1923, MP 7B/284; Daly to Mulcahy 17 Feb. 1923 and Mulcahy to Daly, 18 Feb. 1923, MP 7B/284.
153. MacLochlan to Brennan, 3 Feb. 1923; Brennan to C-in-C, 6 Feb. 1923; MacLochlan to Deasy, 7 Feb. 1923; GOC Limerick to C-in-C with reply from prisoners, 8 Feb. 1923; all in MP P7B/284.
154. Mulcahy to GOC Cork command, 16 Feb. 1923; GOC Kerry to C-in-C, 17 Feb. 1923; C-in-C to GOC Kerry, 18 Feb. 1923; all in MP P7B/284.
155. Mulcahy to each member of the army council, 7 Feb. 1923, MP P7B/284.
156. Army council decision, 12 Feb. 1923, MP P7B/178; also C.1/47, 16 Feb. 1923, MP P7B/243.
157. Cosgrave statement published in newspapers, 17 Feb. 1923.
158. ibid.
159. C/S to all ranks, 9 Feb. 1923, EOM P17/E/45.
160. GHQ memo, no. 10, 10 Feb. 1923, MP P7B/90.
161. A/G to O/C W cmd., 12 Feb. 1923 and A/G to C/S, 19 Feb. 1923, both in EOM P17/E/45; GOC Cork to C-in-C 19 Feb. 1923 and C-in-C to GOC Cork, 19 Feb. 1923, MP P7B/284.
162. Correspondence between GOC Kerry and C-in-C, 17-19 Feb. 1923, MP P7B/284; A/G to C/S, 19 Feb. 1923, EOM P17/E/45.

163. GOC Cork to C-in-C, 19 Feb. 1923, MP P7B/284; and GOC Cork to C-in-C, 22 Feb. 1923, MP P7B/284.
164. Memo. on Con Moylan, 23 Feb. 1923, MP P7B/178; duplicated, with additional points, MP P7B/178.
165. Report of divisional meeting, 26 Feb. 1923, MP P7B/89.
166. De Valera to neutral IRA in reply to theirs of 16 Feb., in *Daily Bulletin*, 22 Feb. 1923, EOM P17/B/1/4; A/G to C/S, 26 Feb. 1923, EOM P17/E/46.
167. De Valera to neutral IRA men in reply to theirs of 16 Feb. 1923, *Daily Bulletin*, 22 Feb. 1923, EOM P17/B/14; A/G to president, 20 Feb. 1923, MP P7B/89; Oifig an tUachtaráin to A/G, 22 Feb. 1923, MP P7B/89; A/G to O/C 1WD, 27 Feb. 1923, EOM P17/E/46.
168. President to A/G, 28 Feb. 1923, MP P7B/89.
169. Mulcahy memo., 1 Mar. 1923, MP P7B/284.
170. General order no. 17, A/G to O/Cs, 8 Mar. 1923, EOM P17/E46; C/S to A/G, 8 Mar. 1923, EOM P17/E/46.
171. Twomey for C/S to O/C 3SD, 12 Mar. 1923, EOM P17/E/46; C/S to A/G, 12 Mar. 1923, EOM P17/E/46.
172. Minutes of executive, 23-26 Mar. 1923, EOM P17/E/47 and MP P7B/89.
173. ibid.
174. ibid. (for February council see above).
175. ibid.
176. See Dáil Éireann, *Report*, 3 May 1923, p.360.
177. Minutes of executive meeting, 23-26 Mar. 1923, MP P7B/89 and EOM P17/E/47; for references by both governments to Aiken, see Dáil Éireann, *Report*, 7 Feb. 1923, col 356; Tallents to Anderson, 27 Feb. 1923, CO 739/17.
178. Dáil Éireann, *Report*, 2 Apr. 1923, cols 62-3; O'Donoghue, *No Other Law*, pp.302-9.
179. C.1/84, 16 Apr. 1923, MP P7B/247.
180 Minutes of executive meeting (adjourned from 26 Mar), 20 Apr. 1923, EOM P17/E/51.
181. ibid.
182. ibid.
183. ibid.
184. Minutes of the government and army council meeting, 26-27 Apr. 1923, EOM P17/E/51.
185. ibid.
186. C/S to O/Cs 27 Apr. 1923, MP P7B/90; de Valera proclamation, 27 Apr. 1923, MP P7B/90.
187. ibid.
188. ibid.
189. See Burke to Mulcahy, 16 Feb. 1923, note for C-in-C 23 Feb. 1923, and interview between Cosgrave and Hannigan and Burke (of the neutral IRA), 27 Feb. 1923, in MP P7B/284.
190. C.1/75 and C.1/78 of 27 and 30 Mar. 1923, MP P7B/247.

191. C.1/78, 30 Mar. 1923, MP P7B/247; report of meeting of subcommittee of the executive council, held on Friday 30 Mar. 1923, attached to C.1/78.
192. Dáil Éireann, *Report,* 2 Apr. 1923, cols 60-64; C.1/81 and C.1/85, 9 and 17 Apr. 1923, MP P7B/247; 'Brief history of events', unsigned, 29 Jan., 2 Feb., 2 Apr. 1923, MP P7B/247.
193. Logue letter to the *Freeman's Journal,* 23 Apr. 1923; C.1/85, C.1/87, C.1/89, C.1/91, 17, 19, 21 and 24 Apr. 1923, MP P7B/247; Loughnane to Curtis, 17 Apr. 1923, CO 739/18; Cosgrave interview, *Freeman's Journal,* 20 Apr. 1923.
194. Loughnane to Curtis, 17 Apr. 1923, CO 739/18.
195. See February memo., 1923 in MP P7B/178; A/G to C/S 12 Mar. 1923, EOM P17/E46.
196. Kennedy memo. to president, 30 Apr. 1923, SPO S 2210.
197. C. Ó hUigín to president, c. 29 Apr. 1923, SPO S 2210.
198. Dáil Éireann, *Report,* 9 May 1923, cols 678-9.
199. ibid., cols 679-81; see also SPO file S 2210.
200. ibid., cols 681-2; for draft Cosgrave to Jameson, 8 May 1923, SPO S 2210.
201. ibid.; see also C.1/102, 8 May 1923, MP P7B/247.
202. ibid., *Report,* Cosgrave to Jameson and C.1/102; see also Douglas memo to president, c. May 1923, SPO S 2210 and Jameson and Douglas to de Valera, 8 May 1923, SPO S 2210.
203. Douglas to president, c. May 1923 (unsigned, undated, but pencilled note saying copy Douglas interview with de Valera) refers to period covered by the negotiations and to views of both Douglas and Jameson after interview; SPO S 2210.
204. IRA executive, 20 Apr. 1923 (adjourned from 26 March), EOM P17/E/51.
205. De Valera/Aiken proclamation, 24 May 1923, copies in MP P7B/90. For the decision see the minutes of meeting held on 13-14 May, 1923, EOM P17/E/51.

Sources and Bibliography

The following is strictly limited to a list of those sources specifically referred to in the text and references. The names and titles used are those which were in use between 1914 and 1923.

A. MANUSCRIPT SOURCES

I. The private papers and/or diaries of:

H. H. Asquith	*Bodleian Library, Oxford*
Stanley Baldwin	*Cambridge University Library*
Robert Barton	*National Library of Ireland*
Michael Collins	*National Library of Ireland*
Lord Derby	*Liverpool City Library*
George Gavan Duffy	*National Library of Ireland*
H.A.L. Fisher	*Bodleian Library, Oxford*
A. Bonar Law*	*House of Lords Record Office, London*
D. Lloyd George*	*House of Lords Record Office, London*
Edwin Montagu	*Trinity College, Cambridge*
R. J. Mulcahy	*Department of Archives, University College, Dublin*
Art O'Brien	*National Library of Ireland*
William O'Brien	*National Library of Ireland*
E. O'Malley	*Department of Archives, University College, Dublin*
Count Plunkett	*National Library of Ireland*
Clement Shorter	*National Library of Ireland*
L. Worthington-Evans	*Bodleian Library, Oxford*

*Reproduced by permission of the Clerk of the Records, House of Lords Record Office.

II. Public Records

Cabinet (CAB)	Records of the cabinet office in the Public Record Office, London
Colonial (CO)	Records of the colonial office in the Public Record Office, London
Dáil Éireann (DE or A-T)	Records of the ministry and cabinet of Dáil Éireann in the State Paper Office, Dublin

R Series and S Series   Files relating to the provisional government and Irish Free State in the State Paper Office, Dublin.

P3269   Microfilm of the minutes of Sinn Féin standing committee in the National Library of Ireland.

B. PUBLISHED SOURCES

I. Newspapers and Periodicals
Belfast Newsletter
Eire
Freeman's Journal
The Free State
The Irish Bulletin
The Irish Independent
The Irish Times
The Morning Post
An tÓglach
Poblacht na hÉireann (The Republic of Ireland)
The Times

II. Official Publications
Dáil Éireann. Minutes of Proceedings of the First Parliament of the Republic of Ireland, 1919-21. Official Record, Dublin
Dáil Éireann. Official Report. Debate on the Treaty Between Great Britain and Ireland signed in London on 6 December 1921, Dublin 1922
Dáil Éireann, Official Report for the periods 16-26 August 1921, and 28 February-8 June 1922, Dublin 1922
Dáil Éireann, Parliamentary Debates, Official Report, vols. i, ii, iii, Dublin, 1922-
Parliamentary Debates, Fifth Series (Hansard):
   House of Commons, 1914-22
   House of Lords, 1914-22
Report: 'Arrangements Governing the Cessation of Active Operations in Ireland, which came into force on 11 July, 1921', 1921, Cmd. 1534, xxix 427
Saorstát Éireann, the Constitution of the Irish Free State (Saorstát Éireann) Act, 1922 and the Public General Acts passed by the Oireachtas of Saorstát Éireann during the year 1922, Dublin, n.d.
Saorstát Éireann, the Public General Acts passed by the Oireachtas of Saorstát Éireann during the year 1923, Dublin 1925
Seanad Éireann, Parliamentary Debates, Official Report, vols i, ii, Dublin 1922-

III. Diaries, personal recollections, biography and secondary material
Anon., *Dublin's Fighting Story, 1916-21,* Tralee, n.d.
Anon., *Kerry's Fighting Story, 1916-21,* Tralee, n.d.

Anon., *Limerick's Fighting Story, 1916-21*, Tralee, n.d.

Anon., *With the IRA in the Fight for Freedom*, Tralee, n.d.

Beaslaí, Piaras, *Michael Collins and the Making of a New Ireland*, 2 vols, Dublin 1926

Birkenhead, Lord, *Frederick Edwin, Earl of Birkenhead*, London 1935

Callwell, C.E., *Field-Marshall Sir Henry Wilson: his Life and Diaries*, London 1927

Jones, T., *Whitehall Diary: III, Ireland 1919-25*, ed. K. Middlemas, London 1971

Kee, R., *The Green Flag: a History of Irish Nationalism*, London 1972

Longford, the Earl of, and O'Neill, T.P., *Eamon de Valera*, London 1970

Macready, N., *Annals of an active Life*, 2 vols, London 1924

O'Donoghue, F., *No Other Law: the story of Liam Lynch and the Irish Republican Army, 1916-22*, Dublin 1954

Riddell, Lord, *Intimate Diary of the Peace Conference and After*, London 1933

Scott, C.P., *Political Diaries of C.P. Scott, 1911-28*, ed. T. Wilson, London 1970.

Taylor, Rex, *Michael Collins: The Lost Leader*, Four Square edn, London 1958

Biographical Notes

Addison, Christopher (50).* MP (Lib.) since 1910, formerly a professor of anatomy. Minister of munitions 1915-16, in charge of reconstruction 1917. President, local government board, 1919. First minister of health, 1919-21. Minister without portfolio, 1921.

AE. See Russell, George.

Aiken, Frank (21). IRA officer. Born in Co. Antrim; educated Christian Brothers, Newry. Joined Volunteers locally 1913; captain, Camlough company, 1918. Officer, Newry brigade, 1921 and commandant fourth northern division. Objected to the treaty; fought in the civil war; became C/S IRA 20 Apr. 1923.

Anderson, John (37). Civil servant. Joint under-secretary to lord lieutenant of Ireland, 1920-22; recommended by Warren Fisher as one who would 'rapidly acquire the real control'. Entered civil service 1905 (colonial office); secretary, ministry of shipping, 1917-19; to the local government board, April 1919; second secretary to ministry of health, 1919. Chairman, board of inland revenue, 1919-22.

Ashe, Thomas. Died on hunger strike 1917. Member of the IRB and IRA. Had commanded successful ambush of British forces in 1916 at Ashbourne, Co. Meath.

Asquith, Henry Herbert (67). MP (Lib.) since 1886. Prime minister, 1908-16. Leader of the Liberal Party since 1908.

Baldwin, Stanley. MP (Con.) since 1908. Joint financial Secretary to the treasury, 1917-21; president of the board of trade, 1921-22; led the Conservative revolt against Lloyd George in October 1922; chancellor of the exchequer, 1922-3; prime minister, 1923. Described by Channon as 'half Milton, half Machiavelli: History may make him out to be a great man'.

*Age in 1919.

Balfour, Arthur James (71). MP (Con.) since 1874. Statesman and former prime minister, 1902-05; leader of the Conservative party, 1902-11; first lord of the admiralty, 1915-16; foreign secretary, 1916-19; lord president of the council, 1919-. Balfour did not 'like the idea of Irish unity' and did not 'wish to encourage it'. It was 'a geographical accident that Ireland was surrounded by sea'.

Barry, Tom (22). IRA officer. Corkman. Served with the British army in the great war. Returned to Ireland 1919. Intelligence officer for IRA and led the flying column of Cork no. 3 brigade. Liaison officer for the martial law area during the truce; objected to the treaty and supported the Four Courts leaders. Officer and member of the IRA executive 1922-3.

Barton, Robert (28). TD (Sinn Féin) since 1918. Gentleman nationalist born in Co. Wicklow. Served in British army during the great war. Subsequently joined Sinn Féin. Member of the Dáil cabinet, 1919. Delegate to the treaty conference 1921. Signed the treaty but subsequently opposed it.

Beaslaí, Piaras. TD (Sinn Féin) since 1918. Journalist and editor of *An tÓglach*.

Beaverbrook, 1st baron. William Maxwell Aitken (40) MP (Con.) 1910-17. Politician and newspaper proprietor of Canadian origin. Educated in Canada and served as Canadian official in great war. Elected to the house of commons for Ashton-under-Lyne in 1910. Chancellor of the Duchy of Lancaster and minister of information, 1918.

Birkenhead, 1st baron. Frederick Edwin Smith (47) MP (Con.) 1906-19. 'Tory Democrat.' Born Birkenhead; sat for Liverpool constituency; solicitor-general, 1915; attorney-general, 1915-19; lord chancellor, 1919-22 — an appointment described by *The Times* as 'carrying a joke too far' and about which the king had doubts. Thought Lloyd George 'alone' in 1918 could 'save this country'.

Blythe, Ernest (30). TD (Sinn Féin) since 1918. Minister of trade in the Dáil government, 1919-22; supported the treaty, minister for finance 1923-31. Born in Co. Antrim and worked as a clerk, a reporter, and an organiser of the Volunteers. Supported with the dourness of the northener the treaty and the Irish language.

Boland, Harry. Died August 1922. TD (Sinn Féin) since 1918. Member IRB and IRA. Honorary secretary, Sinn Féin. In America, 1919-20. Friend of both Collins and de Valera. Opposed the treaty. Acted as mediator but 'joined up' after 28 June 1922.

Boyd, Major-General Gerald Farrell (42). GOC Dublin district; had previously served in South Africa, 1899-1902, and the great war.

Breen, Dan. IRA officer, Tipperary. Involved in the 1919 ambush at Soloheadbeg.

Brugha, Cathal. Charles Burgess (45). Died July 1922. TD (Sinn Féin) since 1918. Born of Yorkshire parents. A candle manufacturer. Member of Gaelic League; vice-president Sinn Féin, 1916; Volunteer C/S 1917; president, Dáil ministry, Jan.-Apr. 1919 (in de Valera's absence); minister for defence, April 1919-Jan. 1922. Opposed the treaty. A republican and a fanatic of whom Collins said 'for his sincerity I would forgive him anything'.

Carson, Sir Edward (65). MP (Con.) for Dublin University, 1892-1918 and a Belfast constituency after 1918. Southern Unionist. Lawyer. Solicitor-general for Ireland 1892; solicitor-general 1900-06; attorney-general 1915; 1st lord of the admiralty, 1917; minister in the war cabinet without portfolio, 1917-18.

Cecil, Lord Robert (55). MP (Con.), 1906-10 and since 1912. Third son of Lord Salisbury. Minister of the Blockade, 1916-18; assistant secretary of state, foreign affairs, 1918; lord privy seal, 1923; in 1918 he would not acquiesce in home rule 'unless it was accepted by Ulster'; and once the cabinet resolved on a bill 'I shall resign'.

Chamberlain (Joseph) Austen (56). M.P. (Con.) since 1892. Secretary of state for India 1915-17; member of the war cabinet, 1918; chancellor of the exchequer, 1919-21; lord privy seal and leader of the house of commons, 1921-2.

Childers, Erskine. Died November 1922. Officer, gentleman and Irish nationalist. Clerk of the house of commons, 1895-1911; served in the great war with the royal navy; secretary, Irish Convention, 1917. Ran arms to Ireland in 1914 and later joined Sinn Féin, assisting with the Dáil's *Irish Bulletin*. Secretary to treaty delegation. Opposed the treaty; fought in civil war, arrested and executed in November 1922 for illegal possession of firearm. Zealot.

Churchill, Winston (45). MP since 1900 (Lib. 1906-, Con. 1900-06); president of the board of trade 1908-10; home secretary, 1910-11; first lord of the admiralty, 1911-15; chancellor of the Duchy of Lancaster, 1915; minister of munitions, 1917; secretary of state for war, 1918-22; secretary of state for the colonies, 1922.

Clune, Most Rev. Patrick Joseph (55). Bishop of Perth, Australia. Born in Ireland. Served as chaplain to the forces during the war and described by Lloyd George in 1920 as 'thoroughly loyal'.

Clynes, John Robert (50). MP (Lab.) since 1906. Junior office during the war.

Collins, Michael (29). TD (Sinn Féin) since 1918. Born and educated West Cork. Worked in London 1906-16 at post office, board of trade, stockbroking firm and trust company. In London joined IRB and by 1914 treasurer London and South England district. Returned to Ireland, 1916. Joined Volunteers and Gaelic League; junior staff captain in the 1916 rising which 'on the whole' he considered was 'bungled terribly, costing many a good life'. Imprisoned. Released from Frongoch, December 1916. Adjutant-general and director of organisation, Volunteer headquarters; for a period director of purchases. Minister for Finance, Dáil government from 1919. Member, treaty delegation, 1921. Supported the treaty and led the new provisional government, 1922. Killed in an ambush in Co. Cork, August 1922.

Cope, Alfred (39). Civil servant. Transferred from the ministry of pensions in 1920 to be assistant under-secretary for Ireland and clerk of the privy council, 1920-22.

Cosgrave, William T. (39). TD (Sinn Féin) since 1917. Chairman of Dublin Corporation's finance committee, 1916 and member of Dublin Corporation, 1919. Minister of local government, Dáil Éireann, 1919-22. Supported the treaty. Member provisional government, January 1922; acting chairman and chairman in succession to Collins. President, executive council of the Irish Free State, December 1922.

Craig, Sir James (48). MP (Unionist) since 1906 for a Co. Down constituency. Had served in the South African war and in the great war. Parliamentary secretary, ministry of pensions, 1919-20; parliamentary and financial secretary to the admiralty, 1920-21; first prime minister of Northern Ireland, 22 June 1922-.

Curtis, Lionel (47). Civil servant. Had served in South African war and was subsequently involved in administration of Johannesburg and the Transvaal. Fellow of All Souls; lecturer in colonial history, Oxford. Secretary to the Irish conference, 1921; adviser on Irish affairs, colonial office 1921-4.

Curzon, 1st Earl (60). Junior office, 1890s. Lord privy seal, 1915-16; president air board 1916; lord president of the council 1916-19; foreign secretary 1919-.

Derby, 17th earl. Edward George Villiers Stanley (54). Director-general recruiting, 1915-16; under-secretary for war, 1916; secretary of state for war, 1916-18; British ambassador, Paris, 1918-20. Met de Valera secretly in Dublin in 1921.

Derrig, Thomas (22). Mayoman. Volunteer and Sinn Féin TD since 1921. Commandant, Westport battalion, Volunteers and later West Mayo brigade. Objected to the treaty; supported Four Courts garrison, 1922; IRA adjutant, Dublin and eastern command, post 28 June 1922; member of IRA executive; captured early 1923.

Desart, 5th earl (71). Desart Court, Kilkenny and London. Barrister. Official positions included assistant solicitor to the treasury, 1878; director of public prosecutions, 1909; British plenipotentiary, London naval conference, 1908-09 and member international court of arbitration at the Hague.

De Valera, Eamon (37). TD (Sinn Féin) since 1917. Born in New York of Spanish father and Irish mother; brought up in Co. Limerick by uncle. Before 1914 Gaelic League member and Volunteer officer. 1916 commandant, occupied Boland's Mills; imprisoned; released June 1917; elected member for east Clare, July 1917; president Sinn Féin, 1917; president, Dáil Éireann, 1919-Jan 1922. In America July 1919-December 1920. Opposed the treaty and styled himself 'president' during civil war.

Duffy, George Gavan (37). TD (Sinn Féin) since 1918. Solicitor and member of the Irish bar. Irish envoy Paris peace conference, 1919 and Rome. Member of treaty delegation, 1921. Signed the treaty. Minister for foreign affairs, 1922.

Duggan, E.J. TD (Sinn Féin) since 1918. Solicitor since 1914. Involved in the rising 1916; IRA officer, intelligence, headquarters staff; friend of Collins; member treaty delegation; signed and supported treaty. Secretary, home affairs and member provisional and Irish Free State governments 1922.

Duke, Sir Henry Edward (64). MP (Con.) 1900-18. Chief secretary for Ireland, 1916-18. Barrister. Chaired royal commissions, 1915. Appointed Irish secretary by Asquith after the rising. Duke believed it would be 'an error . . . to impose . . . military service in Ireland without disposing of . . . home rule'.

Dunraven and Mount Earl, 4th earl. Windham Thomas Wyndham Quin (78). Chairman of the Irish land conference 1902-03 and president of the Irish reform association.

Fisher, Herbert Albert Laurens (54). MP (Lib.) since 1916. Formerly fellow and tutor New College, Oxford. President, board of education, 1916-. Fisher was flattered by Lloyd George's suggestion that he 'gave an intellectual cachet to his ministry, like Morley'.

Fisher, Sir (Norman Fenwick) Warren (40). Civil servant. Permanent secretary to the treasury and official head of the civil service, 1919-39. Chairman, board of inland revenue, 1918-19.

Fitzalan of Derwent. Edmund Bernard Fitzalan-Howard (64). MP (Con.) since 1894. Youngest son of 14th Duke of Norfolk. Chief Unionist whip, 1913-21; joint parliamentary secretary to the treasury, 1915-21; viceroy of Ireland, 1921-2.

Fitzgerald, Desmond. TD (Sinn Féin) since 1918. Director of publicity, Dáil Éireann, 1919-20; editor, Sinn Féin *Bulletin*. Supported the treaty. Dáil minister for publicity, 1922; minister for foreign affairs, 1922; and for external affairs, Irish Free State, 1922-7.

Fogarty, Most Rev. Michael (60). Bishop of Killaloe since 1904.

French, 1st Viscount. Field-Marshal John Denton Pinkstone French (67). Lord lieutenant of Ireland, 1918-21. Joined the navy in 1866 and the army in 1874. Inspector-general of the forces 1907-11; CIGS 1911-14; C-in-C expeditionary forces in France, 1914-15; C-in-C the troops stationed in the UK, 1915-18.

Geddes, Sir Aukland Campbell (40). British ambassador to the US since 1920. Director of recruiting, 1916-17; minister of national service, 1917-19; president, local government board, 1918-19; president, board of trade, 1919-20.

Geddes, Sir Eric Campbell (43). MP (Unionist) since 1917. Director-general, munitions supply, 1915-16; military railways, 1916-17; first lord of the admiralty, 1917-18; minister without portfolio, 1919; minister of transport, 1919-21.

Greenwood, Sir Hamar (49). MP (Lib.) since 1906. Chief secretary for Ireland 1920-22. Born and educated in Canada. Served in the great war, 1914-16; deputy assistant adjutant-general on Derby's staff, war office, 1916. Barrister, Gray's Inn. Under-secretary of state for home affairs 1919; secretary of overseas trade department, 1919-20.

Gretton, Colonel John (52). MP (Con., 1895-1906; Unionist since 1907).

Grey, Viscount. Sir Edward Grey (57). MP (Lib.) 1885-1916. British ambassador to US, 1919-20. Foreign secretary, 1905-16.

Griffith, Arthur (47). TD (Sinn Féin) since 1918. Founded Sinn Féin 1905. Conceded presidency to de Valera 1917. Secretary for home affairs in Dáil government, 1919. Member of treaty delegation, 1921. Signed and supported treaty. President of Dáil Éireann, Jan. 1922 and of Dáil ministry. Died August 1922.

Hankey, Sir Maurice (42). Secretary to the cabinet since 1918. Joined Royal marine artillery in 1895; served in the Mediterranean and naval intelligence, 1899-1907. Assistant secretary, committee for imperial defence, 1908-12; secretary, 1912-38. Secretary war cabinet, 1916; imperial war cabinet 1917; peace conference, 1919.

Hayes, Michael (30). TD (Sinn Féin) in 1921. Supported the treaty. Minister for education, August 1922 and Ceann Comhairle (speaker) Dáil Éireann, September 1922.

Henderson, Arthur (56). MP (Lab.) since 1903. Member of the war cabinet without portfolio. President of the board of education, 1915-16; paymaster-general and labour adviser to the government, 1916. Resigned from war cabinet, 1917. Chairman, parliamentary Labour party, 1908-10, 1914-17. Native of Glasgow who served apprenticeship as moulder at Robert Stephenson, Newcastle.

Hewart, Sir Gordon (49). MP (Con.) since 1913. Called to the bar, 1902. Solicitor-general, 1916-19; attorney-general, 1919-22.

Horne, Sir Robert (48). MP (Con.) since 1918. Called to the bar, 1896. Minister of labour, 1919. President of the board of trade, 1920-21. Chancellor of the exchequer, 1921.

Jameson, Andrew (64). Irish businessman and Unionist. Chairman, John Jameson Ltd, distillers. President, Dublin Chamber of Commerce.

Jeudwine, Major-General Sir Hugh (57). Commanded the 5th division in Ireland, 1919-22. Career in the army since 1882. Served in South Africa and in the great war.

Jones, Thomas. Principal assistant secretary to the cabinet. Welshman. Academic appointments in Glasgow University and Queens University of Belfast. Barrington lecturer in Ireland, 1904-05. Secretary, national health insurance commission (Wales) 1912-19.

Lansdowne, 5th marquess. Henry Charles Keith Petty Fitzmaurice (74). Had held junior office in the 1860s, 1870s and 1880. Governor-general Canada, 1883-8; India, 1888-93. Secretary of state for war, 1895-1900; foreign secretary, 1900-05; minister without portfolio, 1915-16. Described by Chamberlain in 1916 as 'a "pivotal person" for the lords, with great influence . . . the Hartington of to-day'.

Law, Andrew Bonar (61). MP (Un.) since 1900. Prime minister, 1922-3. Born in Canada and educated in Canada and Glasgow. Iron merchant, Glasgow. Leader of the Conservative party 1911-21;

of the house of commons, 1916-21. Secretary of state for the colonies, 1915-16; chancellor of the exchequer, 1916-18; lord privy seal, 1919-21; member of the war cabinet, 1916-19. Lloyd George claimed in 1911 (when Law became leader of his party) that the Conservatives had 'stumbled on their best man by accident'. In 1921 he referred to Law as 'an Orangeman at heart' and said that 'all the Orange fanaticism was there'. Law believed the Irish were 'an inferior race'.

Liddell, Sir Frederick (54). First parliamentary counsel since 1917.

Lloyd George, David (56). Prime minister, December 1916-October 1922. MP (Lib.) for Carnarvon since 1890. Solicitor, 1884. President of the board of trade, 1905-08; chancellor of the exchequer, 1908-15; minister of munitions, 1915-16; secretary of state for war, 1916.

Long, 1st Viscount. Walter Hume Long (65). MP (Con.) Former chief secretary for Ireland, 1905-06. President, board of agriculture, 1895-1900; local government board, 1900-05, 1915-16. Colonial secretary, 1916-18. Long considered by 1918 that circumstances had so altered since 1914 as to justify some concessions on home rule. But there could be no question of full dominion home rule, for its 'inevitable conclusion' was 'practical, if not legal independence'.

Luzio, Monsignor Salvatore. Domestic prelate to the pope. Papal envoy to Ireland, 1923. Educated in Sicily and Rome University; one-time professor of canon law, Maynooth, 1897-1910; subsequent position, university of S. Appollinaire, 1910-18.

Lynch, Liam. IRA officer; commanding officer first southern division 1921-2; chief-of-staff, 1922-3. Died April 1923.

MacEoin, Sean (26). Longford IRA officer. TD for Longford-Westmeath. Supported treaty.

McGrath, Joseph (30). TD (Sinn Féin) since 1918. Carried messages between de Valera and Lloyd George, summer 1921. Supported treaty. Minister for labour in the Dáil cabinet and member of the provisional government, 1922.

McGuinness, Joseph. Longford IRB Volunteer. In 1917, when in Lewes jail for his part in 1916 rising, elected MP for Longford; defeated Redmonite candidate.

McKenna, Reginald (56). MP (Lib.), 1895-1918. Chancellor of the exchequer, 1915-16; president board of education, 1907-08; first lord of the admiralty, 1908-11; home secretary, 1911-15. Not retained by Lloyd George.

McMahon, James (54). Under-secretary to the lord lieutenant of Ireland, 1918-22. Belfast-born Catholic civil servant who became assistant secretary to post office in Ireland, 1913; secretary, 1916.

MacNéill, Eoin (51). TD (Sinn Féin). Historian of ancient Ireland.

MacNeill, John Gordon Smith (70). MP (Nat.), 1887-1918. Professor of constitutional law, 1909; dean of faculty of law, National University of Ireland.

Macpherson, Ian (39). MP (Lib.) since 1911. Chief secretary for Ireland, 1918-20; junior office, 1914-19; minister of pensions, 1920-22.

Macready, General Sir (Cecil Frederick) Nevil (57). GOC, Ireland. Served in Egypt 1882, South Africa 1899-1902 and the great war, 1914-16. Staff appointments the Cape colony, 1902-06; British expeditionary force France 1914-16; member of the army council, 1916, and adjutant-general to the forces 1916-18; commissioner, metropolitan police, 1918-20. Macready had 'a good civilian mind'. He thought 'nothing' but 'a bold dramatic political stroke' would 'solve' the Irish problem.

MacSwiney, Terence. TD (Sinn Féin). Lord mayor of Cork. Died on hunger strike, October 1920.

Maxwell, Major-General Sir John Grenfell (60). Commander-in-chief Ireland, 1916. Recalled. Army career since 1882: Egypt; South Africa; the great war, 1914-15; Ireland, 1916. Maxwell believed in May 1916 that the 'only way now' would be 'to bring all parties together and settle the Irish question . . . by consent'.

Mellows, Liam (27). TD (Sinn Féin) since 1918. Lancashire-born IRB and Volunteer officer who was 'out' in the West in 1916. In the US, 1916-20. Returned to Ireland, 1920; director purchases, IRA headquarters staff; opposed the treaty; belonged to Four Courts garrison. Executed December 1922.

Midleton, 1st Earl. St John Brodrick (54). MP (Con.) 1880-1906. Succeeded father, 1907. Secretary of state for war, 1900-03, for India, 1903-05; served on Irish convention, 1917-18.

Mond, Sir Alfred Moritz (51). MP (Lib.) since 1906. Barrister 1894 and businessman. First commissioner of works, 1916-21. Minister of health, 1921-2.

Montagu, Edwin (40) MP (Lib.) since 1906. Secretary of State for India, 1917-22. Junior office, 1906-16. Financial secretary to treasury, 1914-16; chancellor of the Duchy of Lancaster, 1915;

Minister of munitions and member of war committee, 1916. Montagu had been offered the chief secretaryship for Ireland by Asquith after the rising, but had rejected the post. He had no interest in, no knowledge of, and no liking for, Ireland. Besides, as a Jew he considered there might be a 'race' barrier. By 1918 he had more interest in the matter and believed something should be done.

Moylan, Sean (30). TD (Sinn Féin) 1921. Corkman and IRA officer. Opposed the treaty and commanded a Cork brigade after June 1922. In US, Nov. 1922-Feb. 1923.

Mulcahy, Richard (26). TD (Sinn Féin) since 1918. C/S IRA before the treaty. Supported the treaty. Minister of defence 1922-.

O'Brien, Art (47). Dáil Éireann representative in London, 1919.

O'Connor, James (47). Lord justice of appeal in Ireland since 1918.

O'Connor, Rory (36). Executed December 1922. Engineering graduate and staff officer IRA. Republican idealist. Opposed the treaty and led the Four Courts garrison from Apr. 1922.

O'Donoghue, Florence. Corkman. IRA officer. Belonged to 'neutral' IRA men.

O'Duffy, Eoin (27). C/S IRA Jan, 1922 and 'national' forces. Supported the treaty. Later chief commissioner of the police force.

O'Hegarty, Diarmaid. Secretary to the Dáil cabinet and provisional government. Belonged to the IRB and a member of the IRA headquarters staff before the treaty. Supported the treaty. Commander of the national/Free State forces.

O'Higgins, Kevin Christopher (27). MP (Sinn Féin) since December 1918. Studied initially for the priesthood and then the law. Joined the Volunteers after the outbreak of European war and by 1917 was captain of the Stradbally company, Carlow brigade. Became assistant minister for local government in the Dáil cabinet. Supported the treaty. Belonged to the provisional government and minister of economic affairs in the Dáil cabinet, 1922.

O'Keefe, Patrick. TD (Sinn Féin) since 1918 and one of the secretaries of Sinn Féin.

O'Kelly, Sean T. (36). TD since December 1918. Irish envoy to Paris and Rome, 1919-22. Opposed the treaty. Chief whip republican party.

O'Malley, Ernie (21). IRA officer from 1919. O/C second southern division from spring 1921. Objected to the treaty and supported the convention and the Four Courts garrison, 1922. A/C/S of the IRA during the civil war and O/C northern and eastern command. Captured November 1922.

O'Sullivan, Gearóid. Adjutant-general IRA before and after the treaty. Supported the treaty and remained on army headquarters staff. Involved in the negotiations between the army groups in early 1922. Belonged to IRB.

Plunkett, George Noble, Count (68). MP for North Roscommon, 1917 and TD since December 1918. Barrister and papal count. Minister for foreign affairs in the Dáil, 1919.

Redmond, John MP (Nat.) for Waterford since 1891; for New Ross 1881-85; for north Wexford 1885-91. Chairman of the Irish parliamentary party. Died March 1918, aged 59.

Rothermere, 1st Viscount. Harold Sidney Harmsworth (51). Newspaper proprietor. Air minister, 1917-18. Grand nephew of Lord Northcliffe, to whom his son succeeded.

Runciman, Walter (49). MP (Lib.) for Oldham, 1899-1900 and Dewsbury, 1902-18. Junior office, 1905-08. President of the board of education, 1908-11; of the board of agriculture, 1911-14; of the board of trade, 1914-16.

Russell, George (52). Irish writer and painter. Wrote '*The National Being: Some Thought on an Irish Policy, 1917*'.

Salisbury, 4th Marquess. James Edward Hubert Gascoyne Cecil (58). MP (Con.), 1885-1903. Succeeded his father, 1903. Under-secretary for foreign affairs, 1900-03; lord privy seal, 1903-05; president of the board of trade, 1905; lord president of the council, 1922-3; chancellor of the Duchy of Lancaster, 1922-3.

Salvidge, Sir Archibald Tutton James (56). Liverpool brewer and alderman. Chairman of the council, National Unionist Association of Conservative and Liberal Unionists' Organisations, 1913. President, Liverpool Constitutional Association. Birkenhead explained to Lloyd George in 1918 that 'The Liverpool Workingman's Conservative Association and Salvidge are pivotal . . . We hold every Liverpool seat'.

Samuel, Sir Herbert Louis (47). MP (Lib.) 1902-18; junior office, 1915-19. Chancellor of the Duchy of Lancaster 1909-10; postmaster-general, 1910-14; president of the local government board, 1914-15; postmaster-general and chancellor of the Duchy of Lancaster 1915-16;

secretary of state for home affairs, 1916; high commissioner, Palestine since 1920.

Scott, C.P. (73). Governing director of the *Manchester Guardian* since 1872. Former Liberal MP for Lancashire (1895). Friend and confidant of Lloyd George.

Selborne, 2nd earl. William Waldegrave Palmer (60). MP (Lib., 1885-86; Lib. Unionist, 1886-92). Junior office, 1895-1900. First lord of the admiralty, 1900-05; governor of the Transvaal and high commissioner for South Africa, 1905-10; president of the board of agriculture, 1915-16.

Shortt, Edward. MP (Lib.). 1910-22. Chief secretary for Ireland, 1918-19. Home secretary, 1919-22.

Smuts, Jan Christian (49). Prime minister and minister for native affairs, Union of South Africa, since 1921. During the great war was the South African representative at the imperial war cabinet, 1917-18, and subsequently South African plenipotentiary, with Botha, at the peace conference in Paris.

Stack, Austin (39). Kerryman. TD (Sinn Féin) since 1918. Honorary secretary of Sinn Féin, October 1917. Minister of home affairs in the Dáil cabinet, 1920. Opposed the treaty.

Strickland, Major General Sir (Edward) Peter (50). Commanded 6th division, Ireland 1918-22. Joined the Norfolk regiment in 1888. Served in Upper Burma; with the Egyptian army in the Sudan and at Khartoum; and in Northern Nigeria. Served in the European war, 1914-18.

Tudor, Major-General Sir Hugh (48). Police adviser Ireland, 1920-21. Served in South Africa 1899-1902; in the European war, 1914-18. Commanded 9th division, 1918. Major-general, 1919.

Walsh, J. J. (39). Postmaster-general, Irish Free State.

Wilson, Field-Marshal Sir Henry Hughes (55). CIGS and member of the war cabinet, 1918-22. Career in the army since 1884. The son of James Wilson of Currygrane, Edgeworthstown, Ireland.

Worthington-Evans, Sir Laming (51). MP (Con.) since 1910. Temporary major in the army, 1914-15 and junior office, 1916-18. Minister of blockade, 1918; minister of pensions, 1919-20; minister without portfolio, 1920-21; secretary of state for war, 1921-2. Vice-chairman, National Unionist Association.

Index